the container gardening
ENCYCLOPEDIA

the container gardening
ENCYCLOPEDIA

GREENWICH
EDITIONS

This edition published in 2004 by
Greenwich Editions
The Chrysalis Building
Bramley Road, London W10 6SP

© Salamander Books Ltd., 2002, 2004

An imprint of **Chrysalis** Books Group plc

All correspondence concerning the content of this
volume should be addressed to Salamander Books Ltd.

ISBN 0 86288 656 2

Printed in China

Credits
Edited, designed & typeset: Ideas into Print
Photographs: Neil Sutherland
Decorative borders: Ian Mitchell

Compiler
After leaving school, Sue Phillips worked for a
year on a general nursery before studying
horticulture at Hadlow College of Agriculture and
Horticulture, Kent for three years. For the next
five years, she was co-owner and manager of a
nursery in Cambridgeshire before joining a
leading garden products company as Garden
Adviser. In 1984, Sue turned freelance and since
then has written several books, contributed
widely to various gardening and general interest
magazines and appeared often on radio and TV.

Contributors
The principal contributors for each section are
credited on the contents pages.

Photographer
Neil Sutherland has more than 30 years
experience in a wide range of photographic
fields, including still-life, portraiture, reportage,
natural history, cookery, landscape and travel.
His work has been published in countless
books and magazines throughout the world.

Half-title page: A wirework basket bursting with
summer flowers in white, yellow and orange.
Title page: Ornamental cabbages and violas
combine to create a simple yet stunning display.
Copyright page: A wicker basket is the ideal
container for a vivid display of cosmos and
petunias in shades of pink and purple.

INTRODUCTION

The Grow Anywhere Garden

Containers enable anyone to garden, whether they have soil or not. Pots, tubs and troughs are the perfect way to transform paths and paving into oases of flowers and foliage, and enable balconies to bloom. Spectacular pots create focal points around the garden, highlight hot-spots and add drama to entrances. Boxes underline windows in an old cottage and giant jars add architectural accents to a carpet of colour. The enormous range of containers now available makes it easy to create anything from a fully coordinated and themed patio display to artfully arranged collections of primitive pots that look as if they 'happened' almost by chance. And since pots are portable, it is easy to create eye-catching patioscapes, as plants can be rearranged until you are happy with the effect. With containers, you can recycle a basic collection of plants round the garden throughout the season, and make them into a sequence of ever-changing displays. This book shows you how, and provides the basic grounding and a selection of ideas to get you started. With its help, you can create countless beautiful and innovative plant and container displays of your own that will be enjoyed by family and friends all the year round.

Sue Phillips

CONTENTS

A wicker basket, here bedecked with early spring colour, suits a country garden setting.

PART ONE

CHOOSING CONTAINERS

Today there are containers in every style, shape and size and for every situation. For a coordinated display, choose the containers first, picking ones that match the style of their surroundings, then select plants for the pots. Good-quality containers will last for years and can be given a fresh look by regular seasonal replanting.

CONTAINER OPTIONS

To make outstanding displays, exploit the range of container types to the full. Troughs are long and low, ideal for a more formal arrangement of plants, and perfect for windowboxes. The same long, narrow shape can also look good at the foot of a wall or, planted with a row of clipped rosemary or box, as a low divider rather like a mini-hedge. Hanging baskets look most impressive when teamed with a floor-standing display of containers planted in similar style. Some hanging baskets feature self-watering bases, which help to overcome the usual problems associated with these containers. Wall planters are less showy and more sophisticated. They are available in a much wider range of shapes and styles than hanging baskets, and look their best when several are grouped together at different levels. They are the perfect way to decorate an uninteresting area of wall. Some types can even be hung on trellis to give the impression of a planted wall or an unusual garden divider. But the most widely used containers are floor-standing pots and planters. These are available in a tremendous variety of materials and in a huge range of shapes, sizes and styles, ideal for all kinds of plants in any situation. Supremely versatile, they can be stacked, tiered, grouped or used on their own as architectural features. Some also lend themselves to different kinds of decoration, to add an extra dimension to a plant display.

Left: Wall planters do not have room to hold many plants, so make the most of them by using perfect plants, and squeeze in as many as possible. Keep them well watered, as the roots will be very overcrowded.

Left: In a mild sheltered spot, you can use hanging baskets even during the winter. Plant them with primroses, ivies and winter-flowering pansies. However, do not allow the potting mixture to freeze.

Above: Growing plants separately in individual pots allows maximum flexibility, since displays can easily be rearranged and new plants added to create a fresh look without needing to replant.

Above: Windowboxes bring plant interest right up to the house, merging home and garden. A mixture of annuals creates a cottagey display that gets away from the usual formality of this type of container.

Left: Water plants make fascinating features for the patio. Use containers without drainage holes in the bottom; they are in effect 'potted ponds'. Use them for miniature water lilies, marginals and floating plants.

Getting things into proportion

Here are a few basic tips that may help you when planning a container display.

As a general rule, choose plants one-and-a-half times the height of a tall container, or one-and-a-half times the width of a low wide container. It is useful to know these vital statistics when choosing plants, but do not be constrained by them.

In practice, plants are put in while small and keep growing over the whole season. And a compact pot may well look great displaying an equally compact plant. So always stand the two together when choosing them to gauge the effect.

***Right:** This trimmed box and its pot are in the ideal proportion of 3:2. It will continue looking in proportion during the current growing season, but will probably need a pot one size larger the following spring. By then, root growth will need the extra room.*

In a 'busy' situation with lots of background detail, simple plants and containers stand out best. Conversely, colourful containers are invaluable for adding interest and detail to a part of the garden that is looking leafy after the main shrub flowering season. You can bring a single striking potted shrub to life by teaming it temporarily with a brilliant flowering planter display.

Plastic and clay pots

Clay and plastic pots not only look different, they provide different conditions for plant roots and need a different regime of care.

***Above:** Standard clay (terracotta) containers have large holes in the base that need covering with crocks to keep the soil in, but allow surplus water to drain out. Clay pots have porous walls through which water evaporates.*

***Above:** Standard plastic pots do not need crocking, as the mix is unlikely to escape through the small drainage holes, especially coarse peat- or coir-based mixes. Plastic pots have thin impervious walls that retain moisture.*

15

Left: A 'beehive' jar has such a narrow neck that once planted and filled with root, it would be almost impossible to remove the plant without breaking the container. It is best used decoratively – empty. Pots with wider necks than bases are safest for planting.

Anthemis cupaniana

TERRACOTTA CONTAINERS

There is no limit to the displays that look good in terracotta planters, from traditional arrangements with bedding plants, such as tuberous begonias and lobelia, to a Mediterranean design based on vivid pelargoniums. Terracotta pots dry out more quickly than plastic ones, so herbs do well in them as they are fairly drought-resistant and would rather be slightly on the dry side than too wet. Not all terracotta pots are frost-proof; many will crack if left outdoors in winter with soil inside them. If you want to use clay pots outside in winter, buy good-quality pots labelled frost-proof. Although they are less likely to crack, the pots do not protect plants growing inside them from freezing. During severe weather protect them as described on pages 70-71. Experiment with daring colour schemes and bold plant shapes. You can never really tell how plants will look until you see them together, so buy enough for several containers and try out all the possible combinations before deciding which to plant together. Old terracotta pots have the most character; these are occasionally sold by alpine nurseries or found in junk shops. Scrub them well in warm soapy water inside and out before reusing. Soak new clay pots in water overnight before use. To achieve a weathered effect, lay pots on their side in soil or amongst undergrowth and leave for several months, occasionally damping and turning them.

Right: The terracotta 'chimney pot' has holes in the sides that make ideal planting pockets for lewisias, which are very susceptible to rotting. They grow naturally on edge in rocky crevices, so this container is perfect for them.

Right: An enormous range of terracotta pots is available from garden centres, but you can also find specialist suppliers who keep a truly staggering selection in all colours, shapes, sizes – and prices!

Above: Amphorae and jugs are a great way to add character to a display of plants in terracotta pots, but do not plant directly into them. You could, however, lodge a suitable potted plant into the top of a wide-necked container.

Right: Terracotta wall planters harmonise specially well with old brick or stone walls; but being small and porous, the containers dry out particularly fast, so plants need more attention than usual.

Plants that look good in terracotta containers

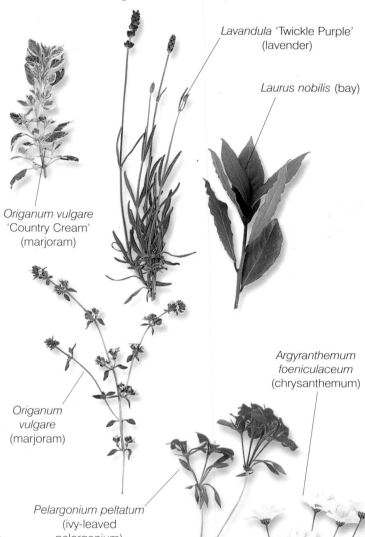

Lavandula 'Twickle Purple' (lavender)

Laurus nobilis (bay)

Origanum vulgare 'Country Cream' (marjoram)

Argyranthemum foeniculaceum (chrysanthemum)

Origanum vulgare (marjoram)

Pelargonium peltatum (ivy-leaved pelargonium)

Fragaria (strawberry)

PLASTIC CONTAINERS

Plastic containers are available in all shapes and sizes, from standard tubs, troughs and planters to windowboxes, wall planters and hanging baskets. You can also buy classical urns and a huge range of ornate containers in every style. They can be left as they are or decorated with a variety of paint effects or 'fake' finishes. Growing in plastic containers is a bit different to growing in terracotta. Plastic is not porous, so the potting mix in it dries out less quickly. This is a benefit on hot summer days, but can be a problem at the start of the season, as small, young plants do not use a great deal of water, especially when the weather is cool. It is easy to overwater them, especially if you use a peat-based potting mixture, which holds much more water than other types. Water with care for the first four to five weeks. Another difference lies in the drainage holes. Plastic pots usually have several holes spread around the base. Because the holes are quite small, there is no need to cover them with crocks, especially if you use a soilless potting mixture, which is more fibrous in texture and less likely to trickle out. Some people prefer plastic containers for plants that only last one season – typically spring or summer annuals. This is probably a throwback to the days when plastic containers were rather poor quality and often became brittle after a year or two out in the sunlight. A hard frost in winter was often enough to make them disintegrate entirely. But nowadays, good-quality plastics are available that last very much better and can be used outside all year round.

Above: Even the plastic boxes that nurseries use for transporting plants and cut flowers can be used for creative displays – ideal for making an instant arrangement of spring flowers, as seen here.

Left: A plastic tub makes a good container for this miniature potted water garden complete with fountain. It is a very safe type of water feature to include in a garden that small children play in.

Right: Plastic is such a versatile material that it is used to make containers in all shapes and sizes. A good range of colours is also available, although the most popular ones are white, cream, terracotta and black.

Suitable plants for plastic containers

Plastic pots are ideal where you need a large container to hold a dramatic display for which a suitably sized 'character' pot would be prohibitively expensive. You can grow almost anything in plastic pots, but they are mostly used for riotous summer bedding displays.

Above: Polystyrene containers offer a certain amount of natural insulation to roots inside them, ideal for plants that stand in a hot sunny spot in summer and are also left outside for the winter.

Left: Plastic pots allow the plants in them to star. And in any case, an ebullient display will quickly hide much of the container.

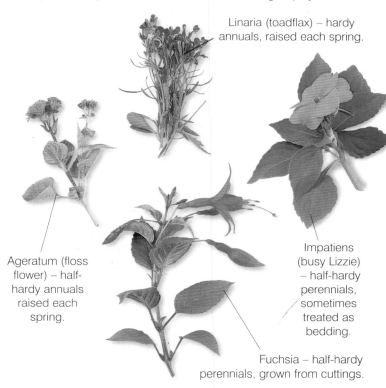

Linaria (toadflax) – hardy annuals, raised each spring.

Ageratum (floss flower) – half-hardy annuals raised each spring.

Impatiens (busy Lizzie) – half-hardy perennials, sometimes treated as bedding.

Fuchsia – half-hardy perennials, grown from cuttings.

Below: Most of the more naturally compact varieties of annual bedding plants are ideal for growing in plastic containers. Look out, too, for dwarf versions of old favourites, such as nicotiana and African marigold.

WOODEN CONTAINERS

Wooden containers come in a variety of shapes, sizes and styles. They range from half barrels and rustic containers faced with rough bark to smart, formal, hardwood tubs and even Versailles planters (painted, formal square boxes with knobs on the corners). Manufacturers of wooden garden accessories, such as fence panels, trellis and pergola poles, often make matching wooden tubs and planters for a totally coordinated look. You can make your own wooden containers, too – in fact, far more easily than any other kind. Timber yards sell bark offcuts that make effective rustic cladding for simple containers, while architectural salvage yards often have deep, moulded skirting boards from which to make a unique planter. All wooden containers need protecting from damp to prevent rotting. Most are already treated with preservative, but a second coat is a good idea before planting. Allow this to weather to remove any risk of fumes affecting plants. It is also worth lining the inside of wooden containers with plastic to keep potting mix away from the timber sides. Push the lining down through the central drainage hole and make sure that wooden containers are well clear of the ground to ensure good air circulation underneath; this also helps to prevent rotting.

Wicker baskets make attractive natural-style containers that suit a wide variety of plants and planting styles. Use them to create stunning tropical-looking displays by teaming them with exotics, such as cordyline palm, abutilon and hardy hibiscus, or make rustic cottagey creations based on unsophisticated annual flowers, such as calendula with herbs. Baskets also look good with tall, linear-shaped plants, such as bamboo, miscanthus or *Arundo donax* 'Variegata'. For a more traditional effect, choose a mixture of striking half-hardy perennials, such as pelargonium, gazania and osteospermum.

Right: Wooden wheelbarrows occasionally feature as 'character' garden containers. This miniature version is perfectly scaled for its cargo of polyanthus, set amidst a carpet of spring flowers.

Left: This ornamental trug is made from wafer thin 'slices' of natural wood, steamed and bent into shape. Team something as pretty as this with very simple flowers to avoid overkill.

Right: Wooden and wicker containers make delightful natural-looking containers for wild and woodland plants as well as more sophisticated displays. Treat them with preservative, stain or varnish.

Above: Wicker makes an unusual wall planter in which to house a changing succession of potted plants. This spring display includes *Crocus* 'Vanguard' and 'Wanda' hybrid primroses.

Above: Plunge pots of seasonal flowers, just approaching their best, into plastic-lined baskets of moss to make instant displays for house, conservatory or garden.

Below: Since wicker is lightweight and will not crack, it avoids many of the drawbacks of some types of outdoor pots.

Plants for wooden containers

For rough oak half barrels, try a mixture of woodland plants, such as violets, lily-of-the-valley and dwarf rhododendron, a collection of hostas or single specimen camellia or pieris. Train clematis up obelisks in large cedar tubs. Symmetrical forms of topiary, such as spiral box or standard bay, and standard-trained citrus trees suit Versailles planters.

Right: Gaultheria mucronata, Choisya ternata *'Sundance'*, a winter-flowering heather and the stringy stems of Chamaecyparis pisifera *'Filifera Aurea'* make an effective plant association for a wooden tub.

Clematis – deciduous climbers

Below: *All sorts of woody and woodland plants look good in wood! Clematis are particularly versatile and underrated plants for large tubs, either trained up walls or a free-standing plant support, such as an obelisk.*

Ivy *(Hedera helix)* – evergreen climbers and trailers

Hosta – herbaceous perennials that die down in winter

Rhododendron – evergreen shrubs that need ericaceous potting mix

Above: The clay colours and naturalistic designs of oriental-style glazed pottery suit all sorts of plants, including many with no oriental connections. Pick out the colour of the container in some of the flowers to make a good match.

Right: The translucent glaze on this beautiful ceramic container gives it the natural weatherworn look of an antique container. Charismatic pots such as this are best planted with simple flowers.'

Below: Another strategy is to choose plants with completely contrasting colours; here a blue container and orange winter cherry make a brilliant combination.

Below: Glazed ceramic containers come in a huge range of shapes, colours, patterns and sizes to suit almost any kind of plant. Look for frostproof kinds for year-round use.

GLAZED POTTERY

Glazed pottery is one of the newer arrivals on the garden scene; surprisingly inexpensive, much of it is oriental in origin, attractively patterned, often available in sets of three or five containers in different sizes, and usually available with matching saucers and pot feet. The most expensive kinds are likely to be more reliably frostproof. Choose pots with striking oriental designs to team with plants on a similar theme; suitable 'plant partners' include bamboos, grasses, hostas, houttuynia, irises, Japanese maple, conifers or evergreens. For more colourful flowering plant displays based on annuals, etc., choose plain colours or very simple designs that do not distract. Or if teaming a flowering shrub with a patterned container, choose a flower whose colouring matches that of its pot. Alternatively, arrange an interesting collection of various types of glazed pottery jars and pots on raised staging, planted with different green foliage plants chosen for their varied shapes and textures, to create a striking display in which the pottery is the focus of attention. Ceramic pots also make good temporary homes for seasonal displays; use them as pot covers for spring bulbs and plants such as polyanthus and primulas, in much the same way as you might use glazed containers on a windowsill indoors. Again, display them on tiered shelves or staging to make the most of them; they would look effective set off against a permanent collection of evergreens, such as *Choisya ternata* 'Sundance', dwarf conifers or rhododendrons.

Right: Ceramic jars are a lovely shape, but avoid using them for long-term plants. If these become pot-bound, they can split the container. Stick to short-term annual planting schemes.

Below: Glossy green tureens look fantastic teamed with brightly coloured gazanias. The reflective surfaces bring out the best in the flowers and blend with the foliage colours.

Glazed dishes for bonsai

Make sure that containers for bonsai plants are frostproof, that they have several drainage holes and that the floor of the pot is level, so that no pockets of water can accumulate in the base. The pots should have feet to leave space for water to drain away. Avoid pots that are glazed on the inside; this is an inhospitable surface for the roots and will cause the soil to dry out too quickly around the perimeter of the pot.

Above: *These tiny coloured pots are similar in shape and quality to full-sized ones. They can become collectors' items in their own right.*

Left: *The vividly coloured leaves of this Japanese red maple are set off well by the blue glazed container in which the tree is growing. A bonsai pot should complement the tree to form a harmonious unit.*

Given the range of glazed containers, it is not difficult to find something suitable for every occasion.

STONEWARE CONTAINERS

Today, real stone containers, such as horse troughs, animal feeding bowls and butler's sinks, are garden antiques and as such prohibitively expensive and rarely sold. However, when available, they make superb plant containers, particularly for alpines and other rock plants, which suit their rough-hewn texture. Reconstituted stone containers are also quite expensive. These are usually formed into classic container shapes and have a more 'finished' look than real stone, but due to price are normally only found as relatively small containers. Containers cast in concrete and cement are a much cheaper alternative and available in a huge range of sizes and styles, including formal troughs and urns. Because the material is cheap, it can be used to make large planting boxes for areas without any suitable soil. These can be largely hidden by tumbling plants if required. Cement can also be artificially 'weathered' to resemble real stone, or used to cast homemade containers in a variety of shapes. The main disadvantage of cement containers is that they are massively heavy and only available in one colour – grey, although it is possible to paint them for a more interesting finish (see page 50). When mixed in equal quantities with coarse sand and peat, cement becomes hypertufa. This can be used as a textured 'plaster' to cover old sinks or pots, giving them a 'stone' finish, or poured into moulds to make artificial stone-effect containers, as described on page 44.

Right: This unusual twist-effect concrete wall planter looks best with a simple planting scheme that emphasises the shape of the container. As space is limited, make each plant count.

Below: Genuine stone butler's sinks look perfect filled with gritty soil and planted with alpines and miniature conifers. The result is almost a miniaturised landscape. The grit topdressing is decorative and provides surface drainage.

Above: Stone urns look good on a formal terrace. They are best planted fairly traditionally with pastel-coloured annuals, such as pelargoniums, lobelia and verbena.

Below: Cast cement containers can easily be painted or given a fake aging treatment for added authenticity. They are available in a wide range of styles.

Below: Hexagons and other geometrical shapes are easily moulded from concrete, making it simple to find innovative shapes to add an extra dimension of interest to plant arrangements.

Above: A classical urn or plinth made of reconstituted stone will be much cheaper than real stone. A pair of these containers would make a grand entrance to a house or driveway.

Plants for stoneware and concrete pots

Concrete and stone are extremely weatherproof materials that can be used outdoors all year round, so are specially suited to evergreens. Classic stoneware containers look best with formal planting displays.

Daboecia cantabrica 'Atropurpurea' – a late summer-flowering heath for acid potting mix.

Potentilla – dwarf sunloving shrubs with flowers in shades of orange, red and yellow.

Patio rose – will flower all summer with regular feeding.

Armeria maritima (thrift) – will tolerate an exposed location.

Sempervivum – a hardy drought-proof plant.

Hebe – many varieties available of this rewarding and versatile shrub.

Sedum spurium 'Atropurpureum' – a tough plant with good flowers.

Above: Because they can be moulded so easily, reconstituted stone containers are particularly good for classical shapes resembling stone carvings.

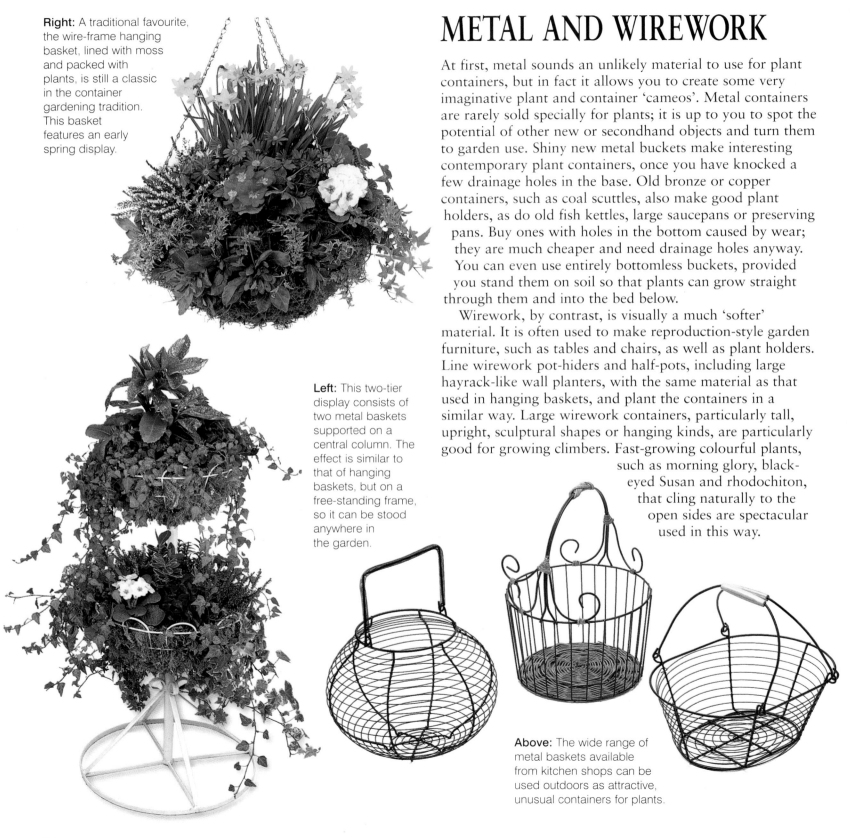

Right: A traditional favourite, the wire-frame hanging basket, lined with moss and packed with plants, is still a classic in the container gardening tradition. This basket features an early spring display.

Left: This two-tier display consists of two metal baskets supported on a central column. The effect is similar to that of hanging baskets, but on a free-standing frame, so it can be stood anywhere in the garden.

METAL AND WIREWORK

At first, metal sounds an unlikely material to use for plant containers, but in fact it allows you to create some very imaginative plant and container 'cameos'. Metal containers are rarely sold specially for plants; it is up to you to spot the potential of other new or secondhand objects and turn them to garden use. Shiny new metal buckets make interesting contemporary plant containers, once you have knocked a few drainage holes in the base. Old bronze or copper containers, such as coal scuttles, also make good plant holders, as do old fish kettles, large saucepans or preserving pans. Buy ones with holes in the bottom caused by wear; they are much cheaper and need drainage holes anyway. You can even use entirely bottomless buckets, provided you stand them on soil so that plants can grow straight through them and into the bed below.

Wirework, by contrast, is visually a much 'softer' material. It is often used to make reproduction-style garden furniture, such as tables and chairs, as well as plant holders. Line wirework pot-hiders and half-pots, including large hayrack-like wall planters, with the same material as that used in hanging baskets, and plant the containers in a similar way. Large wirework containers, particularly tall, upright, sculptural shapes or hanging kinds, are particularly good for growing climbers. Fast-growing colourful plants, such as morning glory, black-eyed Susan and rhodochiton, that cling naturally to the open sides are spectacular used in this way.

Above: The wide range of metal baskets available from kitchen shops can be used outdoors as attractive, unusual containers for plants.

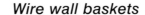

Right: The tall narrow metal buckets used by florists for cut flowers also make unusual containers for plants out in the garden. Patio roses continue the floristry theme, and do well in these elegant containers.

Left: An old copper water tank makes a beautiful 'character' container at this old cottage. All sorts of bargain finds like this can be made at secondhand shops and architectural salvage yards.

Wire wall baskets

Delicate wirework suits period properties. Team with wirework garden seats and pretty cushions whose colours complement those of the flowers in the display.

Right: *Line ornate wall baskets with moss to give modern containers a period air. Choose simple plants that do not fight for attention with ornate containers.*

Below: *Wall baskets range from those like hanging baskets cut in half to those that resemble hayracks. All dry out fast, so check the plants in them regularly.*

Plants for metal and wirework containers

Above: Brand new metal pails, troughs and flower buckets can be found at hardware stores and in the household departments of big stores. Teamed with suitable plants, they make imaginative containers for the garden.

Shiny, solid-sided metal containers, such as galvanised buckets, suit highly coloured plants, especially traditional cut flower varieties, such as dwarf sunflowers, patio dahlias and spring bulbs, for a themed display. Use them, too, for cottagey flowers, such as nasturtiums, to create a pleasing rural backyard scene. For more sophisticated displays, team them with white or cream flowers and plants with silver-variegated foliage that pick out the colour of the container. Consider galvanised buckets and troughs for water plants, as the silvery surface gives a suggestion of water beneath them. Since they do not have holes in the base, buckets are doubly suitable for this type of display, which could be created from marginal or floating plants actually growing in water, or bog plants living in very wet potting mixture. Team copper or bronze containers with warm-coloured plants, especially those with the same pink or reddish-brown tones of the container. In a conservatory, say, old copper kettles or coal scuttles look good teamed with Begonia rex, coleus or brightly coloured tropical flowers. Lead or tarnished copper containers, which have a bluish patina, look brilliant planted with silver, white, grey and blue flowers.

Creative container gardening at its best can produce stunning results like this.

PART TWO

CREATIVE CONTAINERS

You can get great satisfaction from creating your own plant containers. Restore and recycle secondhand containers, or redecorate your own with fashionable paint effects such as stencilling. Or use other paint techniques to give cheap plastic containers an expensive new look as fake stone or leadwork.

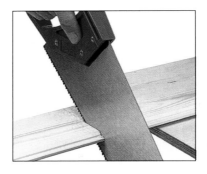

1 Decide on the overall dimensions of the planter and cut enough lengths of cladding to form the four sides. Sand the cut ends smooth to remove splinters.

2 Assemble the sides by interlocking the plank edges. Glue them together as well, using waterproof woodworking adhesive. Squeeze some into the grooves.

3 Assemble the planks to form each side, using a hammer and a cladding offcut to knock them tightly together. If any excess adhesive oozes out, wipe it off with a damp cloth.

MAKING A SIMPLE WOODEN PLANTER

Planting in above-ground containers has many advantages over in-ground gardening. For a start, you can work from a standing rather than a kneeling position, which is a boon for the elderly or partly disabled. Whatever you decide to plant is self-contained, allowing you to keep over-vigorous growth from spreading too far. Weeds are easy to keep under control and you can move the container around if you wish, placing it in sunshine or shelter as necessary. Groups of containers can also be an ideal way of breaking up the featureless expanse of a large patio. You can use all kinds of containers, but wooden planters are some of the most versatile and you can make your own, in virtually any shape or size, using the technique shown here. Tongued-and-grooved cladding is an ideal material for the planter's sides; you simply use as many planks as are necessary to give the height of container you want, and you can easily remove the tongue from the topmost planks to leave a neat square edge. Internal posts form the corners of the container, and the removable base panel sits on battens fixed to the inner face of the side walls. A series of drainage holes bored in the base panel allows the planter to drain freely in wet weather or after watering.

With the planter complete, apply two coats of a suitable microporous paint or wood stain, which will not flake and peel as time goes by. It is particularly important to make sure that the base panel is well treated with preservative; it it here that continual contact with moist planting mixture is most likely to cause the wood to rot away. Use preservatives that will not harm plants once they are dry. Place a pebble over each drainage hole to prevent them from becoming blocked and fill the planter with a suitable planting mixture.

4 Make up the short ends of the planter. Cut two corner posts for each end, then glue and nail the side panels to the posts with the tongued edge uppermost.

5 Use two nails per plank, punching the nail heads just below the wood surface. Disguise the holes with exterior-grade wood filler when assembly is complete.

6 Rest the base of the planter on slim battens glued and pinned to the inner faces of the side walls, flush with their bottom edges. Cut and fix the two battens to the assembled end walls of the planter first.

7 Glue the side walls to the two end sections. Using just adhesive at this stage allows you to align the corner joints and check that the whole assembly is square.

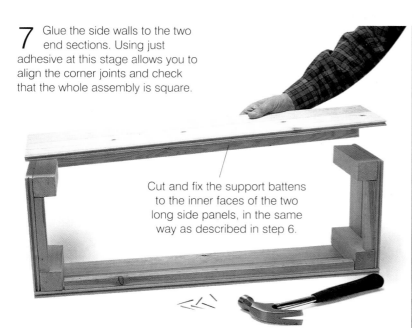

Cut and fix the support battens to the inner faces of the two long side panels, in the same way as described in step 6.

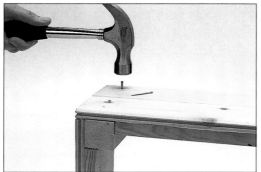

8 Once you have made any adjustments, leave the adhesive to set for a while. Nail the side walls to the corner posts and punch in the nail heads as described in steps 4 and 5.

9 One way of finishing off the side top edges is to cut down some narrow strips of the cladding and glue their grooved edges to the exposed tongues, as here.

Adding the base to the planter

Once you have assembled the planter walls, fit the base – a piece of exterior-grade plywood. Although this fits fairly loosely within the planter, drill some extra drainage holes to prevent waterlogging.

1 To mark the outline of the base, stand the planter upside down on the plywood sheet. Draw round the internal profile of the planter walls.

2 Extend the pencil lines to meet at each corner and cut out the resulting rectangle. Remove the corner squares of waste wood with a tenon saw.

3 Make a series of equally-spaced holes in the base using a flat wood bit in your power drill. Drill through into some scrap wood.

4 Drop the plywood base into the planter so that it rests on the inner support battens. You can pin and glue it in place if you prefer, but this is not essential.

5 You can leave the planter undecorated if it is made from preservative-treated wood. Otherwise, apply paint or wood stain.

MAKING A WINDOWBOX

You can make a simple windowbox using the same general techniques shown on pages 30-31. The aim of this particular project is to make a wooden surround that will enclose a standard-sized plastic trough. These are widely available in a range of colours and sizes. The construction materials are the same as before, but the tongued-and-grooved wooden cladding used here has a more detailed profile that gives the finished box more 'style'. You can choose from several cladding profiles, but be sure to use the heavier weight 'structural' cladding rather than the thinner type supplied for facing surfaces.

There are two plus points in using a plastic trough inside a wooden windowbox. One is that the interior of the box is not in direct contact with the planting mixture and is therefore less liable to rot away. The other is that it is very easy to change the display simply by replacing the trough with another one planted up in a different way. The plastic trough featured here is 60cm(24in) long and this is a convenient size for a small windowbox that will not be too heavy or unwieldy to fix up. The box is particularly sturdy around the end panels and these are the ideal points for support when attaching it to a wall or balcony railing. Advice on fixing up containers is given on pages 36-41.

Be sure to treat the completed windowbox with a suitable preservative stain or paint before using it. The possibilities are endless and it is easy to match existing house or garden colour schemes. Turn to pages 34-35 for guidance on preserving and decorating planters and windowboxes.

1 Use cladding and battens to make a windowbox for this plastic trough that measures 60cm(24in) long and 15cm(6in) wide and deep.

2 Measure and mark the pieces of cladding that will form the end panels of the box. For a snug fit, make these 17cm(6¾in) wide.

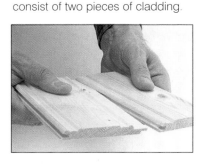

3 Saw the end panels to length and sand the cut edges for a smooth finish. Each end panel will consist of two pieces of cladding.

4 Using a tenon saw, cut off the thinnest part of the tongue on the piece of cladding chosen to form the top of each end panel.

5 Squeeze some woodworking adhesive in the groove of the top piece of cladding and carefully push the two pieces together.

6 Using panel pins or fine nails, attach the bottom edge of the end panel to a batten cut to the same width. Use adhesive to create a firmer bond.

7 Nail and glue battens along each side edge of the end panels. Punch the nail heads below the surface for a neat appearance.

8 Wipe off any excess adhesive with a damp cloth. This is one completed end panel viewed from what will be the inside of the box.

Putting in the base rails to support the trough

Since plants will be displayed in the plastic trough that fits inside the windowbox, there is no need to make a solid wooden floor to the box itself. A good way of supporting the trough is to use pretreated roofing lathes to make two base rails that fit between the battens in the base of the box. Fit these rails edge on to help them resist bending when the plastic trough is full of planting mixture.

1 *Cut two pieces of roofing lathe to fit inside the box, sawing notches at each end so that they rest on the battens.*

2 *Push the support rails down onto the end battens. Screw them in place or leave them loose for easy removal when cleaning the box.*

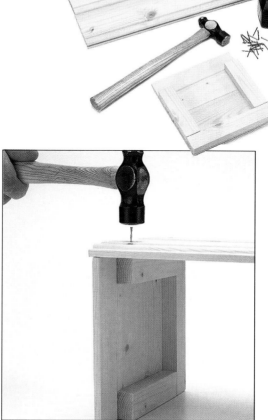

9 Cut long pieces of cladding and assemble them in pairs to make up the side panels. These should measure 63.5cm(25in). You now have two end and two side panels.

10 Add adhesive and attach the side panels to the end panels by nailing through into the battens. The result is a bottomless box that will fit snugly around the plastic trough.

3 *Drop the plastic trough inside the windowbox so that it rests on the two rails. Drill holes in the plastic base to let water drain out.*

Alternative end panels

As a variation, you can make different styles of end panels. Here, they are made of plywood glued and screwed onto four battens that make up a square. Fitting these with the battens facing outwards gives a 'practical' look and convenient handles for moving the box. Battens inside support the base rails as before.

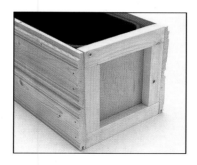

DECORATING PLANTERS AND WINDOWBOXES

Having constructed a windowbox or planter to your own design, you can add all sorts of individual finishing touches. It is now possible to buy preservative wood stains in a wide range of attractive colours. If you prefer to decorate the outside of the box with paint, only use wood preservative on the inside and underneath. If it seeps through cracks to the outside, use a sealant such as aluminium paint followed by universal primer before attempting to apply the top coats, otherwise the preservative colour will keep working its way through to the surface.

One of the easiest yet most striking ways of decorating a wooden windowbox is to use stencils. Many designs are available from shops or by mail order. You can buy special pots of stencil paint, but provided you use paint of a suitable consistency, you can apply artist's acrylics or dilute matt emulsion – even one of the mini 'tester' pots. The beauty of stencils is that you can use different motifs to emphasise whatever mood and visual style you have chosen for your house and garden. For example, heraldic lilies (fleur-de-lis) and medieval stars give a 'gothic' look to the windowbox below. To achieve the patina of age, paint the box with artist's acrylic – here in a shade called Monestial Blue – and apply the gold paint unevenly to make it appear worn.

Another way to add a note of distinction to is to use decorative wood mouldings. Once firmly secured and painted, the effect is of carved wood or cast metal.

Painting and stencilling a seashell windowbox

This wooden box with sides reminiscent of weatherboarding has a strong seaside flavour. The wood was painted using a mini 'tester' pot of blue emulsion paint, diluted down so that it just coloured the wood like a stain, rather than masking it completely.

1 Attach a stencil with small pieces of low-tack masking tape. Use a stencil brush and dilute artist's acrylic paints.

2 You can also achieve a stippled look using a natural sponge. Dab excess paint onto newspaper before applying it.

3 Untreated, the stencil motif and blue 'stain' would soon begin to weather. Use exterior-quality or yacht varnish, described as matt or silk/low sheen. Although colourless, the varnish will darken the paintwork slightly.

Stencilling a gold fleur-de-lis

1 Shake the pot to get a little paint onto the lid. Dip the brush lightly into the lid. Remove excess paint on a piece of paper.

2 For a stippled effect, lightly tap the paint onto the wood. Overlap the stencil as you work. Keep the brush perpendicular.

3 For a more solid coverage, keep the brush in light contact with the wood, making small circular movements.

4 A combination of stippled and solid paint application creates light and shade and an aged, three-dimensional look.

Applying mouldings

You can apply a range of decorative mouldings, including carved beading, to smooth-sided windowboxes using waterproof wood glue. Novelty magnets and mini wall hangings could be used to similar effect. For an oriental look, try split bamboo canes, stained and finished with yacht varnish. Ceramic tiles in a wide range of styles and colours can be applied with waterproof cement.

1 Measure and mark the position of the moulding. Glue it in place and weight it down. When dry, thoroughly seal it with wood or universal primer.

2 Depending on the coverage, apply two or more coats of high-gloss paint, sanding lightly between coats. Paint mouldings on the flat to prevent paint dripping.

Using opaque stains on a windowbox

Left: This water-based stain builds up a good depth of colour on the second or third coat to create a more opaque finish. Always brush in line with the wood grain.

Below: Protected from wind and midday sun, dwarf narcissi and cultivated primroses in a windowbox flower twice as long as plants growing in the open garden.

Staining a wooden windowbox

Some years ago, the only options for staining wood were varying shades of brown. Today, the range of stains and preservative paints is quite staggering. And what is more important, many are water-based, making them more pleasant to apply and safer to use with plants.

Above: *Translucent, water-based wood stains such as these are available in a range of bright colours. They allow the grain of the wood to show through.*

Left: *Use variegated plants and bicoloured flowers to 'pick out' the colour of a bright container. And redecorate old containers in a smart new scheme when you want a fresh look – much cheaper than buying new ones.*

Varnishing a windowbox

Right: *Solvent-based wood stains produce a more traditional finish in shades simulating natural wood colours such as walnut, oak and red cedar. Apply two coats for a solid-looking result. Always allow preservative stains to dry before using the container.*

1 Measure and mark out the pieces that will make up the bracket. This is 50x25mm(2x1in) planed softwood, suitably sturdy to support an average windowbox.

2 Although we will be using a mitre block to achieve accurate saw cuts, it would be wise to draw in the cut marks clearly with a combination square.

3 A mitre block is a great aid to accurate sawing. Hold the piece to be sawn firmly against the block and saw down onto an offcut to ensure a clean edge beneath.

4 To cut the diagonal support for the bracket, use the 45° guide in the mitre block. Cut the other end by using the same angle guide but turning the wood around.

A WINDOWBOX BRACKET

Any wall-mounted container needs to be securely fixed, but this is specially important with windowboxes. They are big and heavy, and when placed on upper-storey windows or above a street, have the potential to cause serious damage or injury if they fall. Metal brackets are sold in garden centres but if you make your own wooden windowbox, you will probably need to make your own support brackets, as ready-made ones may not be big enough. The bracket should be as wide as the depth of the windowbox, plus 2.5-5cm(1-2in) between the box and the wall to allow for air circulation. If possible, fix the windowbox to the bracket to make certain that it cannot slip off. If necessary, attach separate fittings to the wall, and wire or screw the box to these at each end. Check existing windowboxes and their brackets several times each year to make sure that they are still sound and that wooden boxes or fittings are not decaying. (This is most conveniently done when replanting.) Consider also the height at which the windowbox is to be fitted. If a window slides upwards, fit the box just below sill level, allowing the display to be seen from indoors as well as from the street. The window can still be opened – essential for watering plants on the upper storeys. If a window is hinged at the side or top, fit the container about 30cm(12in) beneath it, so that there is enough clearance to open the window above the plant display. This does mean losing the view of the plants from indoors, but the box can still make a dazzling display when seen from the garden or by passers-by.

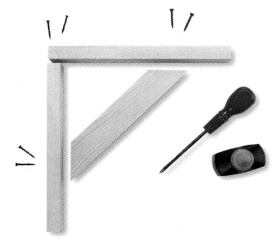

5 These are the pieces that will make up the bracket. Cutting the diagonal support so that it fits edge on makes for a much stronger result. All you need to do now is to glue and screw the pieces together.

6 Drill two pilot holes right through the edge of the top piece. Make these holes just smaller than the screw diameter to help the screws bite as they go in.

7 Apply some wood glue to the top cut edge of the back piece and screw the top piece to it. These screws are designed to make their own way into the grain.

8 Offer up the diagonal support to the assembled top and back pieces and mark the inside faces. Use a combination square to transfer lines onto the outside faces of the top and back pieces as a guide for the screws.

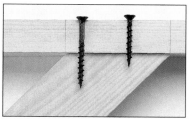

9 This shows how two screws fix the support strut at each end by passing through the outside faces of the top and back pieces. Use one longer screw for strength.

10 Apply wood glue and screw the support strut into place. Secure it with one screw at each end before adding the others and finally tightening up.

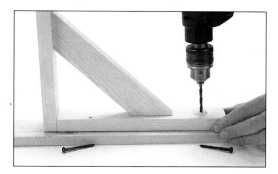

11 Drill holes in the back piece to take screws that will fix it to a wall. Make one of these below the strut (as here) and another to one side of the strut further up. This allows clearance for the screwdriver.

12 Fix each bracket securely to the wall using strong screws. Use wall plugs to stop the screws working loose in a masonry wall. Check with a spirit level to make sure the back piece of the bracket is truly vertical.

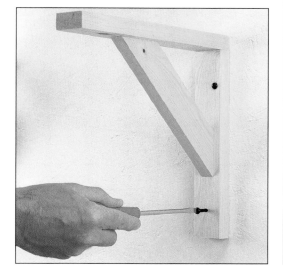

Positioning the windowbox

The best place for a windowbox is on the front of the house where the plants will be seen from the street. If this means that the box will be in shade, then the choice of plants is very limited. Most bedding plants need direct sun for at least half the day and some will relish even more.

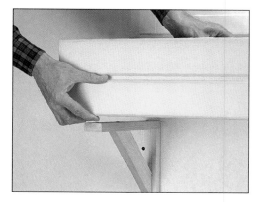

1 Two brackets are fine to support a windowbox 60cm(24in) long, as here. Fix the brackets to the wall first and then attach the box to them. Remember to treat the brackets with a suitable preservative paint or stain before fixing them to the wall.

2 This side view shows that for this window the box is supported well forward of the edge of the sill so that you can take out the inner plastic tray.

3 The windowbox in place beneath the window. Since a full windowbox can be very heavy, it is vital to attach the box securely to the brackets with screws. Drill holes in the arms of the brackets and screw through into the box.

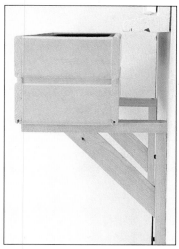

Fixing up a hanging basket bracket

1 Put the bracket against the wall and mark the position of the screw holes. Using a hammer-action drill and the correct sized masonry bit, drill the top hole in the wall.

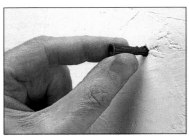

2 Push a wall plug into the hole, making sure that it fits tightly. It will prevent the screw working loose when the bracket is fixed.

3 Fix the top screw loosely so that you can check the position of the second hole. Make any necessary adjustments.

4 Drill and plug the second hole and screw the bracket firmly in place against the wall. Suitable round head screws that match the colour of the bracket are usually supplied in the pack.

Which way up?

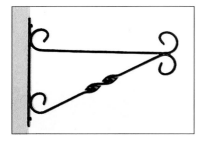

Above: This is the 'normal' way to attach a hanging basket bracket to the wall, with the angled support bar underneath the main strut.

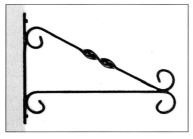

Above: With brackets that have loops curling both ways at the end, you can attach them to the wall with the angle support at the top.

HANGING UP BASKETS AND WALL PLANTERS

Hanging baskets are traditionally suspended by a doorway, a little above head height, where the shape and style of the display can be best appreciated. However, there are plenty of other options. Hang them from the end of pergola poles, from special, free-standing hanging basket support frames – which take several baskets at different heights – or suspend a collection of baskets from brackets to decorate a large plain wall. Wall planters are more often used in the latter situation, but being smaller they are better suited to more intimate spots, where they add fine detail rather than vivid colour. When buying baskets and fittings, choose brackets and containers that not only match in style and colour but scale. A basket too large for its bracket will look even more out of proportion when the container is filled with flowers, and the weight may be too much for a small bracket. Fix everything very securely, as any filled hanging basket places a considerable strain on the two screws that are all that are usually provided to hold it in place. When reusing existing brackets in subsequent years, always check them over thoroughly first; rust quickly weakens both screws and struts. Replace screws as necessary. After four or five years, many brackets will also need replacing to keep them safe.

Wall pots and planters

Containers that attach directly to a wall have one or two holes so that you can hang them on screws or nails protruding from the wall. On some, the moulding will hide the screw heads.

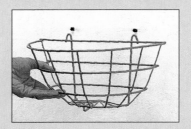

1 Offer the planter to the wall and mark the screw positions. Drill and plug the holes and then simply hang the basket over the screw heads.

2 With the planter in place, the fixing screws are hard to see. When the planter is overflowing with plants, they will disappear completely from view.

Matching brackets and baskets

Above: A small bracket supporting a large hanging basket can look out of proportion and restricts the space available to the plants at the back of the display near the wall.

Right: This large basket looks fine suspended from a suitably large bracket. The basket is in perfect proportion to the supporting bracket.

Above: A smaller hanging basket on the same size bracket not only looks better but allows plenty of room for the plants to spill over the sides when in full growth.

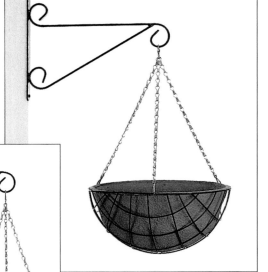

Left: The same large bracket makes a smaller hanging basket suspended from it seem puny and disappointing. However, a large plant arrangement would help to redress the balance.

Creating a three-tier hanging basket

Create a striking 'hanging garden', by joining two or three baskets together. Depending on the size of plants chosen to grow in them, the displays can be completely independent of each other, or look as though they are one big tiered arrangement, or each basket can merge with the one below to make a giant column of flowers. You can either plant the baskets then put the display together, or hang the baskets first and fill them later, whichever you find easiest.

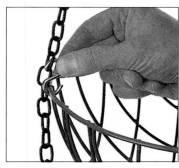

1 *Securely fix a strong support hook in place, here on a pergola. Attach three lengths of heavy-duty chain from the hook.*

2 *Attach each basket to the chains at three evenly spaced points around the edge, using strong metal 'S' hooks.*

3 *Use the largest basket at the bottom of the arrangement. Use three 'S' hooks to suspend the rim of the basket from the last links of the chains.*

4 *The bottom basket should have sufficient clearance from the ground to allow plants to trail over the edge and for the whole display to be seen well.*

A simple wooden 'hanger'

1 You can make a support that fits over the horizontal lathes of a trellis panel with two pieces of 50x25mm(2x1in) planed softwood and a piece of 25x25mm(1x1in).

3 The wooden hanger spreads the load over three trellis lathes and so provides a stable support for a hanging basket. It is simple to change its position.

2 Attach a hanging basket bracket to the support and simply hang it onto the trellis. The horizontal lathes are at the front here so the wooden 'hook' fits well.

Wall planters

This idea can be adapted as a horizontal support for a wall pot, with the 'hooks' turned through 90°. Place two screws in the main strut and hook the planter onto them. This technique works even with terracotta wall pots, which usually come with fixing holes predrilled in the back. Other wall pots are supplied with hooks, allowing them to be slung onto trellis or netting. Hang up plastic pots with wire fittings resembling a circle with two hooks. The pot fits snugly into the wire circle.

FIXING TO TRELLIS PANELS

Hanging baskets, wall planters and troughs fixed to balcony rails or fence tops are a great way of adding an extra dimension to the garden. 'Vertical gardening' is a specially valuable technique for making the most of the available space in a small plot. But it is vital to start with a practical consideration: how to hold raised containers safely in place. Some are fitted with hooks that slip over any straight edge on a narrow wall, fence-top or trellis. Otherwise make your own hangers, as shown here. It is not a good idea to screw containers directly to wooden fences; in time, water will penetrate the surface layer protected by timber treatment, and the wood will start to rot. The biggest advantage of hangers is that they enable you to create and rearrange vertical displays in an instant. Transform trellis 'garden dividers' into a sea of colour, or hang them on trellis or wire netting fixed to a shed wall, to turn a potential eyesore into an eye-catching feature. Add them to an existing background of climbing plants over a suitable framework, or turn patio screens into distinctive features. As always, check container fittings carefully each season, as rotting or weak mountings can be hazardous. And make sure they are adequate for the weight of container and plants they are to hold. Fittings should ideally match the container and its surroundings in style, but by clever use of climbing and trailing plants, more fittings can quickly be concealed by vegetation, so do not feel that your handiwork has to be of 'show' quality.

A hanging bracket

1 To make a trellis bracket that supports a windowbox from underneath, cut and assemble these pieces of planed softwood. Use non-rusting screws and waterproof woodworking adhesive for a strong and durable result.

The base piece is 75x25mm(3x1in) to provide a wider support.

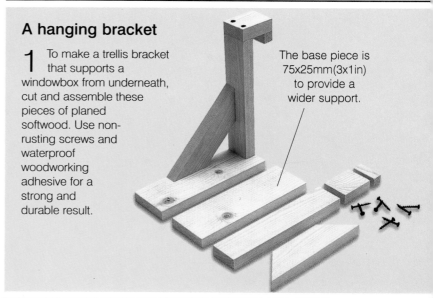

A classic bracket

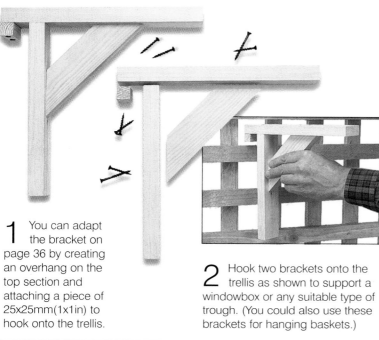

1 You can adapt the bracket on page 36 by creating an overhang on the top section and attaching a piece of 25x25mm(1x1in) to hook onto the trellis.

2 Hook two brackets onto the trellis as shown to support a windowbox or any suitable type of trough. (You could also use these brackets for hanging baskets.)

3 Two brackets hooked onto the trellis panel form a stable platform to support this wooden windowbox. For safety, screw through the brackets into the base of the box.

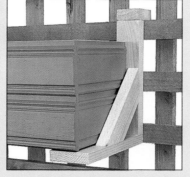

2 The brackets hook over the horizontal trellis bars. This is the lefthand bracket with the diagonal support offset to the left.

3 This is the righthand bracket with the windowbox in place. Move the box by unhooking each bracket and fixing them elsewhere.

Hanging containers on a balcony rail

A balcony rail seems an ideal place to hang planted containers, but making safe and attractive fixings needs more ingenuity. Some brackets are available in garden centres and you can improvise as shown here.

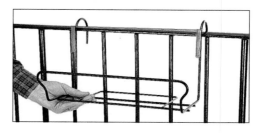

1 *This metal device is designed to hook over a balcony rail and support a trough. The base rests against the uprights and keeps it stable.*

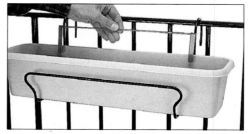

2 *Once the trough is in place, pull down the red restraining bar so that the metal 'tongues' fit inside the trough. This will prevent the container tipping forwards.*

Individual pot hangers

1 *This pot hanger simply hooks over the balcony rail and provides sturdy support for one planted container.*

2 *Find a pot that fits inside the metal framework and set it on the built-in saucer. Changing the display is quick and easy.*

Strap-hanging windowboxes

One way of attaching a windowbox to a balcony rail is to literally hang it from two straps that loop over the top. There are many possible materials you can use, including rope, but do make sure that they are strong enough to do the job. At any rate, hang this on the inside face.

This is hessian webbing sold for upholstery.

Renovating a wooden windowbox

Wooden windowboxes are bound to deteriorate after several years exposure to the weather. But a simple repaint can work wonders.

1 The wooden panels on this new windowbox look fresh, with warm tones in the grain that complement the pastel flowers.

2 After several years in the open, the same windowbox has lost its glow and looks dull and grey. The wood is undamaged but needs a face-lift to recreate its appeal.

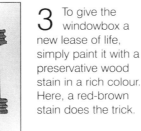

3 To give the windowbox a new lease of life, simply paint it with a preservative wood stain in a rich colour. Here, a red-brown stain does the trick.

RENOVATING AND ADAPTING CONTAINERS

All sorts of creative containers can be made from 'finds' in the garden shed or cupboards around the house. Suitable items can also be bought inexpensively from boot sales or secondhand shops. Anything that will hold potting mix will do, as long as it is big enough to take one or more plants. Old boots, fish kettles, coal scuttles, tin baths, buckets and casserole dishes have all been successfully given a new lease of life in the garden for growing plants. Do not be put off if the chosen container does not hold potting mix; just line it with black plastic before use. Old wicker baskets, cane picnic hampers and woven log baskets can all be treated in this way. (Black plastic or an old potting mix bag used with the black side outermost is ideal; pond liner makes a heavier duty finish.) Otherwise, simply stand plants still in their pots, inside the basket, instead of filling the container with potting mix and planting. It is not only plant containers that can be recycled in this way. All sorts of old furniture can be adapted as novel garden plant stands. Wooden washstands, chests and small cabinets can be stained and varnished, decorated with stencils or artificially aged using paint techniques to transform them into unusual 'objets trouvés'. A cabinet, painted and with plants on the top, is a useful place to keep small hand tools or barbecue equipment so that they are to hand when needed, but can be quickly stored between uses. A group of suitably redecorated old pieces of furniture makes a 'character' outdoor work area for potting plants, trimming potted topiary, etc., and – teamed with containers of plants in keeping with the style – could make a novel 'garden room' of its own.

Petunia

Fuchsia

Verbena

4 With two coats of wood stain, the windowbox looks like new and forms a perfect foil for the vivid shades of these bedding plants in their full summer glory. It will now last for many more years.

Preparing a wooden barrel as a planter

Wooden half barrels are not usually prepared for use as planters. Treat the timber and make drainage holes. Add a waterproof lining to prevent the wood from rotting as it will be in constant contact with damp soil.

1 Drill a hole at least 1.25cm (0.5in) in diameter in the base of the barrel. Alternatively, make a group of smaller holes around the edge of the base.

2 A drainage hole is essential, especially for plants left outdoors in winter. Otherwise, the potting mix in the barrel becomes waterlogged in wet weather.

3 Using a plant-friendly wood preservative, paint the barrel inside and out (including the base) and leave it to dry out completely for a few days.

4 Lay a large piece of black plastic over the top and push the middle down to form a loose lining. Push the centre 5cm(2in) out through the hole in the base.

5 Cut the tip off the plastic protruding through the hole in the base. This allows the excess water to drain away without wetting the wood and causing it to rot.

Painting wicker baskets

New or secondhand wicker baskets need treating to protect them from rotting when left outdoors in all weathers. Since their natural colour soon fades in the sun, stain or paint them first in natural or bright colours, depending on your chosen planting scheme. Line them before planting.

Above: *A wicker wastepaper basket can be transformed with a coat of coloured wood stain. Apply the paint carefully, making sure that you treat all the surfaces.*

Above: *Wicker baskets with loop handles are available in many styles and sizes. Suitably painted, they can make charming planters.*

Above: *Natural wood stains can enhance the tones of wicker as well as provide protection against rot from dampness in the garden.*

Right: *With two coats of pine varnish, this large wicker basket becomes an excellent container for tall plants such as grasses.*

Below: *With two coats of stain, the basket is ready for use as a planter, although it would still be advisable to line it with plastic.*

Below: *With its deep blue finish, this basket would be ideal as a feature in a country-style garden.*

43

1 Select two strong boxes that fit one inside the other, leaving a gap between them of 5cm(2in) all round. The outer box will be the depth of the finished container.

2 Cut a piece of board to fit exactly inside the base of the larger, outer box. Nail in four corks as shown; these will eventually form the drainage holes in the base of the container.

3 Cut a piece of small-mesh chicken wire to cover the inner box completely. Fold the corners to form a loose cage very slightly bigger than the inner box.

4 Slip the smaller box, with its reinforcing wire cover, into the larger box to check for fit. If the wire sticks out at all, bend it down more firmly until it slips in easily.

A HYPERTUFA CONTAINER

As an alternative to genuine old stone containers, you can make your own containers from a fake stone mixture called hypertufa. You can use it to cover an old ceramic sink, provided the shiny surface of the sink is first given a coating of outdoor-quality building adhesive. This gives it a rough surface to which the hypertufa can 'key in', otherwise the mixture just slides off. You can also make your own free-style containers from scratch using the mixture to cover a foundation made of scrunched up small-mesh chicken wire. Or you could try the cardboard box method, shown here, to make a 'stone' sink or trough. Hypertufa takes a long time to dry out, so make the container where you will not need to move it, or put it on top of a firm wooden base that you can lift without touching the sides of the container.

Hypertufa continues to dry for a time after the mould is removed. When it is completely dry it turns a pale grey colour very similar to stone. If you used coarse textured sand and peat in the mix, it will also have a craggy texture. The longer you leave hypertufa containers outside in the open air, the more weathered and stonelike they become. To speed up the aging process, spray the sides with diluted liquid houseplant feed. This encourages lichens and moss to gradually colonise them, creating the look of a genuine aged stone container. Hypertufa can transform an old container, such as a clay flowerpot, into a stone one, just by giving it a new outer finish.

5 To make hypertufa, mix equal parts by volume of cement, gritty sand and moss peat or peat substitute with enough water to produce a sloppy paste.

Cement powder

Peat or coir-based substitute

Coarse gritty sand

6 Remove the inner box and wire netting, and trowel enough of the hypertufa mix over the base to come to the top of the corks. Do not cover them or you will prevent them from becoming the drainage holes.

7 Fit the inner box and wire cover evenly into the outer box. Press down firmly, so that the wire sinks into the hypertufa. Fill the gap between the boxes with hypertufa.

8 Use a piece of wood to ram the mixture well down between the two boxes on each side of the mesh, so that there are no air pockets. These would turn out as holes in the sides of the container.

Do not worry if the sides of the outer box bow out slightly, it will only improve the final shape.

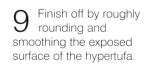

9 Finish off by roughly rounding and smoothing the exposed surface of the hypertufa.

Removing the container from the mould

Allow about six weeks for a large sink or trough made by the cardboard box method to set before you remove the boxes.

1 Remove the inner box by folding it inwards, then lifting out the base one end at a time. Work slowly and do not use force.

2 Carefully cut away the cardboard from the sides of the container. Peel off any loose paper shreds with your fingers.

3 To remove thin paper slivers, wet them and peel them off with a knife, or try wire-brushing. They will disappear eventually.

4 Turn the container over to lever away the cardboard base and the wooden board. The corks will be left in the hypertufa.

5 Drill through the corks to make the drainage holes in the base. This is much safer then trying to drill holes into the hypertufa, which could crumble and split.

6 The container has good drainage holes for its size – something genuine old sinks never have. When it is in its final position, raise it on two bricks to allow surplus water to drain away.

1 This plastic urn was offered at half price as a shop-soiled item. Scrubbing it with soapy water not only cleans off the grime but prepares the surface for painting.

2 The first coat to go on is red oxide primer – the paint sold for priming metal surfaces. It dries to a matt finish and provides an excellent 'key' for the next layers.

PAINTING A PLASTIC URN

Plastic containers are probably the cheapest you can buy, yet with care they can be made to look much more expensive. Choose a classic formal shape, such as an urn, cornucopia, or bowl. If the container is to go on a pedestal later, choose one that is correctly proportioned for its base. Use paint effects to create a fake stone or verdigris finish, but do this long before you intend planting the container, as it takes several coats to achieve the desired result and thorough drying between coats is essential. Give the shiny surface of a plastic container a rough finish before painting, using sandpaper or a wire brush, otherwise the paint will run off. When moving the container before planting, take care not to scratch the surface; any areas of white showing through quickly spoil the effect. Since plastic containers are very light, be sure to weight the base of the urn well down with gravel or crocks when starting to plant them up. These not only allow excess water to drain freely out of the bottom, but also prevent the container rocking in windy weather. For the same reason, avoid top-heavy planting schemes. If you use a plastic pedestal base, weight this down, too, to keep it safely upright. (This is easily done by filling it with stones or water.) Since the finish on a painted container is literally only skin deep, it is likely to need repainting every few years as chips damage the paintwork and spoil the illusion. However, you can take the opportunity to give them a new look at the same time, using a different colour scheme.

This colour forms the first dabbed-on layer.

This colour is used for the final highlights.

3 To build up the look of aged stone or verdigris, you will need three subtle shades of water-based matt emulsion paint.

This colour will form the base coat over the primer.

4 When the red oxide primer is dry, apply the first layer of emulsion paint. This drab grey-brown shade acts as an excellent solid background to the paler tones to be dabbed on later.

5 Use a short-bristled stencil brush to dab the dusky green paint onto the urn when the drab coat is dry. Immediately, you can see how effective this technique is.

6 Even at this stage, with only a two-tone colour scheme, the illusion of a stone urn covered with lichen or a metal urn gilded with verdigris is fairly convincing. You could leave it like this, if it suits your garden scheme.

7 To take the transformation a stage further, use the stencil brush to dab on some of the pale blue-green emulsion paint.

8 To protect the paint from the weather, apply a coat or two of acrylic varnish. It is milky as you put it on but dries clear.

9 When the varnish dries, the urn is ready to be planted up and exposed to the elements. Even at close quarters, it is easy to forget the white plastic urn underneath this stunning paint job.

Making a plinth from a plastic drum

An urn-shaped planting pot usually benefits from being raised on a plinth, which you can make yourself for almost nothing. If you visit your local garage, you should be able to obtain an empty plastic oil drum – one about 50cm(20in) tall is more than large enough for the purpose.

1 Drain the drum and wash the outside with detergent, keeping it upside-down. Apply one coat of blackboard paint, and a second coat an hour later.

A display of penstemons, nicotianas, petunias, verbenas and roses.

2 When dry, stand the drum in position and shorten it if needed, either by cutting off the surplus or digging it into the soil. Place a heavy stone urn on top.

3 Plant ivy close to the drum and fasten the tips down with modelling paste or small strips of strong tape. Pinch out regularly and clip when well grown.

'Luzii' is a compact ivy with mottled variegation.

1 Mix up a small quantity of white, yellow and dark green artist's acrylic paints, adding water until the mixture becomes quite thin and runny. Tilt the planter back slightly and apply the first coat.

PAINTING PLASTIC POTS WITH ACRYLIC PAINT

Nowadays, you can obtain a wide range of plastic terracotta-effect pots. These have the advantage of being unbreakable, frostproof and lightweight. Some are more realistic than others, but all have a rather raw, brand new look about them. Over a period of time, real terracotta weathers and takes on the patina of age. White salt deposits work through to the surface and in damp, shady conditions, a coating of green algae often appears. Using a variety of simple paint techniques, it is possible to mimic this transformation and achieve a realistic effect on plastic containers. Pots and planters with a high relief are the most convincing when painted, as the dark and light shading emphasises the contours. Acrylic paint, mixed and thinned with water, is an ideal medium for this technique as it remains wet and soluble for long enough to work on and allows you the opportunity to correct any mistakes you may make. It then dries to form a durable and waterproof plastic coating.

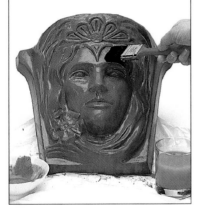

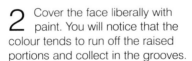

2 Cover the face liberally with paint. You will notice that the colour tends to run off the raised portions and collect in the grooves.

3 If the terracotta does not start to show through soon, use a clean, wet brush over the raised areas again, diluting the paint.

4 Use a piece of absorbent kitchen towel, scrunched up into a pad and dampened slightly, to dab off some of the paint from raised parts of the face. Do this in irregular patches.

5 Once the surface is dry, apply a second coat of acrylic paint. Adjust the mix if the first coat was too dark or light. In this case, extra white and yellow were added.

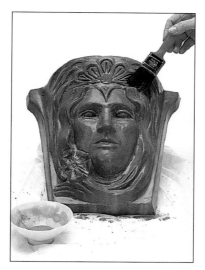

6 The paint runs down in streaks, as though weathered in damp conditions. Pigments separate out, adding to the illusion.

7 When dry, mix up some dark green paint and water. Using a damp natural sponge, work paint into the crevices of the face.

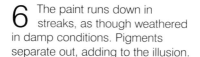

Create a sense of mystery in the garden by half hiding the face on a wall or fence covered in foliage.

8 When dry, plant up the head with flowers and foliage to enhance the weathered face. Soft, old-fashioned and 'neutral' colours work well in a container like this.

Practical tips for using acrylic paint

Artist's acrylic paints are very easy to use and widely available. You can buy them as tubes or little pots. The colour range is huge and includes vivid tones as well as muted shades.

Conveniently, acrylic paints are water-soluble and yet, once dried, they produce a waterproof finish.

You can achieve good results using acrylic paints on plastic containers, even if you have little or no artistic experience. Before working on a large piece, practise the techniques on an old plastic food or drink carton from the kitchen until you are happy with the results.

Before you start decorating a particular container, make sure you have sufficient supplies of the paints you will need.

Do not be afraid of mixing paints to get the required colour. Use a piece of clear plastic over a sheet of white paper as an economical 'painter's palette' that lets you see the colours clearly, but can then be thrown away after use – no washing up!

Buy good-quality paintbrushes if painting intricate decorations by hand. The bristles shed from cheap brushes and stick in the paint, spoiling the effect.

Acrylic paints are ideal for use with stencils, as we show on page 52-53. You can wash the paint off a stencil if you do it very soon after finishing with a particular colour. If you let the paint dry on a stencil, however, it will not blend with the next colour being used.

Given effective paint techniques like this, all sorts of plastic containers can be recycled. Look out for cheap plastic plant tubs

and planters, but also search out boot sales, secondhand shops and builder's yards for old plastic water butts or giant fruit juice containers that might be suitable.

Wide plastic drainpipes can be painted to resemble antique chimney pots and connecting corner pieces of plastic guttering can be made into attractive wall fittings. Be inventive!

Always wash plastic containers well before painting them. Any grease will prevent the paint from sticking properly, and result in flaking and peeling or blistering after a short time.

If the container surface is completely smooth, rub it down lightly with sandpaper to remove the gloss from the surface. This gives the new layers of paint something to key into.

You can get lots of ideas for 'fake' and decorative paint finishes from an interior decorator's book of paint effects.

Once they get chipped or you feel like a change of style, you can easily repaint over containers that have already been treated with acrylic paints. Simply rub the container over with sandpaper to remove any loose paint, wash it well with warm water and liquid detergent and allow it to dry. Then treat as before.

When you have finished painting, replace the caps on tubes and pots and wash the brushes in warm or cold running water straight away. If you leave them to dry, the bristles will stick together and you will find it virtually impossible to use the brush again. If you cannot wash them immediately, leave the brushes standing in plain water until you can clean them properly.

A 'terracotta' tub

At 38cm(15in) tall and wide, this heavy container deserves to form a focal point in the garden, but it looks so much better with a coat of paint that transforms it into an elegant Cretan-style 'terracotta' tub.

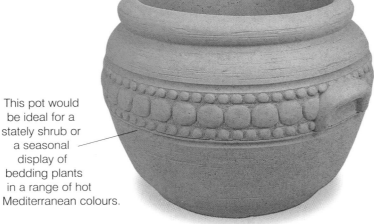

Left: This paint mimics the natural colour of terracotta and is specifically sold for painting on cement and concrete. Simply brush it on and it dries very quickly.

Below: The painted pot is transformed. Such a pot in real terracotta would be far more expensive than a cast cement one.

This pot would be ideal for a stately shrub or a seasonal display of bedding plants in a range of hot Mediterranean colours.

PAINTING A VARIETY OF CEMENT CONTAINERS

Is is easy to overcome the grey drabness of cement and concrete containers, simply by painting them! You can buy paints specially formulated for use on concrete surfaces or you can use those sold for masonry and house exteriors. The latter are also available with added grit to produce a textured finish, which may suit some containers. Follow the manufacturer's instructions when using these paints – some require protective gloves, for example.

The range of colours available is very wide, although generally speaking the more natural 'earth' shades will suit containers better than some of the 'sweeter' hues destined to adorn a country cottage or a seaside home. Using single colours can transform the appearance of cement and concrete containers, especially shades that produce a finish impressively similar to natural terracotta. Even simple white can give an intricate concrete casting a convincing 'alabaster' look. For a more adventurous approach, try several colours on one container. This works well on pots with repeated elements in their design. You can also buy verdigris and gilding paints that add touches of natural age and elegance to appropriate style containers.

Exposed to the weather, the paints may peel after several years outdoors. Since the pots are unlikely to suffer from frost damage, it is worth rubbing down the surface and painting them again, perhaps in a new colour!

A small pot of many colours

This small cement pot with a repeating leaf motif lends itself well to painting in different colours or shades of the same colour. Clearly, you will need a small brush and a steady hand.

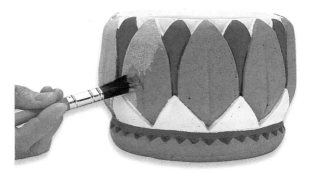

Left: Two shades of terracotta against a background of white create a striking pattern on this pot.

Above: Changing the colours alters the 'mood' of the pot, inviting plants in muted shades of green and yellow.

Left: Gazanias with orange flowers and stark silver-grey foliage are set off brilliantly by the pattern on the pot.

A stylish wall planter

An ornate wall planter becomes even more stylish when painted and gilded. It takes on a sophisticated appearance that belies its humble origins as cast cement.

1 An overall coat of lovat green exterior wall paint immediately softens the harsh rawness of the cast concrete. You can choose from a huge range of pastel tones.

Make sure that your paint reaches into all the crevices.

2 Lightly brushing with gold paint emphasises the intricate detail of this wall planter. Filled with suitable plants, this planter would grace the walls of a stylish conservatory.

The patterns on the cement casting are ideal for picking out in gilding.

The pure simplicity of white

A coat of white masonry paint can transform a cement container. It is particularly effective on elegant castings such as this. The finished result not only looks refreshingly stylish, but its restrained colour also acts a superb foil for an infinitely wide range of colourful plants.

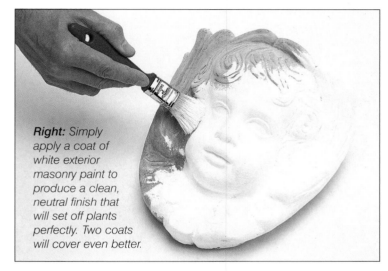

Right: Simply apply a coat of white exterior masonry paint to produce a clean, neutral finish that will set off plants perfectly. Two coats will cover even better.

Creating an 'oriental' pot

This hexagonal cast cement pot is an ideal candidate for the oriental look. With a dark base layer and gold highlights, it gives a convincing appearance of a heavy metal pot. The finished pot would be an ideal container for displaying a dwarf bamboo or conifer.

1 Apply a base layer of black paint, making sure that you cover all the fine details of the casting. This paint is formulated for use on cement surfaces.

2 Using a stipple brush, add touches of gold-coloured pigment to mimic the highlights on a bronze or cast-iron container. The effect is impressive.

PAINTING TERRACOTTA

Decorative paint effects, such as stencils, have been fashionable indoors for some time. Now they are moving outdoors; painted flowerpots are the latest patio accessories. But there is no need to spend a fortune because you can paint your own. It's fun, quick and easy – even for non-artists. Use stencils, handpainted patterns or colour washes to transform plain terracotta pots. Be as traditional or as outrageously creative as you like. Use these techniques to make new pots look much more expensive than they really are, or to give old pots a new look. You can also make raw new terracotta pots look weathered by dabbing shades of green, grey and yellow onto a colour-washed pot with a sponge, to simulate moss and lichen growth. After painting, add a coat of varnish to make the colours weatherproof. But since repainting is so simple, why not just repaint them every year or two? Clean the pots well first and remove loose or flaky paint, then cover with a light colour wash (use two coats if needed to cover the old pattern) and redecorate when completely dry. This is a nice winter job that you can do indoors when there is no growing to do.

Using colourisers with masonry paint

To create new and richer shades, add concentrated colouriser pigments to the basic colours as shown here.

1 Shake the bottle well and add a few drops of the pigment to a small amount of masonry paint in a saucer.

2 Stir the pigment into the base paint until you create the desired shade. Add more pigment or paint as necessary.

3 Use a stencil brush to dab a sample of the mixed colour onto the saucer to show how it will look on the final pot.

Stencilling with masonry paint

Masonry paint is ideal for decorating terracotta pots. Since this paint is designed to protect brickwork and house walls, it will form a weatherproof finish. The only drawback is that the colours are usually in the pastel range, but you can create new, brighter shades by adding colourisers.

1 Attach the stencil securely to the pot with tape and apply the first colour by dabbing carefully with a stubby bristled stencil brush.

2 The first colour dries quickly and then you can add the second one. Make this by adding blue colouriser to basic white paint.

3 To create a contrasting central ring in each flower, simply dab in some white paint. Ensure that the stencil does not move.

4 The final touch in this floral decoration is to add a yellow blob that reflects the pollen-bearing stamens of a real flower.

This terracotta pot has a rough-textured finish that is ideal for masonry paints.

5 When all the colours have dried, peel off the stencil to reveal the finished pattern. Wash the stencil before using it again.

Stencilling with acrylic paints

Acrylics are water-soluble paints that dry rapidly to produce a water-resistant plastic finish. Some types are more suitable for outdoor use than others, but all can be coated with an acrylic varnish to improve their weather resistance. They are easy to use and come in a range of colours.

1 To brighten up this standard clay pot, use a solid colour acrylic paint to coat the rim as a background for a stencilled pattern.

2 This 'wheat ear' stencil will make an interesting border around the top of the pot. Offer it up to ensure it will fit the space.

3 Tape the flexible plastic stencil securely to the rim and apply the yellow acrylic paint carefully with a suitable short-bristled brush.

4 Leave the stencil in place until the paint is dry – about 20 minutes should be fine – and then peel it off to reveal the pattern.

6 The finished design adds interest to a simple container. You may need to coat the rim with a waterproof varnish to protect it.

5 To create a border around the rim of the pot, simply repeat the process. Clean and reverse the stencil for a more interesting effect.

Using coloured washes on pots

Terracotta can look raw and orange when new. You can 'age' the surface quickly using a dilute colour wash of artist's acrylic. As the water is absorbed into the terracotta, an uneven and natural-looking covering of white pigment remains. This is how to create a pink finish.

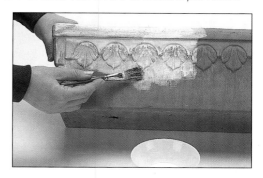

1 *Using diluted white artist's acrylic paint, roughly apply a wash to the surface of the dry terracotta container. The uneven coverage or drips are all part of the distressed look. Blot off the excess paint.*

2 *Mix your colours together, here ultramarine and crimson, with some more white paint. Apply in downward strokes to create darker and lighter 'weathered' streaks. Apply the darker colours cautiously.*

3 *The painted trough comes to life when planted up. Here ivy and pale pink impatiens echo the colour tones of the surface. These plants are ideal for shade.*

Handpainting pots

Right: *If you have a steady hand and an artistic eye, why not try painting directly onto your pots to create informal patterns?*

Simple handpainted patterns can give plain pots a refreshing style.

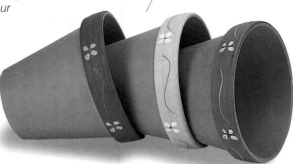

IMAGINATIVE CONTAINERS

Given a bit of imagination, you can find all sorts of unusual containers to add character to plant displays. Old kitchen pots and bowls, fish kettles, garden trugs, household baskets and old tin baths all qualify for the job. As a general rule, the more elaborate or ornate the container, the plainer the plants should be. But like any rule, you can have fun breaking it. This becomes easier to do if you are prepared to experiment with lots of different combinations of plants and containers and learn from your mistakes while you gain experience. The secret lies in finding unusual containers in the first place. They might be ordinary containers given a fresh new look by paint effects, stencils or other decorations. Or things that were never intended to hold plants, that have been given a new lease of life. Do not worry if they do not hold water – stand plants in them still in their pots or line containers with thick black plastic. And solid-based containers like buckets need drainage holes made in them anyway. Finding the right plants to complement unusual containers also takes some doing. Some containers suit strong shapes, bright colours or particular plant personalities. Others just need something very simple to bring out the colour or accentuate the shape. More so than with any other kinds of container, the only way to see what will 'work' is to place the containers and plants together.

Above: Empty clay flowerpots make a novel textured 'floor' surface between large decorative planters. To make more of the pattern they create, gazanias have been planted at regular intervals.

Left: This ordinary clay pot has been decorated with stencils; the reason it looks so good is that the green of the stencil picks out exactly the same shade in the leaves of the nicotiana growing in it.

Right: An old wicker wastepaper basket, given a new paint job, now makes a good temporary home for a flowering hydrangea. Inside, the plant is still in its pot, and will be planted in the garden after the flowers are over.

Boots, barrows and baths

Anything that will hold enough soil for a plant to grow in can become a container – however bizarre. Old cupboards and sheds often yield 'finds', and friends moving house often evict large quantities of useful junk – otherwise hunt in secondhand shops or car boot sales.

Left: *Old gardening boots look good planted up and arranged casually on a step by the back door, but be sure to choose plants that are tolerant of dry conditions, as small containers like this dry out very quickly.*

Right: *A wooden wheelbarrow is a favourite 'character' container, but here it has been planted to look as if the contents were just being trundled out from the greenhouse.*

Below: *An old cast-iron bath can be used in dozens of ways – filled with water plants or, as here, with other 'props' and a screen of annual climbers.*

Above: This decorated container is actually a huge vase, housing an outdoor flower arrangement of classic country garden flowers – an unusual technique but well worth considering for a special occasion.

Right: A conical wall planter does not give much room for plant roots to grow, so restrict yourself to reasonably drought-tolerant plants such as felicia and brachyscome – and water them often.

Argyranthemums and petunias provide an elegant and colourful display.

PART THREE

GARDENING IN CONTAINERS

Container gardening is an intriguing blend of art and science. As well as artistic pairings of plants and pots, the right potting mixes and soil additives, growing techniques, plant food and watering secrets all play their part in creating traffic-stopping container garden displays that keep on looking their best all season long.

POTTING MIXES

Some potting mixes are designed for specific purposes, such as ericaceous ones for lime-hating plants. Others make life easy for people who only grow a few plants, and therefore only want to buy a single bag of something to plant up a hanging basket, for instance, instead of mixing several products together. The most useful mix is a multipurpose one, suitable for virtually everything except lime-hating plants. These are usually peat-based, although alternatives based on coir are available. Soil-based mixes are ideal for plants that will be left in the same pot for several years. This is because soil holds nutrients, especially trace elements, better than peat and does not decompose in the pot as peat does, hence the mix retains its porous structure for longer. All mixes contain some plant foods, but once used up, you need to start liquid feeding regularly to replace them.

General multipurpose mix

This is the most generally useful mix, as it can be used for both propagation and potting. However, if you use a multipurpose mix for repotting established plants, be sure to start liquid feeding soon.

Has a low level of nutrients – seeds, cuttings and young plants are sensitive to strong fertilisers.

Soil-based potting mix

Use soil-based mixes for plants that are to stay in the same pot for several years. Seed formula can be used for propagation and young plants; use stronger mixes for bigger pots and those outdoors.

Several 'strengths' available depending on the amount of plant food in each.

Bulb fibre

This is formulated for growing bulbs in bowls without drainage holes (as often used indoors). If you want to re-use bulbs, pick one containing nutrients, or the bulbs will not replenish themselves ready for flowering the following year. Alternatively, use a normal mix and choose containers with holes in the bottom.

Perlite may be included to create an open texture and also charcoal to keep the mix 'sweet'. Some brands contain nutrients.

Ericaceous potting mix

Suitable for lime-hating plants, such as rhododendrons. Repot plants every 2-3 years and liquid feed regularly using a product containing trace elements, since peat does not retain nutrients well.

Peat-based mix which, unlike normal potting mixes, has not had the natural acid in the peat neutralised with lime.

Hanging basket mix

Peat-based mixes specially formulated for container growing. Ideal for anyone with only a few containers. Alternatively, buy both 'additives' separately and add them to your usual potting mix.

Most brands contain slow-release fertilisers and many also have water-retaining gel crystals to prevent containers drying out fast.

Aquatic plant mix

The heavy and viscous nature of this mix prevents it floating out of the pots when immersed in water. Alternatively, use a high-clay garden soil from an area where no fertiliser has been used.

A mixture of sterilised soils with the addition of a suitable slow-acting aquatic plant feed.

Cacti and succulent mix

These plants are slow growing and need a free-draining mix like this to prevent them being waterlogged and growing lush and out of character, which could happen with normal potting mixes.

Loam, peat and sand mixtures with added grit or expanded clay granules to provide extra drainage.

Tree and shrub mix

This is really intended for planting shrubs, etc., in the ground, but you can use it alone or added to other mixes when growing shrubs (including fuchsias) in containers. Do not use it for young plants.

Contains coarse peat, which is slower than usual to break down in the soil.

Worm compost

Rich organic matter that has been worked by worms and is basically crumbled worm casts. Add at 10% by volume to improve seed and potting mixes or to topdress plants that remain in pots for years.

Contains nutrients, including trace elements. Suitable for organic gardeners.

Growing bag mix

For growing plants – particularly tomatoes and other edible crops – directly in the bag, usually without drainage holes, as a means of avoiding soilborne root diseases. Also good for growing vegetables on a hard surface where there is no soil.

Specially formulated peat-based mix.

Reconstituting a coir brick

The most popular environment-friendly alternative to peat is coir – the shredded and composted outer husk of coconuts. It is often transported as compressed 'bricks' to save shipping costs. Ready-made coir mixes are also available. It holds less water than peat so needs more frequent watering; use special coir liquid feeds.

1 *Place the compressed coir brick in a large container and add tepid water according to the instructions; it will vary according to the size of the brick.*

2 *Leave the brick to soak until all the water has been absorbed and it has swollen up and become soft and crumbly. This may take several hours.*

3 *Break the brick up roughly into pieces, then crumble them between your fingers until all the lumps disappear, leaving fine fibrous material.*

4 *Add more water – see the supplier's notes for quantity. Leave for a few hours until the fluid is absorbed and the fibre expands to its maximum volume.*

5 *When fully reconstituted, each coir brick makes roughly five times its own volume of fibre. Use this to add to sterilised loam, sand and base fertiliser to make your own homemade potting mixtures.*

MIXERS AND MULCHES

Barks, gravels, grits and expanded minerals are used mainly as decorative topdressings, for improving potting mixes, or for plunging pots into to stop them drying out too quickly. All store well, though like any garden products are best kept in the original plastic sacks with the tops rolled down to prevent weed seeds, insects or other organisms getting in. (You can seal the tops with clothes pegs.) If kept in a dark dry place, which prevents algae and moss growing in them, most can be kept for years without harm, so you have them to hand when you need them. When choosing topdressings to give a good finish to pots of plants, consider the type of plant as well as the nature of the container, so that the topdressing 'links' the two visually together. Bark chippings, for example, look best in wooden tubs round rhododendrons and similar plants. Granite chippings, coloured grit, tufa fragments, slate shards and marble nuggets are also very useful to complete a really special container planting scheme.

Ground and composted bark
Use as an alternative to peat for digging into the ground as a soil improver, or add to sterilised loam instead of peat or coir in homemade potting mixtures – especially for large containers.

Has a fine texture similar to peat.

Perlite
Use it to aerate potting mixtures. Larger particle sizes are also available for orchid potting mixes or as an alternative to sand in capillary benches in greenhouses.

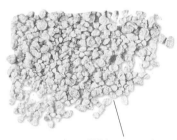

White granules of expanded volcanic mineral with a porous structure.

Gravel
Use coarse gravel in the base of large containers for stability. Gives sharp drainage for alpines and cacti. Add to potting mixes for fruit trees for drainage and weight.

Available in various particle sizes from coarse to fine. Wash thoroughly before use.

Large bark chips
Ideal as a topdressing for plants such as rhododendrons and other woodland subjects in containers (left). In summer, use it to insulate roots from overheating.

Chipped bark from conifer trees; a byproduct of the wood industry.

Cocoa shells
Use like bark chippings to protect plants in containers. Cocoa shell decomposes much faster than bark, but appears to repel both cats and snails – a useful benefit.

Discarded outer shells of cocoa beans. Smell strongly of chocolate at first.

Expanded clay granules
Add to potting mixes for fruit trees, alpines or cacti instead of, or as well as, coarse grit. Can be used instead of perlite in orchid mixes, and in capillary benches and trays.

Baked clay granules. Porous nature opens up the texture of potting mixes, improving aeration and drainage.

Topdressing grit
Adds a decorative finish and improves surface drainage for plants such as alpines and cacti that are liable to rot off at the collar if this part of the plant is in contact with damp potting mix.

A coarse grade of grit available in various shades.

A potted rock garden

Grits and gravels are useful for plants that need good drainage, such as alpines. By using them in containers, you not only create good growing conditions, but also help prevent neck rot by raising plants off damp soil and provide the plants with a natural-looking background.

1 This terracotta pot needs a crock to cover the drainage hole. You will also need some soil-based potting mixture, potting grit and coarse gravel.

2 Put about 2.5cm(1in) of gravel over the crock to prevent soil washing out when you water. It also provides the sharp drainage rock plants need.

Potting grit
Add to potting mixes, especially soil-based kinds and for plants that need better than usual drainage. Also provides extra weight so that top-heavy plants are more stable in outdoor containers.

Vermiculite
Use on its own to root cuttings or sow seeds, but remember that plants need feeding as soon as they grow roots. Also excellent for adding to seed mixes (at 20% by volume) to improve their structure.

A special grade of grit made from expanded inert, lime-free flint particles.

An expanded silica-based mineral with a unique structure that retains moisture and yet aerates potting mixes.

3 Almost fill the container with soil. Add some potting grit and mix the two together. Use 1 part of grit by volume to 6 parts of soil-based potting mix for the rock plants in this display.

You could add a few larger pebbles to the surface for decoration.

Add a topdressing of gravel to finish off the display.

Gritty sand
Can be used instead of potting grit, or to make sand beds for plunging pots to keep them moist. Much used in cold frames for plants in small pots such as auriculas, or on benches in alpine houses for potted rock plants. Do not use sea or building sand.

Sand and fine grit. Use horticultural grade, free from salt and excessive amounts of lime.

4 A well-filled container looks fairly mature straightaway. Deadhead regularly and never allow the soil to be too wet or bone dry; both stress the plants.

Water-retaining gel crystals

Water-retaining gel crystals are a useful way of keeping the potting mix in containers moist for longer. The crystals absorb water, turning into large rubbery lumps that slowly release their stored water back into the mix.

1 Mix the dry crystals with water and stir thoroughly to make a thick gel. Follow the maker's notes on the quantity of water required.

2 As they absorb water, the crystals swell up to many times their original size. When the gel is fully expanded, add it to your potting mix in a suitable tray.

3 Once the gel is combined with your potting mix, simply use it in the normal way. Mix with added gel is ideal for hanging baskets, which are prone to drying out rapidly. The gel lasts the whole season.

WATERING TECHNIQUES

The secret of successful containers lies in regular watering. Check containers daily by testing them with a fingertip or a water meter, and water whenever the potting mix starts to dry out. Keep it as evenly moist as possible for optimum growth. If plants are constantly drying out badly, they will be less able to grow and flower well. In a hot summer, well-filled containers in full bloom may need watering twice a day. Morning and evenings are the best time to water; during the middle of the day water simply evaporates before plants can take it up. Use a watering can or slow-running hosepipe to water. Hanging baskets pose the biggest problems. Being high up, you cannot always reach them easily to water. When you do, they drip all over you and if the mix dries out badly, the water just bounces off the surface without soaking in. Fortunately, there are various products and devices to help if you cannot find the time for regular watering. Try self-watering containers, or add water-retaining gel crystals to the potting mix before planting containers. If you have several awkward baskets to water, it might be worth investing in a long-handled attachment for your hosepipe, or a device for raising and lowering your baskets – you need one for each basket. You can also get watering extensions for pressure sprayers, which are ideal for watering hanging baskets out of reach of hosepipes.

Self-watering containers

Self-watering containers, such as the trough and wall planter shown here, have a reservoir in the base. These containers can keep plants watered for a week or more before the reservoir needs refilling, even in summer.

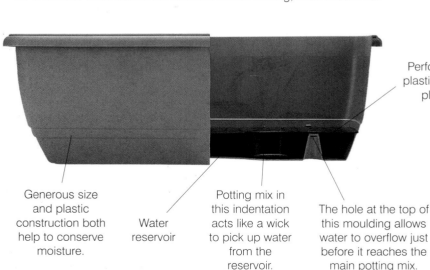

Generous size and plastic construction both help to conserve moisture.

Water reservoir

Potting mix in this indentation acts like a wick to pick up water from the reservoir.

The hole at the top of this moulding allows water to overflow just before it reaches the main potting mix.

Perforated plastic base plate

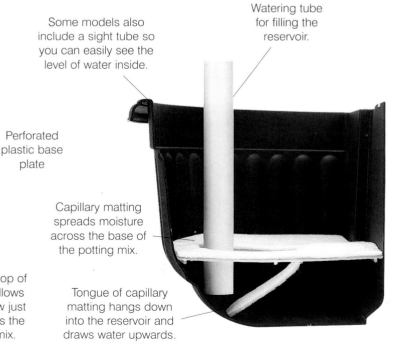

Some models also include a sight tube so you can easily see the level of water inside.

Watering tube for filling the reservoir.

Capillary matting spreads moisture across the base of the potting mix.

Tongue of capillary matting hangs down into the reservoir and draws water upwards.

Watering dried-out potting mix

Potting mix that has dried out can be difficult to rewet, since it shrinks, allowing water to trickle down the sides of the pot instead of being absorbed. This is particularly true of peat-based mixes, which shrink most.

1 When potting mix dries out it forms a hard crust that does not absorb water easily. Water forms into large droplets and runs away across the surface.

2 A drop of liquid detergent breaks up the surface tension, preventing water making large droplets – instead, it stays where it is applied and soaks in.

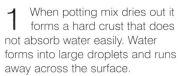

3 Once slightly damp, the potting mix readily absorbs more water. Avoid repeating the treatment too often, as the plants will not like too much soap.

Soaking a dried-out hanging basket

1 If your dried-out container is small and portable, such as a hanging basket, another way of rewetting the potting mix is to start by adding a drop of liquid detergent to a sink or bowl of water.

2 Plunge the dry basket into the water and leave it until the potting mix is completely saturated. Allow it to drain and then stand it in a sheltered, shady place until the plants fully recover.

Reaching high baskets

1 *Easy-to-use pulley systems clip onto the bracket and give access to baskets for feeding, watering and maintenance.*

2 *Reach up to the base of the basket and pull it down. Nudge the basket up to release the lock and push it back up.*

Left: Long-handled attachments that fit onto a hosepipe for watering hanging baskets have an on/off switch on the handle, so you only need to squirt once the nozzle is in position. They are invaluable if you have a lot of high baskets.

Right: An empty plastic bottle is also a useful aid to watering, especially if you just have one or two baskets. It is much lighter than a full watering can and is therefore ideal for overhead watering.

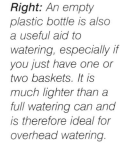

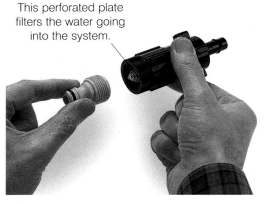

This perforated plate filters the water going into the system.

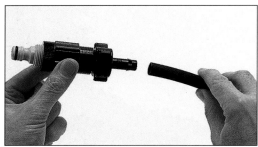

1 The first part of the system is a regulator that reduces the pressure of your mains water supply to a constant low level. You can screw this directly onto a threaded tap or attach an adaptor that plugs into a hose connector.

2 Attach a length of tubing to the outflow pipe of the pressure regulator. In this system, the supply tubing is 13mm(0.5in) in diameter.

3 If you want to run your watering system from a standard hosepipe, first fit a hose end connector and plug in the pressure regulator. Do not turn the water on until the system is complete.

AN IRRIGATION SYSTEM

The most efficient way to take care of watering if you are too busy to do the job daily by hand is to install an irrigation system. For plants in containers, the best strategy is to give each pot an individual watering nozzle connected by small bore tubing to a normal hosepipe. To water, you simply connect the hose to an outdoor tap and switch on. It is a good idea to have one nozzle hanging in an empty glass jar to monitor the amount of water being applied, so you know when to switch off. Although this is much quicker than watering each plant individually, you still have to turn the tap on and off – and it is easy to forget, resulting in a flooded garden. You can add a timing device, or 'water computer', that fits onto the tap and can be set to turn the water on for a period each day and then switch it off. This is ideal when you are away for the weekend, or if you work long hours and are unable to water daily yourself. The cost of a timing device is not great, compared to the cost of the rest of the installation, and the extra expense is justified. You do not need to bother neighbours to take care of plants for you, nor is it obvious to potential intruders that you are away from home, because the system stays in place through the spring, summer and fall. Since the pipes may deteriorate if frozen, especially when water is still inside them, it is advisable to remove irrigation systems in winter, unless the pipework is intended for year round use and is buried under the soil or a surface mulch. Check and flush out irrigation systems regularly, as the nozzles can clog up; you may not discover this until too late, when a plant dries up and dies.

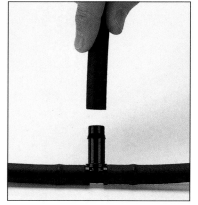

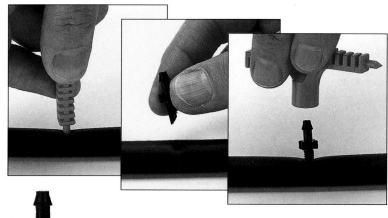

4 You can control the flow of water to various parts of your system by fitting these taps. Simply cut the supply tube and push the ends over the flanges on the tap.

5 To create a 'branch' line in the supply tubing system, fit a T-connector as shown here. Use elbow connectors to turn corners and straight ones to make joins.

6 To connect lengths of smaller diameter tubing to the system, punch a hole in the supply tube with the plastic tool, insert a narrow tube adaptor and screw it in with the socket part of the tool. Fully screwed in, the adaptor creates a watertight seal with the supply tube.

7 Push the end of the narrow tube – in this system 4mm(0.17in) in diameter – onto the adaptor in the supply tube. For the system to work efficiently, make sure these 'micro' tubes are no longer than 1m(39in).

Capillary matting

Any material with tiny pores will soak up water through capillary action, as happens with a sponge. You can turn this characteristic to your advantage by using capillary matting to deliver water to your plants.

Right: *It is easy to set up a capillary watering system in a greenhouse. Lay the matting on the staging and overlap the edge into a length of plastic guttering. Keep this filled with water and the plants will thrive.*

8 You can plug various drippers, sprinklers and spray nozzles into the micro tube. The flow from this dripper can be adjusted by rotating the cap. Used inverted, it is ideal for hanging baskets.

Left: *You can use a strip of capillary matting to keep a single container, such as a hanging basket, watered while you are away from home. Soak the strip and place one end in the basket and the other end in a large pot of water.*

9 This fixed-output dripper is a good way of providing slow and steady irrigation for containers and growing bags. Support the micro tube on a plastic stake to allow the drips to fall.

Creating a humidity tray

Below: *Plants in the home flourish in a humid microclimate. To create this around single plants, fill a large saucer with clay pebbles and add water to just below the top of the pebbles. Put the plant on top and water will evaporate around it.*

10 Once you have set up your system, flush water through it and then close off the supply tubes with these end sleeves.

11 Push the tube through, fold it over and pull it back to trap the folded end in the sleeve. To remove, simply reverse the steps.

Slow-release feeding pellets

If you do not have the time or are apt to forget regular liquid feeding, use slow-release feeding pellets. Insert these into the potting mix at planting time. They last the whole season, releasing feed when plants are watered. The amount varies according to the temperature.

Below: When plants are watered by capillary matting or drip irrigation, it is easy to overlook feeding. Add slow release fertilisers to the potting mix before planting.

Above: Slow-release fertilisers are available as tablets and pellets. Add them to the potting mixture as directed by the manufacturer.

Soluble feeds

Dilute soluble feeds in water following the directions (do not exceed the recommended strength), and use the solution as you would a liquid feed.

Right: Keep powdered feeds in a closed container, as they take up moisture from the air. To keep feeding simple, find a good general-purpose product and use it for everything.

Below: Liquid feeds allow you to feed more often when plants are growing faster. Tomato feed (shown here) is useful for all fruiting and flowering plants.

FEEDING METHODS

When plants grow naturally in the open ground, their roots are free to spread out in all directions, covering a wide area in search of everything they need. But when confined in a container, the roots are constricted, so the plant is totally dependent on what is provided for it. Plants need three main nutrients: nitrogen, phosphate and potassium in the largest quantities (the N, P and K on plant feed labels). Several other minerals are needed in moderate amounts, including iron and magnesium (which are vital components of chlorophyll), and dozens of trace elements, which are only needed in minute quantities, such as molybdenum, boron and copper. A good brand of potting mixture will provide everything a plant needs, but after a time all the available nutrients will be used up. From then on, regular liquid feeding is needed. This restores nutrients to optimum levels, essential for the plant to grow and flower or fruit well. But even regular liquid feeding is not enough to keep the balance of trace elements in the soil exactly right, and potting mixtures lose their open texture in time. So plants that are grown in the same pots for a long time need completely fresh potting mix every few years. Either repot them into a pot one size larger or put them back into new mix in the same container after shaking off the old mix.

When to start feeding

The length of time that can elapse before you need to start feeding newly potted plants varies with different brands of potting mix, so check the maker's directions. Generally speaking, soil-based mixtures 'hold' more nutrients than peat-based types, so you do not need to start feeding so soon after potting. The rate at which plants 'consume' nutrients varies with the rate of growth. In warm weather, when plenty of water and fresh air are available, plants are growing at their fastest and need more nutrients to maintain the production of new cells. As conditions get colder, the rate of growth drops and plants need less feed. This is why you should feed mostly during the growing season. In winter, plants are barely 'ticking over'; too much feed then can trigger them to produce lush soft growth easily killed by frost.

Above: You can spray foliar feeds directly onto the leaves.

Feeding ericaceous plants

Acid-loving plants need iron and other nutrients, which are chemically locked up by lime in the soil. If lime is present, leaves turn yellow due to iron deficiency. Feed container plants regularly.

Soluble feed for acid-loving plants. Dissolve in water and use regularly in the growing season.

Granular sequestered iron supplies iron in a fast-acting, easily assimilated form. There is also a liquid form that needs diluting.

Solid ericaceous fertiliser. Scatter it around plants and water in. Use each year in spring and to improve soil before planting.

Right: The foliage of this pieris is turning yellow (chlorosis) due to lack of iron, locked up by lime in the potting mix. It will recover with a 'tonic' of sequestered iron. Use ericaceous mix for best results.

Feed for water plants

Water plants take most of their nutrients from the water around them, but you can also add feeds specially designed for water plants. Do not use ordinary plant feeds, etc., otherwise they will make the water go green.

Fertiliser in small bags

Powdered fertiliser

Feeding deficiencies

If underfed, plants can suffer poor growth, few blooms or pale leaves. However, it is rare for the lack of one nutrient to be responsible. Feeding little and often with a feed that contains the main nutrients N, P and K plus minor nutrients and trace elements is the way to avoid deficiencies.

Left: *Towards the end of the growing season, tomato plants may show signs of magnesium deficiency, usually caused by high-potash (potassium) feeds.*

Below: *Yellowing leaves, as on this fuchsia, are often linked to a lack of feed. Give plants a general balanced feed with a variety of trace elements.*

Above: *The red leaf edge is a sign of phosphate deficiency.*

Left: *The likeliest cause of leaves browning around the edge is shortage of water. If you are sure this is not the case, it may be due to lack of potassium. Liquid tomato feed is rich in this nutrient and ideal for all flowering and fruiting plants as well as tomatoes.*

LINING HANGING BASKETS

Wire-framed hanging baskets need to be lined before they will hold potting mixture and plants. When choosing a liner, think about practicalities as well as looks. Moss and moss substitutes look prettiest, but they dry out quickly and are difficult to rewet. Thick synthetic basket liners provide good insulation, useful for protecting the roots of winter displays from freezing. For summer baskets, a liner that retains moisture better than moss is a great asset. Various absorbent liners are available, or you could use capillary matting or woollen fabrics that act as an extra moisture reserve. For the best of both worlds, line a basket first with black plastic, then add an inner water-retaining lining of, for instance, capillary matting. Rigid pre-formed liners effectively turn a wire basket into a solid one, which can only be planted through the top, not through the sides as well, so will never make such a spectacular display, although they are easier to look after. Flexible liners allow planting through the sides. Cutting slits in thin materials, such as black plastic, means you can push plants through the holes; tougher liners such as those of coir or 'whalehide' are made of overlapping flanges so they can be fitted into the shape of the basket.

Right: A thick layer of this green-dyed natural coconut fibre has good insulating qualities that help to keep the potting mix inside it at a more even temperature, by day and night.

Left: Many of the liners used for hanging baskets are made of recycled or waste materials, such as this coir matting, a byproduct of the coconut industry. Push plant roots through the slits between the panels.

Left: Fibre liners are made from recycled paper. They soak up water, which helps to keep the potting mix moist, and are less porous than moss. The disadvantage of rigid liners is that you cannot plant through the sides and base.

Above: Baskets lined with a flexible foam liner do not dry out or drip as much as mossed ones. Press the liner down and overlap adjacent panels for a good fit. Place a circle of plastic in the base to prevent water dripping straight out through the bottom.

Below: This flexible material, made of fibre tufts 'crocheted' in plastic, combines the best of both worlds: a natural, almost mosslike appearance on the outside and a moisture-retentive inside.

Right: The overlapping panels of a flexible 'whalehide' liner adjust to different models of hanging baskets of the same width. The white fibre circle helps to retain water.

Below: Lay a recycled wool liner into the basket and press it into place, folding the fabric as necessary. Trim off the excess with sharp scissors.

Cheating with moss

A traditional moss-lined hanging basket is tricky to make up and dries out fairly quickly. This technique uses a lining of fine green netting, the kind sold to protect fruit from birds, to help contain the moss in the first place. Putting a disc of black plastic or an old saucer into the bottom of the basket before filling it helps to reduce dripping and rapid drying out later.

1 Stretch a length of fine, flexible green netting over the basket. Knot the ends and use clothes pegs to secure the edges of the net around the top of the basket.

2 Place a circle of plastic in the middle of the basket base. This one has been cut from an old potting mix bag that is black inside. Use it black side outwards. Alternatively, use an old saucer.

3 Add moss, potting mix and plants. When you have finished, remove the pegs. The contents of the basket will hold the net firmly in place.

SEASONAL CARE

In summer, the main concern of container gardeners is keeping tubs and baskets adequately fed and watered during hot dry weather, especially during holiday times when owners are away. But now that all-year-round container planting schemes and winter/spring bedding have become popular, container gardeners need to learn a new set of skills: how to care for containers of plants left outside during the cold winter months. From autumn throughout winter and well into early summer of the following year, plants grow slowly, if at all, and rarely need watering. (Check them weekly in dry spells, though.) Indeed, during wet weather, containers need protecting from excess wet. If left standing in puddles or under leaky gutters, the roots of even the hardiest plants can rot away. Strong winds are another problem; if tall plants keep blowing over they can be bruised or broken, and their containers become scratched and chipped or are smashed. So in autumn, for dual protection, collect together all planted-up containers and group them to make new seasonal displays in a well-sheltered spot, say on the patio, under a car port or in front of a high wall. If necessary, secure tall plants to wall ties to keep them upright. Raise floorstanding containers up on pot feet or bricks. During the coldest spells, containers need extra protection to prevent the potting mixture freezing solid. There are various ways of doing this, but if a cold or frost-free greenhouse is available, move the most susceptible plants under cover during the worst weather. In extreme conditions, plants can even be moved temporarily to a shed or garage where they are in the dark, but only for a few days at a time.

Protecting pots from frost damage

Protecting plants

During long spells of freezing weather, take extra precautions to avoid frost damage. Roots of all plants in containers, even dormant ones, need protection from the dehydrating effects of continuous freezing. Frosted plants may appear undamaged after the thaw, but root damage often leads to rotting later on.

Left: In a severe frost, the tender 'hearts' of upright, single-stemmed plants, such as the cordyline palm, will die, but new shoots may grow from lower down the stem.

1 Using raffia, tie the leaves into a loose cone. The foliage creates an insulated layer around the delicate central growing point.

2 Wrap fleece loosely around the top of the plant – this is good for extra protection, but avoids the risk of excess humidity.

Left: Porous pots, especially terracotta ones, can crack, chip or shatter if left outside in freezing weather, as water within the walls expands. Frostproof terracotta is less likely to be damaged.

Right: Place pot feet under containers left standing outdoors in winter to help surplus water run out of the potting mix; it also avoids any risk of a container standing in a puddle of water. If too wet in winter, plant roots may rot.

3 Wrap several layers of bubble plastic round the sides. Leave the bottom uncovered so that after the thaw, moisture can drain away.

4 The plant can be left like this for several weeks, but unwrap it and let the air in as soon as the severe conditions have passed.

Sinking pots in the ground

1 Another way of insulating containers is to sink them to their rims in a vacant sheltered spot somewhere in the garden, and let the soil act as its own insulation. This is how plants growing freely in the garden survive.

2 Make a hole very slightly larger than the pot. Sink the pot to the rim, then fill round the edges with loose soil. For extra protection, you can place a layer of bark chippings over the surface as a mulch in very cold weather.

Maintaining a basket during a summer break

If no-one is available to water your baskets while you are away for a few days, saturate the soil with water and put the baskets in a shady spot at ground level. For longer periods, either set up some kind of automatic watering system, say using the capillary wick method, or 'plant' any baskets lined with moss or other porous material in a shady border.

1 Find a spot in a sheltered, shady part of the garden and dig a hole large enough to accommodate the base of the basket up to planting level.

2 Water the hole thoroughly and soak the basket in readiness for planting. You must ensure maximum saturation before you go away.

3 Sprinkle a few slug pellets into and around the hole and in the top of the basket to protect against attack. Check for slugs on your return.

4 Lifting trailers clear of the base, lower the basket into the prepared hole. Rest the hanging chain on the surface and then backfill with soil.

5 Drastic though it may seem, you must remove all the flowers. Bunch together the stems of small-flowered plants and cut them back near the base. Take off any blooms that have just started to open and would be over on your return. Water the basket and surrounding soil once more.

1 This moss-lined hanging basket has been rather neglected; not only is the soil bone dry and the moss yellow, but the flowers need deadheading, trimming and tying up into place.

RESCUING A DRIED-OUT HANGING BASKET

Containers need attention little and often to keep them looking their best. The important thing to remember is that containers need more water as the plants in them grow bigger. Large plants use more water and feed than small ones, and once their roots fill the soil, they dry out even faster. If you miss the odd watering, feeding and deadheading, it is amazing how quickly the display suffers. But do not feel too bad about it – it happens to all of us once in a while, especially when we are busy or away from home a lot. As long as the plants are not completely dead, the container can usually be revived. The first problem is to get some water into the soil. Unless you used water-retaining gel crystals in the soil before planting, you will find that dried-out potting mix is very difficult to rewet. In fact, it is virtually waterproof. If you pour water into the top of the container, it just runs out around the sides without wetting the centre. As explained on page 63, try adding a tiny drop of liquid detergent to the water as a wetting agent. The simplest solution is to stand the container in a deep bowl of water for a couple of hours and let it soak until the soil is saturated. Here we show how to rescue a typical 'lost cause'.

2 Start by snipping off the dead flowerheads – this makes the basket look better straightaway. Remove any dead, damaged or browning leaves at the same time.

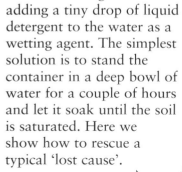

3 Where there are no buds on the same shoot to follow on, cut complete stems back close to the base to encourage a new crop of shoots and buds.

6 As you tidy the basket, you will remove a lot of material. The basket will look better for it, however, and it is quicker than trying to revive nearly-dead pieces.

4 Untangle trailing stems to see which ones are worth keeping and cut old, yellowing shoots with no new buds back to where they branch from a healthy shoot.

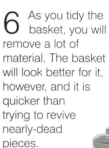

5 Tie back healthy green shoots with plenty of flower, using twist ties. Trailing and climbing plants look best growing up the chains or trained round the sides.

7 Stand the basket in a deep bowl of tepid water for at least an hour and spray more water over the plants to revive them. This also makes it easier for bone-dry potting mixture to start absorbing water.

8 Top up the basket with a watering can until it is fully saturated. Do not feed dry plants; wait a few days until they have had a chance to recover.

Watering in situ

If it is not practical to lift down a dried-out hanging basket to soak it, use a pencil to make a few holes in the potting mix between the plants. Trickle in a little water and allow it to soak in. Do not flood it, as the water will simply run off over the edges. Repeat the process every half-an-hour until all the potting mix is moist. Fill the holes with fine grit or a similar material that will allow water to soak in more quickly in future.

Rescuing a lopsided basket

To prevent container plants growing unevenly if they are close to a wall, turn the basket every week or two, so that both sides have a spell in the light. Choose well-shaped bushy plants and regularly nip out any out-of-place shoots. Cut straggly or one-sided growth back quite hard to encourage branching out from lower down, producing several shoots where there was one.

1 *This hanging basket was growing close to a wall, with one side in deep shade. Because it was not turned, the plants have all grown over to one side.*

2 *Tidy up the hanging basket and snip off the dead flowerheads. With fuchsias, take off the heads where the flower stems join the main stem.*

3 *Remove any dead, yellow or disfigured leaves, as they spoil the display. Remove old pelargonium leaves, as here, at the base of the leaf stalk.*

4 *Tie trailing stems evenly over the underside of the basket to create a sphere of flowers.*

5 *The finished result may not be perfect but it is much better than it was. To maintain the improvement, tie in new stems regularly to keep the display in shape.*

73

DESIGN WITH CONTAINERS

Although tubs of flowers are traditionally used on the patio, various combinations of plants and containers can be used creatively all round the garden. A large striking terracotta olive oil jar makes a good focal point at the end of a view; potted topiary brings a touch of glamour to a formal 'garden compartment' enclosed by neatly clipped hedges, while bright flowering displays are just the thing to add a touch of instant colour to a background of evergreens or out-of-season shrubs. Part of the secret of using containers successfully lies in looking for unusual places to put them. Small pots can easily look untidy if stood haphazardly together on the ground, but raise them up in a row on a wall or stand them on steps or a Shaker-style boot locker, and they suddenly become a display. Medium-sized containers make most impact in a large open space when several are grouped together. An odd number (especially three or five) always makes the best display. Use containers of similar style but in different sizes to group together – hence the popularity of 'nests' of oriental ceramic pots – and choose a similar theme to run throughout the planting scheme. Large containers, especially if they are strongly patterned, textured or architecturally shaped, can often look best with subdued plantings. Team a large jar or urn shape with plain trailing plants or very simple flowers, for example, that do not detract from its impressive shape.

Full stops
A container of trimmed box (right) accentuates the corner of a geometric bed; use pots such as this in formal herb gardens and potagers or, as in this cottage garden, to contrast with haphazard flower beds, attractively edged with Victorian tiles.

Highlights
A collection of containers grouped round a seat (below) makes a good focal point when seen from a distance, and adds much to the ambience when you are sitting there. Change the display throughout the seasons.

Vertical gardening
Many odd spots round the garden can be improved with a few pots. Steps (left) provide a natural change of level that turns a row of pelargoniums into an uncontrived but strikingly tiered display.

Creating contrasts
An imposing architectural shape, such as a textured Cretan jar (right), contrasts strongly with the surrounding plant material. To accentuate the difference, leave it unplanted. Use it upright in a formal setting, but in a wilder scene it could lie on its side or tip forward to look as if it has been abandoned, perhaps with trailing plants growing over part of it.

Hanging baskets in design

Hanging baskets are a useful way of extending a container display upwards to complete a complex picture, but they can also be used imaginatively in a wide range of situations all round the garden to add stunning splashes of colour, instantly, wherever they are needed.

Softening straight edges
Pots arranged at the edge of a patio or deck help to blend in the hard landscaping with the surrounding garden, especially if, as above, the two displays have a similar theme so that they subtly combine. Use attractive pots to contrast with the foliage.

Adding height
Containers are a great way of lifting plants to make them stand out. The tall jar (above) makes a fine setting for the crown imperials, so they show up better, too.

Making an entrance
A pair of matching formal-style plants in containers, such as these spiral trimmed box (below), outlines an important feature – here the front door – and adds a note of distinction to an already impressive entrance. Box are ideal for this as they only need trimming once or twice a year. Bay trees make a good alternative, although they cannot be so tightly trimmed.

The coordinated look
One really spectacular hanging basket and a trio of matching wall pots added to the existing climber make a complete and colourful frame around a window (above), producing a picture book cottage effect.

Instant effect
A few really good hanging baskets suspended from pergola poles (below) make a quick and easy way to decorate this shrub garden with brilliant colour. The garden lighting below each basket picks them out at night.

PLANTS AND CONTAINERS

Like plants, some containers have a strong character of their own, while others are more easy-going and team well with most things. When choosing plants and containers to go together, the knack is to find a common factor. Use this to determine a 'theme' and then follow it through. Terracotta pots with strong architectural shapes or a raised pattern have a Mediterranean air that suits drought-tolerant plants such as grasses and the sort of flowers that enjoy sun and heat, such as osteospermum and pelargonium. Glazed ceramic containers, especially those with oriental designs, are natural partners for oriental-style plants, such as *Acer palmatum dissectum*, conifers or cloud-trimmed evergreens. Classical containers, such as Versailles planters, suit similarly elegant plants, including standard-trained citrus trees or pyramidal trimmed bay. Sometimes a plant's natural habitat will give you a clue. For instance, woodland plants, such as dwarf rhododendrons, look most 'at home' in wooden tubs, while tiny rock plants are happiest in a stone or fake stone tub. Water plants look brilliant in glazed azure-blue ceramic bowls. If you are still unsure, test plants and containers together, even if it means taking your existing tubs to the garden centre on plant-buying trips.

Planting a narrow-necked jar

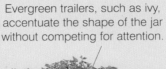

Evergreen trailers, such as ivy, accentuate the shape of the jar without competing for attention.

To avoid filling the whole jar with potting mix, wedge a hanging basket snugly into the neck of the pot, plant with ivies and simply lodge it in position. It can be easily and safely lifted out when the plants need to be replaced or given fresh potting mixture.

Novel ideas
Do not feel bound to use containers the way they were intended – experiment with unusual ideas. A stack of clay flowerpots (below) makes a tower of violas; the result is a much more eyecatching feature than the same containers simply standing in a group on the ground.

Seasonal displays
Vary container displays through the year. Here, ornamental kale and cape heaths (left) are grouped with *Gaultheria procumbens* and *Skimmia japonica* 'Rubella' for late season colour. Garden centres stock exciting plants all year round.

Colour schemes
Plants and pots in complementary colour schemes (above) are easy on the eye. Blue, mauve and purple; pink, mauve and purple; or terracotta, red and orange team up well, and turn a simple display into something really special.

Planting themes

For maximum impact, carry the same planting theme through a complete display. *Phormium tenax* in a pot (above), anthemis in the raised bed and grasses in gaps in the paving form a drought-tolerant, striking perennial display.

Creating cameos

When the garden lacks interest, place colourful tubs (below) adjacent to flowering shrubs (such as this camellia) to turn two separate features into one distinctive 'cameo' that looks more than the sum of its parts.

Repetitive patterns

Patterns that repeat themselves are particularly soothing and help to create a tranquil environment, perfect in a garden designed for relaxation. You can also use repeated patterns to create a slight air of formality, or to contrast with naturalistic or textural backgrounds. The end result is striking but easy to create.

Geometric shapes

Container displays need not rely on riotous colour for their impact. A collection of differently sized potted box spheres (right) makes a minimalistic display with a hint of oriental style.

Enjoying scents

Fragrant plants, such as these scented-leaved pelargoniums (below), are perfect along the edge of a path, as their perfume is released every time you brush past them. The simplicity of the plants and pots accentuates the detail of the path itself.

Framing the picture

An architectural alcove makes a natural frame for a row of identical pelargoniums in pots (right). Keep it simple in this situation; a complicated display would easily overpower its surroundings. To create a similar effect along a plain wall, use perspective trellis with a mirror behind and a windowbox full of plants in front.

BEDDING IN CONTAINERS

'Bedding' has come to mean annual summer flowers, but it actually refers to the art of putting out plants temporarily to make seasonal displays. Annual summer flowers are the traditional favourites, but a good many of the plants bedded out in summer containers are half-hardy perennials, such as fuchsias and pelargoniums, that are killed by frost but can be kept from one year to the next if brought under cover for the winter. (True annuals die after flowering.) As well as summer bedding, bulbs and many small early-flowering plants, such as primroses and polyanthus, are used temporarily in containers for spring colour. Winter bedding, too, is gaining ground: winter-flowering heathers, small evergreen berrying shrubs, such as *Gaultheria procumbens*, and subshrubs such as santolina, can be used temporarily in tubs and hanging baskets. Plant them with skimmia or winter-flowering pansies to make mixed winter displays or use them in containers all planted with the same type of plant. Climbers are incredibly versatile as container plants. Annual kinds, such as morning glory, provide colour and fast cover for trellis or screen walls, but they can also be trained over arbours and arches or used to disguise the bare stems of a climbing rose. Large tubs and troughs are quite adequate for growing even the biggest annual climbers, provided they are kept well watered.

Above: Plants such as petunia, fuchsia and ivy-leaved pelargoniums are popular half-hardy perennials that go well together in outdoor containers in summer. Over-winter plants by keeping cuttings on a window indoors.

Left: Striking dwarf sunflowers grow to about 60cm(24in) tall and make unusual cottage-style flowers for pots. They are best grown against a wall; as they are top-heavy, they tend to blow over a lot in an exposed situation.

Right: A large tub containing a glorious mixture of plants (here, helichrysum, argyranthemums, lobelia, and both scented-leaved and variegated zonal pelargoniums), makes a good foil for the *Abutilon megapotamicum* in a pot behind it.

Left: Surfinia petunias must be the single most spectacular hanging basket plants ever, and are specially stunning used on their own. Well fed and watered, they flower prolifically all season. This variety is called 'Blue Vein'.

Below: Large annual climbers such as *Thunbergia alata* (black-eyed Susan, left) and *Tropaeolum peregrinum* (canary creeper, right) can be grown up canes in large pots to add height to a display. You can grow them in troughs and train them on trellis up a wall, or train them round topiary frames to create flowering 'fun' shapes.

Mix and match bedding combinations

It is not only annuals and frost-tender perennials that can be used for bedding out into containers. Any kind of plant can be used temporarily in this way. You can use garden perennials, evergreens, small shrubs or conifers, spring or summer bulbs, and even houseplants. Use them on their own or team them with more conventional container gardening plants to produce striking, unusual planting combinations.

Right: Spring bulbs are a popular subject for containers, invaluable for adding splashes of seasonal colour wherever they are needed. Plant dormant bulbs in the autumn or plunge pots of bulbs just coming into flower into tubs for an instant spring display.

Below: All sorts of plants can be teamed together in containers; this trough contains hardy perennial plants, evergreens, houseplants and bedding to make a complete cottage garden in a windowbox.

PERENNIALS, GRASSES AND ROCK PLANTS

Most of the more naturally compact perennial plants make good subjects for pots. The most successful for creating good durable displays are those that also have long flowering seasons, superb foliage or bold shapes. There are so many different perennials that it is not hard to find something special to suit any style of garden. Grasses, including bamboos and dwarf varieties of miscanthus, have an architectural quality that suits contemporary patios or decks behind modern-style houses. Rock plants, which are themselves only small perennials, like well-drained conditions. If you want something to trail down over the sides of a container in a hot sunny spot, try New Zealand bur, *(Acaena* sp.) a carpeting plant with dense, silvery or glaucous blue leaves, studded with red or bronze burs in the summer. For a more traditional effect, country garden perennials, such as *Anthemis cupaniana*, lamium and ajuga, always look good in containers. Or use the opportunity to turn a collection of choice cottage flowers, such as auricula, double primroses, gold-laced polyanthus or cultivated celandines, into a novel temporary display while they are in flower by 'staging' them on shelves in the manner of an old-fashioned auricula theatre. The possibilities are endless; all it takes is a good supply of plants, pots and imagination.

Left: A trio of perennial grasses in terracotta pots makes a striking but understated plant group that will keep looking this good from late spring until autumn. These plants are ideal for a hot, dry sunny spot or as part of a low-maintenance patio scheme.

Above: Move pots around the garden to brighten up a shrub background. This 'hot' scheme consists of rudbeckia, coreopsis, helichrysum and white sunflowers.

Below: *Diascia rigescens* is a large rock plant or small perennial, whose sunloving, drought-tolerant nature makes it ideal for growing in a hypertufa-clad fake stone sink.

Rock plants in containers

In really hot, dry, sunny situations, choose the most drought-tolerant kinds of rock plants for containers, such as sempervivums and sedums. Or grow them on their own in a small shapely pot in the middle of a group of plants on a scree garden or raised bed.

Below: *Origanum 'Kent Beauty' is not a herb, but a small perennial with hoplike flowers. Given very good drainage, it does well in large pots.*

Above: Hostas are fine perennials for pots. These varieties are (from the left) 'Wide Brim', 'Frances Williams', and 'Gold Standard'. Smear the pot rims with plant protection jelly to deter slugs.

Left: Hardy cyclamens look totally natural when grown in a wide, shallow container, such as this old butler's sink. They are good plants for light shade, and do not need fresh potting mix for several years.

Below: *Rock plants are miniature perennials; a huge range is available, perfect for stone sinks or large terracotta pans. Grow them in a soil-based mix with extra grit, and raise the container up on bricks for added drainage.*

SHRUBS IN CONTAINERS

Many kinds of woody plants – trees, shrubs and climbers – make good container subjects. Their great advantage is that, being hardy, the same plants can be left in containers for many years. Shrubs form the basis of low-maintenance year-round displays, but some are more suitable than others. The best plants are those that are naturally dense and compact, and offer several seasons of interest, not just one short burst of flower. Evergreens are universally useful, particularly those with coloured or variegated foliage. Variegated hebe, *Choisya ternata* 'Sundance' (a form with golden leaves) and variegated pieris are specially good. Evergreens with linear leaves, such as phormium and bamboo, are also invaluable tub plants. Thanks to their strong foliage shapes, flowering evergreens, such as camellias and dwarf rhododendrons, and berrying evergreens, such as skimmia, also make good year-round plants. Even when not at their peak, they still make a good foliage background for tubs of seasonal flowers. Climbers, too, can be used; clematis are specially striking grown in large tubs up pagodas. Conifers and heathers need special care, as both tend to die very quickly if they dry out just once – and this happens easily in pots. The best kinds to choose here include junipers, which are very drought-tolerant, and the winter-flowering heathers.

Left: Potentially large evergreens such as holly make stunning container specimens when trimmed into shapes such as pyramids or standards. This also makes it easy to keep them small enough for tubs.

Right: Clematis are one of the few woody climbers that do well in containers. Here, they are planted one per hanging basket with the stems trained around the wire framework. The roots need protection from freezing in winter.

Left: A group of skimmias grown for winter berries, flower buds and evergreen foliage makes an attractive seasonal display. Stand them together in pots or plant them all in one large container.

Above: Patio roses are one of the very best flowering shrubs for containers. They can stay in the same pots for years if you replant them back into fresh potting mix in spring every few years.

Growing shrubs in the right potting mixture

Growing shrubs in pots enables you to grow plants that would not thrive in your garden. If you have chalky soil, you can grow lime-hating plants, such as rhododendrons, in pots of ericaceous mix. This is also a good way to grow blue-flowered hydrangeas, which turn pink on chalky soil. Stand the pots on paving; do not plunge them into the ground, as the roots will grow into the 'wrong' sort of soil and plants soon suffer.

Right: *This planted container makes a good specimen pot placed out of too much direct sun; hydrangeas also thrive in full shade. Feed regularly for best results; do not deadhead hydrangeas until early spring.*

Below: *Dwarf rhododendrons make excellent plants for pots as they remain naturally compact and bushy. This variety is 'Percy Wiseman'. Team it with plants such as hostas in light shade.*

Above: Evergreens make good, all-year-round container displays; use them alone in a striking container, or as a background to tubs of seasonal flowers.

Left: Dwarf conifers have good shapes for containers, but do not let the roots dry out or freeze. This *Chamaecyparis pisifera* 'Boulevard' will reach 90cm(3ft) in a large pot.

83

EDIBLE PLANTS

Edible plants can be surprisingly decorative as well as useful, so consider growing suitable kinds in containers all round the garden. Pots of evergreen and flowering herbs are good dotted along paths, where they release their fragrance as you brush past them, or in an ornamental vegetable plot or formal herb garden. Group favourite culinary herbs where they are convenient for the kitchen – suspended in a herbal hanging basket, perhaps. Save valuable patio places for plants that need sun and heat, such as tomatoes, peppers and aubergines; citrus plants, such as oranges and lemons, enjoy this situation, too. In a small garden, use tubs and troughs to turn paths or paving into productive vegetable gardens. A wall or fence, covered with netting or trellis, is the perfect way to support a thriving crop of beans, edible-podded peas or trailing courgettes. Use a large container to keep yourself conveniently supplied with a selection of salad leaves, such as cut-and-come-again lettuce, rocket, purslane, watercress and buckler-leaved sorrel. By growing without chemicals, and picking within an hour of eating, the flavour of homegrown produce is far better than anything you could buy.

Below: Here, three terracotta pots have been placed one inside the other to show off the colours, shapes and textures of the mint collection planted in them.

Above: *Salvia officinalis* 'Tricolor' (tricolour sage) retains its aromatic leaves all year round, although they dry out on the plant and turn a duller colour in winter.

Below: Peppers and aubergines do well on a warm sunny patio. Pick aubergines as soon as they are big enough to use; peppers while green or leave them to ripen.

Right: A strawberry planter allows you to pack in plenty of plants into a very small space. For early strawberries, move the planter into a cold or slightly heated greenhouse in mid-winter; the fruit will be ready to pick several weeks earlier than usual.

Above: This unusual terracotta pot houses two kinds of thyme, tricolour sage, a dwarf lavender and a houseleek, all of which have had herbal uses in the past. Houseleek was reputed to deter lightning!

Below: Citrus fruit, such as this calamondin orange, can be stood outdoors in a sunny, sheltered spot such as the patio in summer. If kept too cool or shady, they will not fruit. Keep frost-free in winter.

Above: Apple trees, such as this 'Gala', grown on ultra-dwarfing rootstocks form naturally compact plants. You could have an entire potted orchard, in miniature.

A container vegetable garden

When there is no room for a vegetable plot, why not grow a selection of vegetables and salads in containers? Good choices include tomatoes, peppers, aubergines, cucumbers, climbing and dwarf beans, edible-podded peas and lettuce, all of which are productive and pretty.

1 Put in the plants more closely together than if they were in the garden, as they are growing in richer soil – it is, in fact, potting mix – and they will be receiving more intensive care.

2 Tie tomatoes loosely to their canes, adding extra ties as they grow taller. All except bush varieties must have their side shoots rubbed out, too.

3 Never allow the potting mix to dry out completely. Regularly feed all container vegetables with liquid or soluble feeds to keep them growing fast and cropping well.

Tomato 'Alicante' produces a heavy crop of medium-sized, round, red fruit, with good flavour.

Runner bean 'Streamline' is a reliable, well-flavoured variety, with a heavy crop of pods 38-45cm (15-18in) long.

'Little Gem' has an excellent flavour. It is all heart and grows to about 20cm(8in).

85

CONSERVATORY PLANTS

A conservatory makes it possible to grow a huge range of plants that could not conveniently be accommodated anywhere else. True conservatory plants are mostly large shrubs, such as datura; climbers, such as bougainvillea; or small trees, such as *Cupressus cashmeriana* and oleander, that need good light, warmth and humidity, but are too big to grow indoors as houseplants. The conservatory is not only a good place to house specialist collections of cacti, orchids or bromeliads, but also a huge range of slightly tender plants and bulbs, either permanently or just over winter. Many houseplants also do well in a conservatory if winter heating and summer shading are sufficient to keep the conditions suitable. Seasonal flowering plants, including azaleas, poinsettia, cineraria and cyclamen, are useful to brighten up a background of green plants. If you aim to grow a mixture of plants, make sure they all enjoy similar conditions to avoid problems. Since growing conditions are so good inside a conservatory, plants – even houseplants – will need feeding and watering more often than if grown elsewhere, as they receive more sun and so dry out faster in summer.

Right: Many palms make good conservatory plants; the areca palm, *Chrysalidocarpus lutescens,* needs bright light (but not strong direct sun), heat and humidity.

Below: Few permanent conservatory plants flower in winter, but seasonal houseplants, such as this poinsettia, give a year-round display a temporary 'lift'.

Right: A collection of flowering, columnar and spiny cacti makes a fascinating display for a sunny spot. Plants need a cool dry rest period in winter and plenty of sun and generous watering in summer.

Weberbauerocereus johnsonii

Stenocereus griseus

Mammillaria spinosissima

Parodia schlosseri

Rebutia krainziana

Parodia ayopayana

Mammillaria bocasana 'Pink Flower'

Left: Hippeastrum have huge striking flowers in winter. The fat buds appear first from the dormant bulbs; most leaf growth takes place after the flowers are over.

Carnivorous plants

Carnivorous plants catch flies, which they digest to obtain nutrients. Water them with clean rain water or boiled, filtered water after it has cooled. Do not give them plant feeds – let them catch their own flies. Grow them in special carnivorous plant potting mix.

Right: *In a conservatory, grow nepenthes, the tropical pitcher plant, in a hanging pot. Give it high humidity, and do not let it dry out.*

Below: *In the conservatory, grow these insectivorous plants in a bowl without drainage holes and keep the potting mix very wet, or grow them in individual pots standing in a bowl with 5cm(2in) of water.*

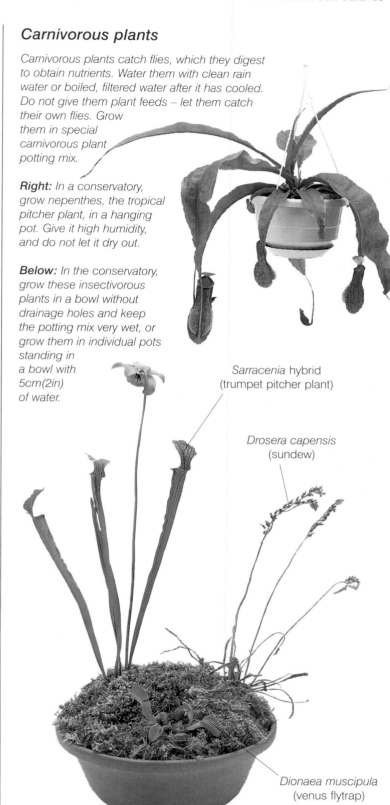

Sarracenia hybrid (trumpet pitcher plant)

Drosera capensis (sundew)

Above: To flower well, aeschynanthus needs high humidity and plenty of water in summer, followed by a drier winter 'rest' at 13-16°C (55-60°F). Cut back the old stems after flowering. This cultivar is 'Mira'.

Left: Miltonia orchids look very exotic but are not difficult to grow. Keep plants warm (19°C/66°F) and humid, mist-spray daily, and give them a weak feed every three to four weeks. Do not overwater or let plants dry right out.

Right: Datura (now brugmansia) is a fast-growing plant that makes a large shrub, standard plant or small tree depending on how it is trained. Flowers may be scented, but the leaves have a rank odour if touched. The plant is poisonous.

Dionaea muscipula (venus flytrap)

A white windowbox graced with the varied shades of pelargoniums in bloom.

PART FOUR

WINDOWBOXES

The perfect way of adding colour and interest to a house front, windowboxes can also create the illusion of bringing the garden indoors. They make the perfect finishing touch to a country cottage or town house, as well providing high-rise garden displays for apartments where there are no proper gardens at all.

1 A perforated base plate separates plants from the reservoir below. To avoid the risk of overwatering, drill seepage holes in the sides of the trough just above the base plate.

Other plants

Other plants that associate well with herbs and enjoy similar conditions include miniature and scented-leaved pelargoniums, mesembryanthemums, portulacas and *Sedum spathulifolium* 'Cape Blanco' or 'Purpureum'.

WINDOWBOX DISPLAYS

Choose short stocky plants and compact trailing ones for windowboxes, as they do not grow too big and cut out the light. It is also a good idea to choose fairly drought-tolerant plants, since windowboxes do not hold a large volume of potting mix and, being raised up in a sunny spot, tend to dry out quickly. Most herbs are drought-tolerant and make excellent subjects for containers, especially if you forget to water regularly. There are many attractive foliage forms with coloured or variegated leaves, as well as plants with attractive flowers, and most combine easily with flowering bedding plants and tender perennials. In this plastic windowbox, an interesting mix of textures has been created by blending the rounded shapes of the pelargoniums and pansies with the feathery upright shoots of rosemary and low mounds of golden oregano. Other shrubby herbs that would provide an attractive foil for flowers include lavender, hyssop, curry plant (*Helichrysum italicum* – its leaves smell strongly of curry!), cotton lavender (*Santolina chamaecyparissus*), several of the silver-leaved artemisias and sage, especially the highly ornamental *Salvia officinalis* 'Icterina', which has gold variegation, and the purple sage (*S.o.* 'Purpurascens'). Low-growing alternatives to oregano for the front of the box might include double-flowered chamomile (*Chamaemelum nobile* 'Flore Pleno'), with its creamy pompon flowers and feathery foliage that smells sweet and fruity when disturbed, or the golden, creeping lemon thyme (*Thymus* x *citriodorus* 'Aureus').

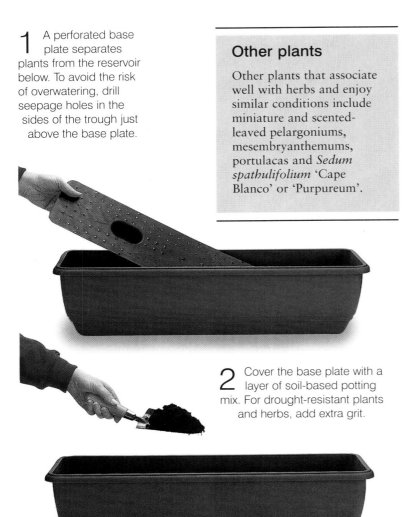

2 Cover the base plate with a layer of soil-based potting mix. For drought-resistant plants and herbs, add extra grit.

3 First plant a row of pelargoniums at the back, one at each end of the trough and one in the centre. Remove any yellow or brown leaves from the plants first, and nip out the growing tip of any long straight shoots to encourage better branching.

4 Interplant the pelargoniums with rosemary. If the herb growth is thin, trim the shoot tips to encourage bushiness.

5 To soften the front edge of the trough, plant five equally spaced golden oreganos. Gently squeeze each rootball into an oval shape to allow more room for the pansies that will come next.

6 Add sparkle to the display with cream-coloured blooms. Fill the gaps between the plants, both at the front and back of the box, with as many pansies as you can fit in.

7 Keep this display in a brightly lit spot. Feed, water and deadhead regularly, and pinch back rosemary shoot tips to keep growth compact.

Origanum vulgare 'Aureum'

Rosmarinus officinalis 'Miss Jessopp's Upright'

Pelargonium Century Series Orchid F1

Pansy F1 hybrid

Diascias in a classic-style trough

1 *Plastic containers usually have the drainage holes marked on the base. Drill them out with a large screwdriver.*

2 *Add gravel for drainage, cover with potting mix and plant the diascias in a row along the back.*

3 *Silver foliage plants make the perfect foil for the salmon-pink diascias. Trim the foliage occasionally with scissors.*

Diascia 'Salmon Supreme'

Lotus berthelotii

Plecostachys serpyllifolia

Houseplants in a green plastic trough

Chlorophytum comosum 'Variegatum'

Right: *White flowers and variegated foliage create a cool, sophisticated, yet inexpensive scheme that looks well against the dark green plastic trough.*

Nicotiana F1 hybrid

Impatiens F1 hybrid

Hedera helix cultivar

1 Protect wooden containers from rot by using a plastic inner liner. There should be enough room to grip the ends of the box with your fingers for easy removal.

2 Cover the holes in the liner with fine plastic mesh to prevent soil loss, or tape small pieces of mesh over individual holes before adding the gravel.

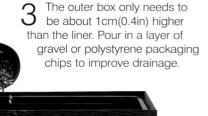

3 The outer box only needs to be about 1cm(0.4in) higher than the liner. Pour in a layer of gravel or polystyrene packaging chips to improve drainage.

4 Fill the back of the box with miniature roses. Feed with a liquid fertiliser for flowering plants and remove dead heads regularly.

PERIOD WINDOWBOXES

It is very easy to achieve the Gothic and Victorian-style effects featured on these windowboxes (see page 34). The planting was also chosen to be reminiscent of olden days; the Gothic windowbox is filled with roses, double primroses and ivy, which all have a long history as garden plants. You would not normally see roses flowering at the same time as primroses, but in spring the houseplant sections of garden centres often have miniature roses that have been forced into bloom early. These much prefer to be grown in a cool, airy situation and can be acclimatised to outdoor conditions quite quickly if given frost protection.

In a formal garden, symmetry and architectural form will feature strongly. In the Victorian-style windowbox, a traditional topiary shape has been used as the central focus. Clipped geometric shapes, such as cones, spirals, pyramids and ball-headed standards, would also work well, but the sphere is the easiest shape to clip. Dwarf box *(Buxus sempervirens* 'Suffruticosa') is ideal, as the foliage is fine and densely packed and specimens can be kept small enough to remain in the windowbox permanently. Another plant that produces a symmetrical outline and does well in containers is the cabbage palm, *Cordyline australis,* which produces an airy fountain-shaped spray of foliage. There are variegated and purple-red leaved forms, but these are not as hardy as the species. Cordylines grow quickly and are useful for creating a partial screen for a window.

Hedera helix cultivar (variegated ivy)

5 Plant a row of equally spaced double primroses in front. When they are over, replace them with, say, double red busy Lizzies.

6 Fill the gaps between the primroses with a compact, small-leaved ivy. Trim long trails to avoid obscuring the design.

Miniature rose

Primula 'Miss Indigo' (double hardy primrose)

7 Regularly remove fading flower heads and yellowing leaves from the primroses. Use secateurs to deadhead the roses. Feed and water the box regularly and keep a watch for aphids.

A Victorian-style windowbox

You could be fooled into thinking that this white windowbox was an example of Victorian cast-ironwork. For details of how to achieve the look, see page 35. Put in a plastic liner and prepare it as before.

1 Add gravel and potting mix and try the largest plant for size. Leave a gap between the mix and rim of the liner for watering.

2 With the clipped box sphere in position in the centre of the box, arrange the marguerites evenly to fill the two empty halves.

3 Soften the edge of the box with trailing Plecostachys serpyllifolia *(often sold as Helichrysum microphyllum).*

4 Plant a couple of pots of white-variegated ivy at either end of the windowbox. Choose a variety with finely cut foliage.

5 Deadhead and trim back the marguerites. Plecostachys will also need cutting back occasionally to keep it neat.

Buxus sempervirens 'Suffruticosa' (dwarf box)

Argyranthemum frutescens (marguerite)

Hedera helix cultivar

Plecostachys serpyllifolia

1 Silver-leaved plants and herbs need good drainage. Cover the drainage holes in the liner with fine plastic mesh to prevent soil from clogging them up or trickling into the outer cover.

2 Add about 2.5cm(1in) depth of gravel over the mesh. This will also help to filter out soil particles from the drainage water, as well as preventing waterlogging.

3 Before planting, arrange the shrubs on the ground to find the best combination. Put the brachyglottis in the centre; add the euonymus to soften the hard edge.

Be creative

Consult an interior design book on decorative paint effects and adapt ideas for marbling, stencilling or sponging windowboxes using outdoor quality paints instead of those recommended for indoor use. You can also achieve good effects quite easily by spraying aerosol paint very lightly over a contrasting or toning background colour on plastic, wood or metal boxes.

SCHEMES AND THEMES FOR WINDOWBOXES

The colours and designs with which you decorate your windowboxes often lend themselves to a particular planting scheme. A seashell motif, for example, suggests a seaside theme and many plants that are resistant to salt-laden winds would look good in this pale blue container. Shrubs, herbs and grasses with silver-grey foliage are worth looking out for because they often perform well in this environment. Their colouring results from the foliage and stems being covered in light-reflective hairs, or wool, which protect the plant from rapid moisture loss. Succulents and plants with small, glossy leaves, such as euonymus, hebe and dwarf cotoneaster, also do well. During summer, hebe, lavender, brachyglottis and cotton lavender (santolina) will all flower, adding white, blue and yellow to the scheme. For extra spring colour, you could interplant with one of the dwarf early *Crocus chrysanthus* varieties, *Scilla siberica* or a dwarf iris such as *Iris histrioides* 'Major' or the cultivar 'Harmony', all of which would look well against a gravel mulch and silver-grey foliage backdrop.

Be inventive with decorative effects and planting. Team stone-effect windowboxes with dwarf alpine plants, half-timbered boxes with cottage flowers, blue-stained and varnished containers with dwarf conifers as boxed bonsai, or log-effect boxes with hostas and ornamental grasses for a country-style scheme. Or use even more decorative boxes with striking foliage plants that allow the container to take centre stage.

4 Plant the cotton lavender in the back corner. Try to avoid arranging the plants in a straight line, as this does not look natural. Add the low-growing hebe.

5 Finally add a lavender. Work the soil round the rootballs to avoid air pockets. Use a soil-based mix with extra grit for drainage.

6 Add a decorative mulch of gold-coloured gravel to set off the plants and to protect the stems and lower leaves from water.

Choosing the right colour scheme

For a restful look, choose a pastel container and 'pick up' the colour in plants of a similar shade. For a startling effect, use contrasting or even unrelated colours, but team plants and containers with colours of similar strength; avoid pastel flowers with containers in bright primary colours.

Verbena 'Blue Cascade'

Osteospermum 'Sunny Girl'

Above: *Mint-green shows off the silver-and-green foliage of* Senecio cineraria *and* Helichrysum petiolare *'Variegatum'*

Deadhead petunias regularly to maintain a good show of bloom.

Above: *The white centres of the petunias are echoed throughout the planting in the variegated edges of the ivy leaves and the pink and white fuchsia flowers.*

Brachyglottis Dunedin Hybrids Group 'Sunshine' (syn Senecio 'Sunshine')

Hebe pinguifolia 'Pagei'

Lavandula x intermedia Dutch Group. This is a compact, bushy lavender specimen.

7 Fix up the windowbox in full sun. Trim the lavender lightly after flowering. The hebe should not need attention. Prune other plants hard back if necessary in spring.

Santolina chamaecyparissus (cotton lavender)

Euonymus fortunei Emerald Gaiety (variegated euonymus)

A temporary display of primroses

1 This windowbox has a plastic trough inside to protect the wood from damp. Part fill with light-weight peat- or coir-based mixture.

2 Use cultivated primroses just coming into bloom and stand the lightest or darkest one in the middle, plunging the pot to its rim.

3 Plunge in one more pot at each end of the box. Arrange the leaves so they hang over the sides and mask the hard edges.

4 Make two pot-sized holes in the remaining gaps and tuck in the last two plants, carefully easing the leaves so that they rest over those of their neighbours without breaking them.

5 The finished display takes only a few minutes to make, yet in a cool spot protected from strong sun the plants will keep flowering for six to eight weeks or more. The pots can then simply be lifted out and replaced.

WINDOWBOXES WITH INSTANT SPRING DISPLAYS

Whenever you want to give the garden a quick face-lift, the simple solution is to create instant container displays. Using ready-grown plants just coming into flower, a few minutes work is all it takes to add splashes of colour in strategic spots around the garden. Containers will accommodate seasonal impulse buys and transform a small number of plants, such as primroses, ranunculus, polyanthus and narcissi, into a 'designer' arrangement. These are traditionally planted in containers during the autumn. A common problem with this is that plants and bulbs put in at the same time do not all grow at the same rate or flower together. By waiting till spring and buying plants already in bloom, you can choose those at the same stage for a truly perfect display. When creating temporary seasonal displays, there is no need to tip plants out of their pots; just plunge the pots to their rim in a suitable medium. Put them as close together as possible to maximise the display. Subsequently, you can lift out individual pots and replace them as flowers go over, or renew the whole display. Use the same idea for summer bedding; this way you can redesign window displays several times during the season when you feel like a change (ideal for a tiny patio garden, balcony or terrace). Or create a fringe of properly planted ivies, lobelia or helxine along the front of the box and 'mix-and-match' an ever-changing selection of potted houseplants, bedding or perennials, especially those with a short flowering season.

Changing the planting scheme

1 If there is room for a taller display, substitute the central primrose for a taller plant in a large pot, which makes a good centrepiece, and balance it with two similar plants in smaller pots.

2 For a more substantial display, add an entire back row of taller plants in small pots. This requires twice as many plants and is more expensive to create.

Narcissus 'Tête-à-Tête'

Potting mixtures for temporary displays

It is not essential to use fresh potting mix in a windowbox where plants are left growing in their original pots. If the box was planted with summer flowers, pull out the old plants, remove as much of the root as possible and loosen the remaining mix with the points of a fork. Allow it to dry out slightly if excessively wet, or dampen if bone dry, before recycling. But replace with fresh potting mixture before planting with longer-lasting plants, such as the next crop of summer annuals. Alternative temporary windowbox fillings include gravel or bark chippings.

A red windowbox with evergreens and narcissus

The predominantly red and yellow scheme demonstrates a useful labour-saving approach to windowboxes. This is to use a backbone planting of evergreens and swap over the seasonal element – bulbs, bedding or flowering herbaceous perennials – as the display finishes.

1 Place a plastic liner in a wooden box, cover the holes with fine plastic mesh and add a layer of gravel for drainage.

2 Put in peat- or soil-based potting mix and add three equally spaced specimens of Euonymus japonicus 'Aureus'.

3 Plant two clumps of miniature daffodil 'Tête-à-Tête' between the shrubs. This multiheaded variety flowers early.

4 Fill in the gaps with gold-variegated trailing ivy so that the stems fall over the two ends of the box as well as the front.

Narcissus 'Tête-à-Tête'

Euonymus japonicus 'Aureus' makes a foil for the daffodils.

Blue-flowered Vinca minor has a cooling effect on the scheme.

Hedera helix cultivar

1 This wooden windowbox has its own rigid plastic liner. It prevents the wood being in contact with damp soil, which could cause the wood to rot. There are no drainage holes.

2 Arrange the plants in front of the windowbox. Place 2.5cm(1in) of soilless potting mix in the plastic liner and make a small depression for each pot to stand in.

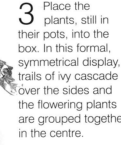

3 Place the plants, still in their pots, into the box. In this formal, symmetrical display, trails of ivy cascade over the sides and the flowering plants are grouped together in the centre.

VERSATILE WINDOWBOXES

Windowboxes are on show all the time and if one plant is past its best, the whole display can easily be spoiled. To avoid this, fill the container with potting mix and 'plunge' in the pots up to their rims instead of taking plants out of their pots and planting them normally. Individual plants can be replaced without disturbing the others, so in this way, windowbox planting schemes can be changed quickly and easily throughout the year. Plant a permanent wreath of foliage such as trailing ivy around the edge, and leave the centre of the container clear for plunging in seasonal plants. Try spring bulbs and polyanthus for instant spring colour and then replace them with annuals, pelargoniums, or fuchsias or a mixture of culinary and scented herbs in summer. From autumn until spring, the best plants for colour are winter-flowering pansies, heathers or ornamental cabbages, mixed with foliage plants such as ivies or euonymus. In the centre of big cities, the microclimate is often mild enough to allow some of the hardier indoor plants, such as cyclamen and azaleas, to be grown outside in sheltered windowboxes. (To avoid any risk of killing your plants, see if other people in your area succeed at this before trying it yourself.) It is also worth leaving foliage plants in their pots, so that they, too, can be replaced when necessary. Besides ivies, small upright conifer trees and many leafy houseplants, such as asparagus fern, can be used in windowboxes. Regularly feed and water plants 'plunged' into a windowbox. Do not just water the soil in the pots, but also the mix around them. This creates a useful 'bubble' of humid air around the plants, which helps to keep them in good condition. Check them every few days, since windowboxes are high up in the airstream and dry out especially quickly in a sunny or breezy spot. The potting mix only needs to dry out once or twice for flowering to be affected and some of the lower leaves to turn brown.

4 Fill the space between the pots with more potting mix. This helps to keep the pots in place and retains moisture, acting as a reserve from which the plants can draw as needed.

SUITABLE PLANTS

Campanula carpatica
Double primroses
Forget-me-nots
Lavender
Polyanthus
Pots of dwarf spring bulbs
Ranunculus
Rockery plants
Rosemary
Santolina

Trailing ivy

Swan River daisy (Brachyscome)

Pelargonium

Ageratum

5 It is easy to lift out fading plants and replace them with fresh ones. Experiment with new 'looks' or alter the composition for a change.

Ringing the changes

Here, just the brachyscome and two ageratums have been lifted out of the middle of the display and replaced with a tuberous-rooted begonia to show the effect that a small change has on the whole arrangement.

Begonia

Houseplants as an alternative

In mild city centre locations, some of the hardier houseplants often thrive outdoors in a sheltered windowbox. Plunging them in a box filled with potting mix provides valuable insulation from the cold.

1 Cover the drainage holes in the base with crocks. Add 2.5-5cm(1-2in) of coarse gravel to allow rainwater to run off quickly without 'drowning' the plants.

2 Stand the most striking plant in the centre. Adjust the gravel to bring the edge of the pot just below the rim of the windowbox, so it is out of sight.

3 For a formal display, place a pair of matching plants one at each end of the windowbox. Position each plant so that its best side faces forward.

4 Fill the spaces between the pots with peat or potting mix and finish with a gravel topping. This sets off the plants and adds extra drainage – vital in winter.

Chrysanthemum

Solanum. Allow long branches to trail over the front.

1 Put a drip-tray in the base of the box to protect the wood from the long-term effects of damp. Then line the whole windowbox with black plastic.

2 Trim off the excess plastic with a pair of sharp scissors. Next, add a layer of drainage material and cover that with a layer of potting mixture.

3 Plant out an evenly spaced row of *Felicia amelloides* (variegated kingfisher daisy) along the front of the lined windowbox.

A CHILD'S WINDOWBOX

The secret of making gardening fun for children is to find a way for them to get dramatic results for very little effort. They love to watch seeds germinate but are impatient to see the results. Hardy annuals, such as nasturtiums, candytuft (*Iberis umbellata*) and pot marigolds (calendula), are ideal, since the seed is quite large and relatively easy for little fingers to handle, germination is rapid and the plants produce plenty of large bright blooms. You can raise seeds in individual pots on the windowsill and plant them in the box when they are large enough to handle or, where plants resent disturbance, such as the Californian poppy (eschscholzia), sow them direct. Mixed packets of hardy annuals are also fun for children; the results may look chaotic to you, but they will love the variety. To overcome the problem of small seed and difficult germination, buy bedding as plug plants or baby plants in net pots. Children can pot the plants up separately and take care of them until they are large enough to plant out. Most of the common bulbs are also very reliable in containers. Buy a selection of dwarf and low-growing types with bright flowers that will bloom from late winter to late spring and help the children to fill the box in layers according to the planting depth stated. Cram in as many as possible for really impressive results. This box was made from sawn-down fencing planks. The wood was given a hint of colour by painting it with a mixture of rich blue and black artist's acrylic paint. This makes the perfect foil for the sun-loving zinnias and brightly variegated kingfisher daisies. For a similar effect, use dwarf dahlias or daisy-flowered arctotis.

4 Tilt the kingfisher daisies slightly forward as you plant them, so that they cover the rim of the box and soften the straight edge with a fringe of flowers and foliage.

5 Next, add the row of zinnias and fill the spaces in between with more potting mixture. Space the plants an equal distance apart.

Below: Children enjoy brightly coloured flowers, such as these *Rudbeckia* 'Toto' and striped French marigolds 'Mr Majestic'. A container like this would be fun for a child to look after, with their own watering can.

A rustic log windowbox with topiary cat

This cat figure sitting in its bed of pansies is sure to appeal to children! This windowbox with a log finish is too small to take a rigid plastic liner, so to help prevent rotting, treat it with wood preservative and line it with black plastic. Cut holes in the bottom of the liner so that excess water can drain away through holes in the box. Add a layer of multipurpose potting mix. As an alternative to the pansies, mixed French marigolds or, for shade, Mimulus 'Calypso', would also work well.

1 Place a topiary cat in the centre of the windowbox. You can buy two-dimensional frames in a variety of animal shapes, either ready planted with ivy (as shown here) or to make up yourself.

2 Plant alternate blue and yellow pansies at the base of the cat, working soil around the rootballs and checking that all the gaps round the plants have been filled with soil.

6 Stagger the flower colours for variety. Zinnias will continue to bloom on side shoots produced once the terminal bloom has been removed. Be sure to deadhead regularly to sustain flowering.

Zinnia Dahlia-flowered mixed

Felicia amelloides (variegated kingfisher daisy)

F1 hybrid pansies

Hedera helix 'Sagittifolia'

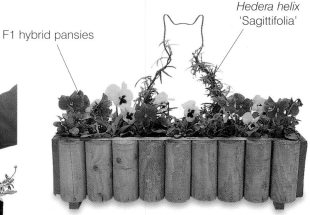

3 Give the box a good soaking. Remove fading flowers and stalks with sharp scissors, and feed and water the display regularly.

1 Three pink-flowered osteospermums and six silver-leaved *Senecio cineraria* plants complement this silvery green windowbox perfectly and will be enough to fill it up.

PINK OSTEOSPERMUMS IN A GREEN WINDOWBOX

Green is the traditional colour for windowboxes; being the colour of leaves, it is the one colour that can be guaranteed to go well with anything you plant with it. But as a change from leaf greens, experiment with other shades, such as deep blue-greens, pale yellow-greens, bronzy greens and silvery sea-greens, when decorating windowboxes. (Consult a decorator's paint chart for further inspiration.) Team them with plants whose leaves echo these paintbox shades for subtle yet interesting plant combinations that will always 'work' regardless of flower shades. Take a colour swatch, made by brushing a wood offcut with some of the same paint, with you when visiting a garden centre to be sure of choosing exactly the right shade of green. And to bring in greater variation, add touches of silver foliage to 'lift' a sea-green box. Cream-variegated leaves will do the same for a yellow-green container; use a few red-bronze leaves in a green-bronze colour scheme, and glaucous foliage, such as that of some hostas, for deep blue-green containers. In the scheme shown here, the plants are all removed from their pots and planted into the liner filled with potting mix. The alternative is to stand the potted plants inside the container. Proper planting does not allow you the flexibility of altering the display in minutes, but it does mean less watering, since there is a much greater volume of potting mix in the windowbox, so it takes longer to dry out. Opt for the latter technique if you are out at work or away from home often, for easier care.

2 Put a plastic liner inside the windowbox. Drill holes in the bottom for drainage; this is essential with these plants as they all dislike moisture lingering round the roots and could rot.

3 This homemade windowbox has two struts in the base to support the inner plastic liner, but is otherwise open. This prevents it rotting when water drains out through the base of the tray.

4 Fit the plastic liner in place and fill it to within 2.5-5cm(1-2in) of the rim with potting mix, leaving just enough room to take the nine plants. Use a trowel to make planting holes for them.

5 Place the osteospermum with the strongest colour in the middle. This will attract the eye and dominate the scheme. If used at one end with paler colours elsewhere, the arrangement would look lopsided.

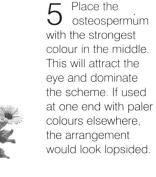

6 Plant the paler osteospermums on either side of it to form a tight group. The flowers mingle and appear to be different shades of bloom coming from the same plant, which produces a natural look.

7 Tuck the silver cinerarias in at either end of the windowbox, spacing them out in order to fill the remaining space neatly. Angle them outwards slightly so that they grow out over the edges of the box.

8 Use a small narrow trowel to top up the mix in between the plants. This makes extra root room and looks more attractive.

9 The finished scheme has a slightly domed outline, which looks as if the plants have grown naturally in these positions. Keep them well fed and watered.

Osteospermum

Senecio cineraria

Windowboxes in sun or shade

Most windowboxes only get direct sunlight for half the day or less, which suits many bedding plants. In hot sun, mesembryanthemums (Livingstone daisies) and herbs such as thyme and sage (including the decorative red and variegated kinds) will thrive. Some plants, such as impatiens (busy Lizzies) and fuchsias, actually prefer a situation where they are shaded from strong midday sun. In even shadier spots, try small trained box trees and ivies for a classic style windowbox display.

Left: *Petunias are one of the most reliable, free-flowering plants for summer containers. The magic formula to keep them flowering from early summer until autumn is shade around midday, frequent watering and feeding (use weak liquid tomato feed), and regular deadheading.*

Above: *In places that are in shade for half the day or more, a collection of variegated foliage plants and violas will thrive. In a sunnier spot, the plants would be at risk of scorching.*

1 This wooden windowbox has been designed to fit around a plastic planter, and acts as a decorative cover for it. The liner protects the wood from contact with damp potting mix and prevents rotting. Sit it inside the box.

A YELLOW WINDOWBOX

Cheerful windowboxes can transform a house, giving it a warm, sunny look even on dull days. But when working with bright colours, be sure to coordinate them carefully; the wrong combination can look awful. To avoid too much of the same bright colour, which could look overpowering, choose flowers that tone with the windowbox and contain merely hints of the same colour. The paprika reds, yellows and orange of the mimulus team well with this windowbox to create a sunny effect. Green leaves and the white petals of the argyranthemum cool down a potentially hot combination. The result looks striking but is easy to live with. Since the plants are not planted into potting mixture but are left in their pots, the display can easily be changed. Individual plants can be replaced in case of accidents and when most of the flowers are over, a completely different planting scheme can be installed in minutes. This type of truly instant display is the ideal solution to the problem of brightening up the garden in a hurry or for a special occasion. You could use almost any bushy, compact or trailing bedding plants or half-hardy annuals, but avoid tall or wide plants that would obstruct the windows or grow out of proportion to the container. You could even stand short perennial plants, bought in flower, temporarily in a windowbox before planting them out permanently into the garden, thus getting two uses from the same plants. Winter bedding could be used in the same way for an out-of-season scheme. If required, pack the spaces between pots with bark chippings or moss for insulation, to create humidity around the plants or to prevent the potting mix drying out too fast.

2 Put 2.5-5cm (1-2in) of gravel into the base of the container. This raises up the pots, so that the rims are level with the edge of the windowbox. It also provides stability and helps with drainage.

3 Bed the 'key' plant (here argyranthemum) into the gravel in the centre. Its yellow 'eyes' echo the colour of the box. A formal display suits windowboxes.

4 Place mimulus on either side of the central plant. Its flowers also contain hints of yellow and help to achieve a well-coordinated effect. (Picking out the colour of a bright container in this way works equally well with other colour schemes.)

5 If the box is wide enough, stagger the planting rather than make a straight line. However, in time, the plants will fill the space so well that there will be no gaps.

6 This box holds four mimulus and one argyranthemum, all in 9cm(3.5in) pots. Leaving the plants in pots makes it easy to replace individual plants when they are past their best.

Argyranthemum

Mimulus

A winter display

Evergreens and small pot-grown conifers make a good backdrop for winter-flowering pansies. These will stop flowering in severe conditions, so a sheltered site is essential. Protect the soil in the box from freezing solid; place the box under cover in prolonged freezing conditions.

1 *Put drainage material and potting mix into the base of the box. Place the most striking plant – here, variegated euonymus – in the middle, towards the front.*

2 *Add a matching pair of small flame-shaped conifers. They will not be there long enough to outgrow their space; this box will be replanted in early summer.*

3 *Fill the spaces in the windowbox with winter-flowering pansies, planting them as close together as possible for a full display. The weather will soon be too cold for them to grow any more.*

Dwarf conifer

Variegated euonymus

Above: *Balance the colours evenly, so the final effect does not look lopsided. Water thoroughly after planting and do not let the mix dry out thereafter.*

Winter-flowering pansy

A RED WINDOWBOX

This smart windowbox is made from tongue-and-grooved cladding, topcoated with high-gloss burgundy-red paint. When using gloss paint, it is important to prepare the surfaces well, sanding them down as smoothly as possible and wiping off the dust. Prime the wood and then apply one or two coats of the recommended undercoat. With dark colours such as this, you will need at least two top coats. Coat the inside and base with anti-rot preservative, and drill holes in the base to allow water to escape. A plastic liner raised slightly off the base keeps damp soil away from the wood, and a piece of fine-mesh plastic windbreak netting over the holes in the liner prevents potting mix leaking out with the drainage water.

As an alternative planting scheme to the one show here, try using bulbs. As well as dwarf daffodils (such as *Narcissus* 'Tête-à-Tête'), deep blue hyacinths, grape hyacinths (*Muscari armeniacum* cultivars) or *Scilla siberica* and red early dwarf tulips, such as 'Red Riding Hood' or *Tulipa praestans* 'Fusilier', would all work well. Bulbs often perform best in their first year, so as soon as flowering has finished, either deadhead and lift the clumps, transferring them to the garden to finish ripening, or discard them.

Above: This terracotta trough makes a fine windowbox; its porous sides help to create a cool environment for hart's tongue fern and busy Lizzie. These and variegated ground ivy (*Glechoma*) are ideal for a shady spot.

1 Wooden boxes last longer if you treat the insides and underneath of the box with wood preservative or water-proof sealant. Before applying a topcoat of paint, seal with aluminium primer.

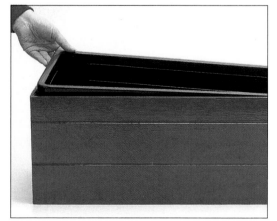

2 Use a plastic trough as a liner. Construct the decorative box so that you have room to grip the liner at each end to remove it for replanting or replacement. The liner should be slightly raised off the base of the box.

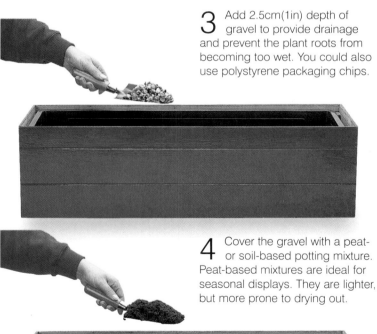

3 Add 2.5cm(1in) depth of gravel to provide drainage and prevent the plant roots from becoming too wet. You could also use polystyrene packaging chips.

4 Cover the gravel with a peat- or soil-based potting mixture. Peat-based mixtures are ideal for seasonal displays. They are lighter, but more prone to drying out.

Alternative colour schemes

When using a strongly coloured windowbox like this one, many colour schemes that would look good in a neutral container just will not work. For best results, stick to complementary and/or contrasting colours.

5 Try the largest plant (here a heuchera) to check the depth of the potting mix. Leave a gap at the top of the box for watering.

6 Pot-grown ajugas provide soft, bronze-purple trails. The foliage separates the red of the box from the red impatiens.

Left: Team red and pink flowers with silver and green foliage for bags of impact in a bright sunny spot. Small touches of white and silver add sparkle to an already brilliant windowbox display for town or country.

7 Plant one large (or several smaller) red-flowered busy Lizzies on either side of the heuchera. Or try red petunias, such as the Junior Strain, zonal pelargoniums, such as Century hybrid, dwarf dahlias or tuberous begonias.

8 All these plants thrive in full sun or light shade. Deadhead the busy Lizzie flowers and watch for aphids on the ajuga. heuchera flowers are long-lasting and add height without spoiling the final display.

Heuchera pulchella 'Rachel' (alum root)

Impatiens F1 hybrid (busy Lizzie)

Ajuga reptans 'Atropurpurea'

Above: *Red, deep pink and purple may not at first sound like an ideal colour combination, but when these flowers (begonia, petunia and lobelia) are growing together the overall effect is striking rather than shocking.*

1 Position the brightest or most strongly coloured plant in the centre. This prevents the display looking 'lopsided' later on.

HOUSEPLANTS IN A SHELTERED WINDOWBOX

Because they are regarded as high-value plants, houseplants are traditionally only grown outdoors in the windowboxes of apartments and town houses, where normal gardening is impossible. However, in practice, anyone can use the hardier houseplants outside in containers in much the same way as summer bedding. Tolmiea and chlorophytum, glechoma (ground ivy), cissus and rhoicissus are sometimes used as foliage plants in hanging baskets and other containers. Flowering plants, such as miniature roses, exacum, pot chrysanthemums and torenia, would be equally happy. However, in autumn, winter and early spring, houseplants can only be used outdoors where the climate is exceptionally mild, say in large city centres where the microclimate keeps the air virtually frost free. Here, indoor cyclamen, soleirolia (gold- and silver-variegated, as well as plain green), primula, winter cherry, kalanchoe, cape heath (*Erica gracilis*) and cineraria provide seasonal colour. As houseplants are quite expensive, they are usually 'diluted' with foliage plants that can be reused in displays throughout the year. Ivies, small pot-grown conifers and euonymus are the most popular, but fatshedera, fatsia and aspidistra are all suitable. In window-boxes, aim for a fairly formal look, so alternate foliage and flowering plants to create a balanced arrangement. Choose plants that are tall enough to be seen from indoors, but not so big that they cut out too much light.

2 Add two 'secondary' plants at each end. This creates a formal, evenly balanced display. Even if not exactly the same colour, the end plants should look similar.

3 Fill the gaps between the flowering plants with ivy; its trails soften the sides of the windowbox, and it can be used outdoors all year round.

4 If there are still any spaces towards the back of the display, tuck in a few small pots of euonymus. Space them out evenly to fill any dips in the 'horizon'.

5 Use a narrow-bladed trowel to trickle potting mixture between the pots. It not only makes them more stable, but also helps to keep them moist and provides insulation from excess heat or cold.

Houseplant displays

It is easy to replace windowbox displays of plants that are plunged temporarily into position in loose peat or potting mix. There are plenty of near-hardy houseplants that do well outside in a sheltered spot.

1 Cover the drainage holes in the base with crocks to prevent the potting mix trickling out. Spread 2.5-5cm (1-2in) of peat or potting mix evenly over the base.

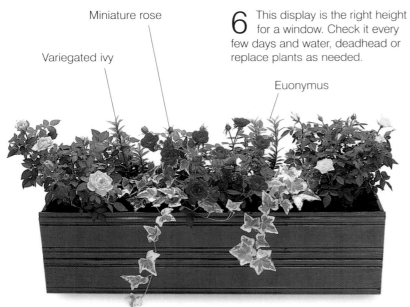

Miniature rose

Variegated ivy

Euonymus

6 This display is the right height for a window. Check it every few days and water, deadhead or replace plants as needed.

2 Put in a cyclamen so that the rim of its pot is very slightly lower than the edge of the windowbox. Adjust the depth of mix if necessary and firm down.

3 Place a contrasting foliage plant on either side. This soleirolia and the cyclamen are virtually hardy, but need a mild spot to look their best outdoors.

Miniature cyclamen

Soleirolia soleirolii

4 Add more flowering and foliage plants alternately until the box is full. A formal look suits windowboxes. You can vary the scheme but use low plants.

Repotting houseplants before planting

When you buy houseplants, their pots are usually full of roots and the supply of nutrients is just about exhausted. Before plunging them into a windowbox display, where they will be expected to last for several months, it is a good idea to repot them. Knock them carefully out of their original pots and tease out the roots, shaking off much of the old potting mix. Replace them in a pot one size larger, using fresh mix. Add slow-release fertiliser granules and water-retaining gel crystals, following the directions. Water well and allow the surplus to drain before placing the plants in the windowbox.

Orange pansies and yellow primroses set off a crown of variegated ivy.

PART FIVE

WALL PLANTERS

More sophisticated than hanging baskets and available in a far greater range of styles, wall planters enable you to garden vertically as well as horizontally. They also offer plenty of creative opportunities for decorating town gardens, beautifying a shed or adding detail to any large uninteresting wall space.

BEDDING PLANTS IN A PLASTIC WALL POT

In a wall planter potting mixes dry out very quickly, but wall planters with solid sides are generally more practical. Even so, they dry out quite quickly compared to containers at ground level. To keep displays looking their best in such potentially difficult circumstances, plants for wall planters need to be naturally drought-tolerant; evergreen herbs, pelargonium, felicia, gazania and osteospermum, or succulent rock plants such as sedum are ideal. In larger planters or where time permits more frequent watering, the full range of annual bedding plants are possible. (Even so, adding water-retaining gel crystals in this situation is a 'must'.) In shady situations, wall planters can be used for plants that thrive in indirect light, such as ivies, helxine, impatiens and trailing fuchsias. Due to the size and style of wall planters, compact and trailing varieties are invariably the best plant options; choose a mixture of plants or several of the same kind according to taste. Wall planters are usually placed in a 'key' position where they are highly visible, so use only the very best plants in them.

Below: A dark green plastic wall planter sets off a vivid display of heliotrope, petunia, fuchsia and the long-tubed flowers of solenopsis.

1 Stand the wall pot on its base while you plant it up. If this is a problem, hang it in position and fill it almost to the rim with potting mix.

2 Formal plantings suit these pots. Here, the centrepiece is a striking *Solenostemon* (coleus). Choose a well-shaped specimen.

3 The back row is made up of bedding salvias. From a box of 15 plants, four of the same shape and size were chosen to maintain the symmetrical shape of the design.

4 The front row consists of four French marigolds placed in pairs on either side of the coleus. Choose the best plants and use up the rest in other containers.

5 Avoid breaking up the root-balls as you plant them. If space is tight, squeeze the roots slightly to make them fit in. This is no problem if you are careful.

6 As the container is relatively small but well filled, water it two or three times, allowing the water to soak in well before adding any more.

7 The finished arrangement will dry out more quickly than a container at ground level, so check it twice daily and water as needed.

Salvia 'Vanguard'

Coleus hybrid

French marigold 'Aurora Fire'

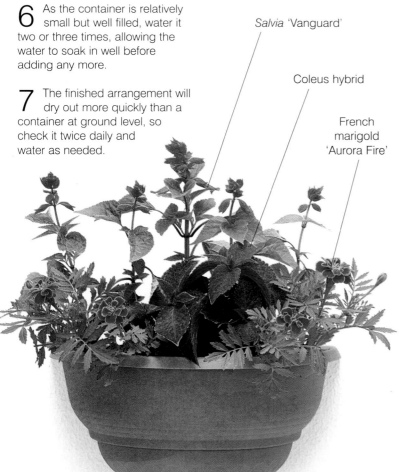

Removing plants from trays

Young plants are sold in a wide variety of pots, boxes and containers, all of which need to be removed, leaving a bare rootball ready for planting. Once pots are well-filled with root, plants can be very difficult to remove without doing damage. Polystyrene trays in which plants grow in individual 'cells' are amongst the trickiest to deal with.

Below: *Bedding plants on sale at a garden centre. Allow the trays to dry out slightly as this makes the plants easier to remove.*

Above: *Push a pencil or short piece of cane into the base of each cell and press upwards until the block of mix lifts out.*

Removing plants from plastic pots

1 Plastic pots are easier to remove. Tap the base of the pot sharply or knock it down on a hard surface to loosen the rootball.

2 Slide the rootball gently out of the pot into your hand. Be prepared to hold it together to prevent the mix falling apart.

Left: *To remove plants from plastic 'cell' trays, shake them to loosen the plants (such trays are often too fragile to tap down) and 'pop' the plants out using your thumbs.*

1 This type of wall basket is designed for use indoors or out; for outdoor use, first make holes in the base. Tap through the weak points marked on the base with the tip of a screwdriver.

STRIKING WALL PLANTERS

The key to a good wall basket is matching the plants to the location. Walls are often in shade for much of the day. In this case, plants such as mimulus, busy Lizzie, ivies, fuchsias, *Begonia semperflorens* and campanulas are the best choice. Provided they are already in flower when you plant them, they will carry on quite happily. In a hot sunny spot, go for real sunlovers; mesembryanthemum, lampranthus, echeveria, portulaca and other succulent plants are naturally drought-proof. Herbs, too, are a good choice for wall baskets in sunny positions; they look particularly good in terracotta containers. But for a position that gets sun for about half the day, the usual range of summer-flowering annuals – the same sort of thing you would plant in a hanging basket – are ideal.

The plastic wall baskets featured here show what different effects can be achieved. In the terracotta-coloured container, vivid but carefully matched colours immediately catch the eye. The dark green trough, on the other hand, makes an excellent foil for the bright lime-coloured trails of creeping Jenny (lysimachia), a pink spiraea and the delicate white-flowered trailer *Sutera cordata* 'Snowflake', also sold as bacopa. Overall the colour scheming is quite subtle, but on a white wall, the result is cool, leafy luxuriance.

2 Half-fill the basket with a peat-based potting mix that will retain moisture in such a small, densely planted container. Set out your plants.

3 This display is based on a pink and mauve scheme. Place the darkest colours in the middle, with the lighter plants towards the outside.

4 Knock the plants out of their pots and plant the rootballs as close together as possible. The denser the planting, the better it will eventually look.

A cascade of white and gold

The pink-red flowers of the spiraea provide quite a long display, but it is the bright leaf colour contrasting with the bronze-tinted new growth that is the main attraction. Kept well fed and watered, this basket will look fresh right through into the autumn.

1 Make holes in the base of the trough for drainage, add gravel to prevent clogging and then multipurpose potting mix.

2 Soak the rootball and place the spiraea in the centre of the trough. A dry rootball cannot draw up moisture from the soil.

3 Add more potting mix to raise the level around the spiraea, then add pots of the gold-leaved creeping Jenny.

4 Fill the gaps with sutera or blue or purple lobelias, cerise-pink and red fuchsias or Begonia semperflorens.

5 Feed and water the basket regularly. Snip off the dead spiraea heads and trim plants to shape if they grow out of proportion.

5 Even if the gap is tiny, try to make room for just one more plant. Put plants of different colours next to each other, so that each one stands out.

6 Water the finished basket very well. Wall planters dry out even faster than hanging baskets, so check the planter twice daily.

Ivy-leaved pelargonium 'Butterfly'

Petunia 'Purple Pirouette'

Ivy-leaved pelargonium 'Summer Showers'

Impatiens 'Accent Lilac'

7 Tease out the trailing stems of ivy-leaved pelargoniums over the front of the planter. Hang the planter in a sheltered, sunny spot.

Spiraea japonica 'Magic Carpet'

Sutera cordata 'Snowflake'

Lysimachia nummularia 'Aurea'

TERRACOTTA WALL POTS

1 Terracotta wall pots in sunny positions rapidly lose moisture, so line them with black plastic to prevent evaporation through the sides. Cut a hole in the base in line with the drainage hole.

2 Put a flat stone over the hole to ensure that it does not clog up with potting mixture. Then add a shallow layer of gravel to provide good drainage for the plants.

3 Cover the gravel with good-quality potting mixture. Always use fresh potting mixture and never garden compost or soil, which contains too many pests and diseases.

The same terracotta wall basket with classical-style relief sets off these two very different displays. One is a rich blend of jewel-coloured primulas and red hyacinths, while the other is a subtle blend of herbs and white verbena. The advantage of buying plants in single colours is that colour scheming in mixed arrangements is so much easier. There are several, equally effective ways to approach colour scheming; one is to stick to just one colour of flower, but to vary the form and texture of the plants as much as possible, say an all-white or all-yellow scheme. Another is to pick two strongly contrasting colours, such as orange and blue, purple and yellow or cerise-pink and lime-green. This wall pot illustrates another option, namely a blend of related colours and shades. The reverse 'cool' option to the one illustrated would be blues, purples, silver-white and lime-green.

Herbs add significantly to the range of foliage plants that you can use in baskets. They also smell good, so hang them where people can gently rub the foliage and release the aromatic oils.

SPRING SCHEMES

Silver cineraria, pale blue pansies, white polyanthus.

Velvet-red pansies with *Heuchera* 'Palace Purple' and dark green ivy trails.

White heather with *Lamium* 'White Nancy'.

Festuca glauca with red bellis (double daisies).

Slate-blue polyanthus, cream viola and *Euonymus japonicus* 'Aureus'.

4 Place the hyacinths against the back of the pot, leaving space for the primulas in front. You may need to shake some of the mix from around the roots to create more room.

5 Fill the remaining space with the primulas. Do not worry if the hyacinths look a little awkward at first; the primulas will soon cover up the base of the bulbs.

Thyme, sage and verbena

Variegated and coloured-leaved herbs make attractive additions to baskets and wall planters. They often perform better than more conventional basket plants in hot, dry summers, thriving in the well-drained conditions and not minding the occasional missed watering.

6 Squeeze the rootballs into an oval shape so that you can fit in as many plants as possible for maximum impact.

7 If regularly watered and deadheaded, the primulas will last for several weeks. Once the hyacinths have faded, cut off the heads, but keep the leaves intact.

1 *Plant the gold-variegated lemon thyme in the centre of the wall pot to soften the edge. Add a variegated sage behind and slightly to one side. The sage will need pinching out to keep it bushy and in scale with the pot.*

2 *Plant a white trailing or upright verbena in the centre and another sage on the opposite side. Deep cerise-pink, scarlet, purple or golden-yellow flowers would work equally well.*

Reddish pink hyacinths

Primula 'Wanda' hybrid

3 *Fill in the gaps at each end with verbenas. Most trailing types need cutting back occasionally to keep them under control, but the blue-purple cascade variety has more delicate foliage and flower.*

Salvia officinalis 'Icterina'

Thymus x *citriodorus* 'Aureus'

Verbena 'Sissinghurst White'

4 *Hang the pot on a wall that is in sun for at least half the day. Feed and water regularly. If the verbenas show any signs of powdery mildew, spray them with a systemic fungicide.*

DECORATIVE TERRACOTTA WALL PLANTER DISPLAYS

Wall planters do not need many plants to fill them and yet it is easy to achieve quite distinctive results. A traditional plant arrangement could feature bedding plants such as tuberous begonias and lobelia, as here, or a Mediterranean design based on pelargoniums – the trailing ivy-leaved sort are specially suitable for a wall planter like this. You could use herbs for a scented mixture or try a half-hardy trailing perennial called *Scaevola aemula;* a single plant is enough to fill a container of this size on its own. (It has flowers like mauve-blue fans with yellow centres.) A single mauve osteospermum with two small *Ozothamnus microphyllus* are all that is needed to fill the terracotta planter on page 119. Experiment with daring colour schemes and bold plant shapes. You can never really tell how plants will look until you see them together, so buy enough for several containers and try out all the possible combinations before deciding which to plant together. For striking results in a container like this, it is vital to pack it full of plants. This means, of course, that it will dry out very quickly, so check it regularly and water it as often as necessary to prevent the soil from drying out. Deadhead old blooms regularly and feed at least once a week. In this way, the display will continue to look good throughout the season and right up to the first frosts.

1 A pot with a rounded base will not stand upright, so fix it to the wall before filling it almost to the brim with soilless potting mix.

2 The centrepiece is a rose-pink flowered tuberous begonia. Plant it in the middle of the pot without damaging the rootball.

SUITABLE PLANTS

Begonia sutherlandii,
Trailing tuberous begonias,
Diascia, Trailing fuchsias,
Lobelia richardii,
Lotus berthelotii,
Solenopsis (formerly
Laurentia) *axillaris,*
Sutera (formerly *Bacopa*)
cordata 'Snowflake',
Trailing verbenas.

3 Add trailing lobelia to fill the rest of the space. The blue of the lobelias will form a vibrant contrast to the deep red begonias.

Non-Stop begonia 'Rose'

Trailing lobelia 'Crystal Palace'

4 By midsummer, the container will be a mass of flowers. Water it often, as a porous terracotta container does not hold much soil and dries out quickly.

Canary creeper
(*Tropaeolum peregrinum*)

Solenostemon hybrid (coleus)

French marigold 'Aurora'

Right: Why not experiment with a new planting idea like this? The trick in mixing such brightly coloured material is to choose flowers that 'pick out' one of the minor colours in the coleus leaves.

Below: Terracotta wall pots with raised patterns, staged at various heights, create a delightful display in which the plants are almost a bonus. The flower-filled containers beneath complete the scene.

1 Wall planters are the ideal way to display plants with a naturally floppy habit of growth, which can spill out over the edges. Part-fill the planter with potting mixture and place the largest plant (here an osteospermum) carefully in the middle.

2 Tuck in a pair of identical plants (here Ozothamnus microphyllus) on either side to create a symmetrical display.

3 Fill the gaps between the rootballs towards the back of the display with a little more potting mixture. Then water well.

4 Hang the planter on a warm sheltered wall that receives direct sun for at least half the day. Water the plants daily in hot weather.

Osteospermum

Ozothamnus microphyllus

Livingstone daisies

Take half a box of Livingstone daisies and plant them without breaking apart the block. Turn it so that the flowers fall over the edge of the container. Plant densely. Fill any gaps around the roots with a little more of the same peat- or soil-based potting mix, trickling it carefully down between the sides of the container and the roots. Hang the planter in a sunny spot.

Mesembryanthemum criniflorum

WALL POTS IN A MEDITERRANEAN STYLE

Vibrantly coloured portulacas are the perfect choice for this little Mexican-style wall pot. These succulents thrive in a sun-baked position; in shade or if the sun goes in, they close up their flowers. Other sun worshippers that behave in the same way are the daisy-flowered osteospermums, gazanias, arctotis and the Livingstone daisy (*Dorotheanthus bellidiformis* syn. *Mesembryanthemum criniflorum*). The latter would be a good substitute for the portulaca, with its drought-resistant fleshy leaves and low, trailing habit. Deadhead it regularly, otherwise the plants go to seed and stop flowering. Portulacas tend to be sold in midsummer as mature plants in flower. Pots often contain a blend of different shades, which gives a very rich effect. The flowers are grouped in tight clusters at the shoot tips. It is quite difficult to remove spent flowers individually without damaging the buds, so wait until the whole cluster has flowered and then cut the stem back to a side shoot. Take care not to overwater succulent plants such as these; it is better to let them dry out slightly between waterings than to keep them constantly moist. For this reason, if you want to mix portulacas with other foliage, choose similarly drought-resistant types, including helichrysum, *Senecio cineraria*, sedum, *Festuca glauca*, pelargoniums, plecostachys and *Lotus berthelotii*. There are many varieties of sempervivum (houseleek) with fleshy rosettes in various colours, from almost white to dark purple-red. An alternative group of succulents with similar looks are the frost-tender echeverias, available in the houseplant section of garden centres.

1 A layer of gravel in the base of the pot ensures adequate drainage and helps to prevent the hole from clogging with soil.

2 Use a soil-based potting mix with extra grit if necessary. A peat-based mix drains less freely and is difficult to rewet if it dries out.

3 Try the first plant in the pot and adjust the soil level as necessary. Tilt the rootball slightly so that the arching stems hang over the side of the pot to create a pleasing shape. Soak the rootballs well before planting.

4 Add the central plant, again tilting it a little so that the stems hang down over the front of the pot. Leave room at the back for another plant to go in. Press the rootballs tightly up together to create extra space.

5 If you squeeze the rootball of a potgrown plant into a flattened oval without damaging the roots, you can pack more plants into the same space and achieve a greater concentration of colour.

6 Balance the shape of the wall pot display by adding a third plant on the lefthand side. Add the final plant at the back of the pot to achieve a really concentrated display.

Portulaca grandiflora

Glazed wall pots need adequate drainage, as excess moisture cannot escape through the sides as in plain terracotta.

7 Fill in any remaining gaps with potting mix. Hang the pot where it will receive sunshine for most of the day.

Grass and succulents in terracotta

Planting schemes invariably work best when the flowers and foliage complement the container. Here a sunloving houseleek, kalanchoes and the steely blue grass Festuca glauca *fit together perfectly.*

1 The blue-leaved fescues provide excellent foliage contrast in baskets. Plant the houseleek at the front, tilting it slightly so that you can see the rosette. Offsets will grow and trail over the edge.

2 Plant the first of the kalanchoes at the back of the basket, filling in the space between the blue grass and the houseleek with extra soil-based potting mixture. This mix suits these plants very well.

3 Add the second kalanchoe, tilting it out slightly to balance the shape. Alternatively, use the succulent trailer Sedum lineare 'Variegatum'.

Kalanchoe blossfeldiana (flaming Katy)

Festuca glauca (fescue)

Sempervivum 'Feldmaier'

WINTER WALL BASKETS FOR MILD AREAS

The festive-looking winter cherry arrives in the shops during late autumn and makes an ideal subject for a basket by the front door over the holiday period. Here, pure white cyclamen, which are readily available at this time of year, and white-variegated ivy provide a foil for the orange-red berries. For a richer combination, you could try scarlet-red cyclamen and dark green ivy. Although these varieties are thought of as houseplants, they will grow outdoors in mild, city centre microclimates, provided they have a sheltered, frost-free position; the warmth given out from house walls and shelter from an overhead or enclosed porch, carport or unheated conservatory may be sufficient for this kind of arrangement in areas where the winter is fairly mild.

Ivy is quite drought-tolerant and cyclamen should be allowed to dry out slightly between waterings to prevent rotting. Do not water overhead; instead use a watering can with a long narrow spout to avoid wetting the cyclamen corms. Remove faded cyclamen flowers and dead or yellowing leaves with a pair of sharp nail scissors.

3 Guide the trails of ivy carefully through the bars, resting the rootball on top of the soil. This arrangement uses four pots of ivy.

4 Pack in more sphagnum moss around the neck of each clump of ivy and continue to build up the moss lining until it reaches the top of the basket. Plant two winter cherries towards the back, leaving a gap at the front.

1 Line the back and base of the basket with plastic, and the front and sides with sphagnum moss. Use a thick, tightly packed layer to act as insulation and to prevent soil from seeping out.

2 Add potting mixture to fill the base of the basket to just below the level of moss shown in the photograph. Break up pots of rooted ivy cuttings ready for planting through the bars of the basket.

5 When planting the cyclamen, tilt it slightly forward so that the marbled foliage hangs over the edge of the basket. Tilting also helps to prevent water from collecting in the crown, which could cause the cyclamen to rot.

Propagating winter cherries

When buying winter cherries, look for bushy plants, well-clothed in dark green leaves and with plenty of unripe, green berries; these will turn orange and provide colour until late winter. Keep the rootball constantly moist, otherwise the berries tend to drop prematurely.

You can collect seed simply by splitting open ripe berries and teasing out the seeds. Let them dry. In spring, sow them in a seed tray 1.25cm(0.5in) apart and just below the surface of moist seed sowing mixture. Place the tray in a plastic bag or propagator and stand it in bright, indirect light until the seeds germinate two to three weeks later. Once they have germinated, remove the cover, keep them warm and when they are large enough to handle, pot them on into 7.5cm(3in) pots. Repot as necessary and pinch out the tips to encourage a bushy growth habit.

Care of winter baskets

Hang winter wall baskets in a sheltered situation in good light. On cold nights, move them under cover temporarily or wrap several layers of protective 'fleece' around the plants and baskets for insulation. Keep the potting mix just moist and avoid feeding, as this would encourage soft growth that is less hardy.

Right: *This wooden swallow's nest-style planter contains a mixture of cultivated primroses,* Gaultheria procumbens, *ivies and euonymus for a long-lasting display.*

Trailing ivy is an excellent way of hiding the edge of wall planters and providing interest at the margins of the display.

Solanum pseudocapsicum 'Thurino'

Cyclamen persicum

6 Fill the gaps between plants with more soil and cover the surface with moss to prevent erosion when watering. Water thoroughly and allow to drain.

Hedera helix 'Hvid Kolibri'

Hedera helix 'Adam'

Left: *This elegant two-tier wire planter is lined with moss before being planted up. The top tier contains euonymus, primroses and ivies, and in the bottom are gaultheria and winter-flowering heathers.*

123

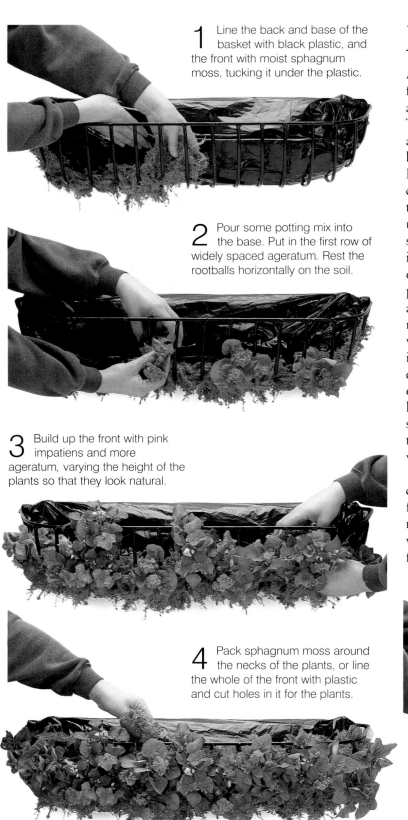

1 Line the back and base of the basket with black plastic, and the front with moist sphagnum moss, tucking it under the plastic.

2 Pour some potting mix into the base. Put in the first row of widely spaced ageratum. Rest the rootballs horizontally on the soil.

3 Build up the front with pink impatiens and more ageratum, varying the height of the plants so that they look natural.

4 Pack sphagnum moss around the necks of the plants, or line the whole of the front with plastic and cut holes in it for the plants.

MANGER BASKETS

A large, manger-style basket can create an impressive wall feature to brighten up a bare expanse of brickwork. It could also be used like a windowbox, fixed beneath the frame. Though not very wide, there is room along the length for a good assortment of plants, and because there are gaps between the bars, you can plant through the front easily. Large containers such as these give far greater scope for combining plants creatively; generally speaking, the bigger the container, the more types of flower and foliage you can use to fill it, especially if you choose a fairly tight colour scheme. When selecting plants for a container, it pays to imagine what size and shape they will be after several weeks of growth. That way you will avoid the situation where one plant becomes out of proportion with the rest. This is not always easy, since the information on the plant label can be rather sketchy and most young plants are of a similar size when you buy them. You will often need to trim back individual plants and it is better to control vigorous types early on. For example, you will need to pinch out cinerarias occasionally to keep them bushy, as well as remove over-large leaves or shoots in the coming weeks. The two schemes featured on these pages show how easy it is to give the same container a whole new look, simply by choosing very different plants to fill it.

The polyanthus used in the spring scheme are the exact colour of wild primroses and to take the wild theme a step further, the spaces between all the plants were filled with moss, giving the impression of a bank in the hedgerow filled with spring flowers. With the exception of the tulips, the flowers in this basket will keep blooming for weeks, as long as they have been looked after properly. Water, feed and deadhead them regularly for best results.

5 Cover the rootballs with potting mix. Be sure to work it in well between the plants to avoid leaving air pockets.

6 Plant three zonal pelargoniums at the back. Look for plants labelled CVI, which have more flowers of a better size and colour.

7 Cut-leaved cinerarias tilting forward to cover the basket edge add a splash of silver and provide strong textural contrast.

8 Add F1 hybrid petunias between the cineraria and pelargoniums. These are compact, free-flowering floribunda types.

Pelargonium (F1 hybrid PAC 'Fox')

Petunia (F1 hybrid 'Mirage Series')

Senecio cineraria

Impatiens (F1 hybrid 'Novette Series')

Ageratum (F1 hybrid 'Blue Danube')

9 Work potting mix into the gaps and cover with moss. Water. Hook the basket onto a sunny wall with two large protruding screws.

A spring display

1 Line the basket as before. Break up bedding strips of violas and plant them at different heights. Fill gaps with potting mix.

2 Put three pots of tulips along the back, breaking the roots apart so that the bulbs can be planted in more of a straight line.

3 Add the yellow polyanthus and double daisies. Firm in potting mix around the plants, cover with moss and water in.

4 Once the tulips fade, replace them with more potgrown bulbs and spring-flowering herbaceous plants.

Polyanthus 'Crescendo Primrose'

Viola

Tulipa kaufmanniana 'The First'

Bellis perennis (double daisy)

WIRE WALL PLANTERS

Romantic wirework baskets are back in fashion and you can now find a range of elegant designs. The plants in this scheme were chosen to match the delicate framework. Zonal pelargoniums would have been too heavy-looking, with their solid flower heads and large rounded leaves. Ivy-leaved pelargoniums are far better suited; their wiry stems, covered in attractive foliage, create a much more open and airy effect. Since most baskets are viewed from below, some foliage or flower detail in the sides of the basket is essential. The kingfisher daisy, *Felicia amelloides,* is a good choice here, as it enjoys the same conditions as the pelargoniums and never gets too vigorous. Its sky blue flowers sometimes appear later in the season and these would complement the crimson-red pelargonium flowers.

To create the impression of a fuller display, team several plain wirework half baskets together on the same stretch of wall. For a more interesting design, use a staggered row, rather than making a straight line. Or arrange them in a 'flight', with each one just below the level of the one ahead. For maximum effect, 'link' the display in the baskets with other containers or flower beds nearby. Or try a more mixed display, where the same plant or colour appears in each basket, even if only in a small way. Adding trailing plants in the sides and base of a basket means that it will dry out even more quickly than usual, so frequent watering is essential.

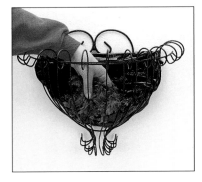

1 Line the back and base with plastic to prevent the wall becoming damp. Trim off the excess or tuck it behind the frame.

2 Line the front with clumps of moist sphagnum moss. Tuck some between the wire and the plastic for camouflage.

3 Firm down the moss. Add potting mixture up to the point where you intend to plant through the front of the basket.

4 Guide the shoots of the felicia between the wires, resting the rootballs horizontally on the soil. Vary the planting heights.

5 Add more moss around the plants, making sure they are far enough inside the basket to avoid the risk of drying out.

6 Now add the first of the ivy-leaved trailing pelargoniums, arranging the trailing stems so that they point out to the side. Deadhead the flowers as soon as they start to fade.

7 Finish planting the top of the basket with more pelargoniums. The aim is to achieve a balanced display that is wider at the top than at the base.

Ivy-leaved pelargonium Barock

Variegated *Felicia amelloides*

SUITABLE PLANTS

Alonsoa warscewiczii 'Compacta', *Campanula carpatica*, *Fuchsia procumbens*, *Heliotropium*, *Lantana*, *Lavandula dentata*, *Lippia citriodora*, *Lotus berthelotii*, *Pericallis lanata* (*Senecio heritieri*), *Tropaeolum majus* 'Hermine Grashoff'

8 Fill in any gaps with potting mixture and water the arrangement thoroughly. Hang it up by hooking the frame over two screws fixed into a sunny wall.

A symmetrical display

Wall baskets are invariably rather narrow, so fairly formal, symmetrical arrangements suit them best. A typical formal display is based on a larger 'star' plant in the middle, with smaller plants at the sides.

1 Line a traditional wire-framed wall basket like this with a preformed liner or a piece of plastic. Fill the container almost to the rim with soilless potting mix. The centrepiece is a cascading begonia. Deadhead it regularly to keep it flowering.

2 Plant one ageratum on each side of the begonia. Add a cineraria at the back; its silver foliage adds sparkle to an arrangement with a lot of similar-looking green leaves. Remove any flowers that appear on it.

Senecio cineraria (*Cineraria maritima*)

Cascading begonia 'Finale'

Ageratum

3 Water the basket well and tuck in any flowers or foliage overhanging the back of the basket so they do not get trapped. Hang the finished container on the wall.

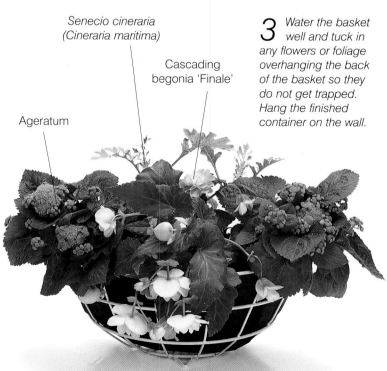

127

1 Line the back of the basket with plastic cut from an old potting mix bag. Turn up a lip at the base to act as a water reservoir.

2 Line the front with a thick layer of moist sphagnum moss, packing it tightly to avoid losing potting mixture through the bars.

3 Turning the plant on its side, feed the stems of the lamium carefully through the bars so that it covers the front of the basket.

4 Add potting mix to support and cover the rootball. Then build up the moss lining across the front and sides of the basket.

5 Split up a tray of bedding begonias. Feed them through the bars around the lamium. They will soon cover the moss.

6 Add an asparagus fern (hardened off outdoors in advance), leaving a gap at the front. Trim off any sections of leaf that bleach or lose their needles.

ROMANTIC WALL BASKETS FOR A SHELTERED SPOT

Tissue paper begonias and airy asparagus fern give a wall basket the feel of a bouquet of flowers, and a rose-pink colour scheme adds to the air of romance. A display like this needs a site sheltered from wind and the bleaching effect of strong sunlight, where the luxuriant foliage and flowers can continue to grow unscathed. Large-leaved tuberous begonias are normally sold singly, in flower, making it easy to choose just the right shade. The F1 hybrid variety Non-Stop is always a good choice and widely available, but it requires a little attention if it is to look its best. The main task is to remove the two single female flowers with their winged flanges that lie on either side of the central male flower. This will help the plant to produce much larger and more showy double flowers. Also remove dead flowers and leaves regularly to reduce the risk of botrytis (grey mould).

Busy Lizzies are invaluable for baskets as they come in such a wide range of colours, from almost fluorescent reds, pinks and purples to soft pastel shades and white. There are varieties with white-striped petals, pale varieties with darker 'eyes' or picotee types such as the one featured on the right, which has darker-edged petals. Single F1 hybrid varieties tend to give the best performance outdoors.

7 Fill in any spaces in the basket with more bedding begonias. Plant the large-flowered begonias and then add sufficient soil and sphagnum moss to cover the plant roots.

Begonia x tuberhybrida (tuberous-rooted begonia)

Asparagus setaceus

Begonia x tuberhybrida

Begonia semperflorens 'Olympia Pink' F1

Lamium maculatum 'Pink Pearls'

MORE HOUSEPLANTS

Asparagus densiflorus Sprengeri Group, *Asparagus plumosus*, *Begonia sutherlandii*, *Chlorophytum comosum* 'Variegatum', *Saxifraga stolonifera*, *Soleirolia soleirolii*, *Solenostemon*, *Tradescantia zebrina*

8 Water the basket well and do not allow it to dry out. It soon fills out; trim the lamium to keep it bushy. You can overwinter the begonia tubers in a frost-free place and bring the asparagus fern indoors as a houseplant.

A pink basket for cool shade

In this arrangement, soft pink busy Lizzies have been selected to highlight the pink-splashed leaves of the variegated tradescantia. These houseplants perform well outdoors in a sheltered, shady spot.

1 Line the back and base of the basket with plastic. Camouflage it with a thick layer of moist sphagnum moss.

2 Line the front with moss, leaving a gap near the top for planting. Fill the base with a hanging basket potting mixture.

3 Plant the sides with bedding impatiens. Push the rootballs horizontally through the gaps and cover them with more moss.

4 Add more impatiens and a variegated tradescantia in the top. Arrange the trails so that they cover the moss at the front.

5 Add tradescantias to fill the basket or plant extra impatiens, which will give the display a more circular outline. Fill in gaps with soil and water well.

Tradescantia fluminensis 'Tricolor'

Impatiens 'Super Elfin Swirl' F1

1 Cut a large square of plastic (here we have used bubble plastic for insulation) and press it loosely down into the basket, getting it well into the corners.

2 With the plastic roughly in place, begin filling the basket with potting mix. The weight will make the liner sink down into all the crevices. Firm it gently down.

WICKER WALL POTS

This pair of wicker baskets make ideal containers for a simple but effective winter display. However, they will need to hang in a particularly well-sheltered spot, as small containers such as these are very much at the mercy of the weather. Plants need protection from wind and wet, but even in a sheltered site, cold can still be a problem. If the potting mixture in a container freezes solid, the plants will suffer badly (oddly enough from drought, since all the water in the mix is frozen and so unavailable to them). If the mix stays frozen for long, it can kill plants completely. So it is a good idea to use thin bubble plastic to line winter containers instead of your usual liner or black plastic. Bubble plastic is sold in garden centres in autumn and winter for greenhouse insulation, but you will often be able to get enough to line a basket if you save up the small pieces that are used as packaging when you buy fragile goods or when such items are sent by mail. Alternatively, move containers under cover for the duration of the worst weather. (This is one great advantage of container gardening in winter – your display is portable.) They make a good splash of seasonal colour in a porch, carport, conservatory and many similar situations where there is reasonable natural light but not much heat. The same wicker containers can be replanted later in the year with summer annuals and other flowers. For a 'themed' display, team wicker wall pots with a group of similar wicker floor-standing containers planted in a matching style.

3 Do not trim the liner first, as it is hard to judge how much overlap to leave to allow for sinkage. When the liner is well bedded down, trim it tidily, leaving an overlap of about 2.5cm(1in).

4 Roll the edge of the liner over to make a neat finish, and tuck it in down the sides of the basket. When it is planted up, the potting mix will keep it in place and the plants will disguise it.

5 Put in the largest plant first, placing it centrally at the back of the basket. Slightly mound up the soil around it to make it stand out better from the plants that will go in front of it.

6 Tuck smaller plants, such as these pansies, in round the sides. For a good effect, choose shapes that contrast with the main plant, but have a complementary colour scheme.

7 Pack as many plants as possible into the display. The plants will not grow much more since this is a winter arrangement. Angle plants round the edge outwards to create a fuller look.

A winter display

1 Loosely line the basket with black plastic (here, a piece cut from a potting mix bag). Partly fill the basket with potting mix.

2 When the liner has settled, trim the sides, leaving a 2.5cm(1in) overlap. Roll the edges over and tuck them in.

3 Put the biggest plant at the back, with the rootball right against the back of the container to leave room for planting in front.

4 Knock the pansies out of their pots without breaking up the rootball. In winter they will not be able to grow new roots.

5 Plant adjacent pansies so that their rootballs are pressed close together. Get in as many plants as possible.

Winter heather

Pansy

Euonymus

Pansy

Right: For maximum impact team two similar containers together, and plant them so that although each one is different, they both have something in common – in this case, the winter pansies.

The display must look finished right from the start for the best effect.

1 Ivy is mostly used as a foil for flowers, but this blend of plain and variegated *Hedera helix* becomes a feature in its own right, creating the effect of silver-streaked hair.

PLANTING UP CHARACTER FACE WALL POTS

A wall pot decorated with a carved face adds a theatrical touch to the garden. These ancient craggy features and untamed beard merely needed some wild locks to frame them and what better plant to choose than trailing ivy? Other 'hair' alternatives include the evergreen grasses and grasslike plants, such as *Carex* species and varieties – try 'Snowline' or 'Evergold' – and the blue-leaved fescues *(Festuca* species). Whatever you use, keep the planting of such pots as simple as possible to highlight rather than compete with the decoration. Double the dramatic effect by using two identical pots on either side of a doorway or, for a classical look, try mounting a single head at the top of a trellis 'pillar' to provide a focus for a bare piece of wall. Wall pots are often made from terracotta or cast cement, which looks like carved stone. They are usually quite small, with room for just a few plants and because they only hold a limited volume of soil, plants tend to dry out quickly. Pick the largest possible container and line unglazed terracotta with plastic to prevent excessive water loss through the sides. Choose plants that withstand occasional drying out – succulents and silver-leaved plants are ideal for pots attached to a hot, sunny wall

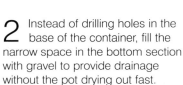

2 Instead of drilling holes in the base of the container, fill the narrow space in the bottom section with gravel to provide drainage without the pot drying out fast.

3 Cover the gravel with potting mixture, filling the wall pot but allowing space on top for the ivies. Try one of the plants for size and adjust the depth if necessary.

The ivy varieties used here are 'Sagittifolia Variegata', 'Golden Ester', 'Adam', 'Meta', 'Mini Heron' and 'Goldchild'

4 Squeeze the rootballs into oval shapes so that you can plant as many different kinds of ivy in the top as possible to make a thick head of hair.

5 As the basket will be hung against a wall, arrange some plants so that they stick up at the back. Other trails will become wisps of unruly hair.

Left: When using few plants, avoid overformality and plant thickly. Blue ageratum suits this 'king' and the trailing *Sutera* 'Pink Domino' at one side gives the head a slightly rakish air.

Keep it simple

When using classical or elaborate pots, keep the planting scheme simple. This is particularly true when lack of space makes it impossible to fit in many plants. The display then looks sophisticated and plants complement their containers rather than attempting to outshine them.

Right: Here, the queen's head has been given a silver 'crown' of *Senecio cineraria*, plus jewel-shades of fuchsia, *Begonia semperflorens* and lobelia to complete the regal (and more feminine) theme.

Left: The head of David is given a classical Roman slant when crowned with a 'laurel wreath' of primroses. Plants can be left in their pots, to make frequent quick changes possible during the season.

Below: A lion mask, leaning informally against a wall at one side of a collection of terracotta pots, looks effective planted with two types of flower with the same shade of pink, but different flower shapes.

6 Fill the gaps between the plants with more potting mixture, and water the plants. Hang the pot on two screws fixed into the wall.

133

A classic summer hanging basket display rich in vibrant colours and flowing shapes.

PART SIX

HANGING BASKETS

These most popular of containers team perfectly with tubs and troughs to make brilliant coordinated displays, and are the only way to grow trailing plants (and some climbers) to perfection. But they can be difficult to water and to keep in prime condition all season long unless you know the tricks of the trade.

Hedera helix 'Mini Adam'

WIREWORK BASKETS

A chicken basket planted with moss and small-leaved ivy demonstrates a simple but very effective technique that you can apply to other hanging shapes, including spheres, which are made by joining two ordinary wire hanging baskets together. You can either plant in the top of the basket and train foliage to cover the outside, as shown here, or using small rooted cuttings, plant directly through the sides. Baskets made in this way are more tricky to keep, especially during very hot weather, as you really need to keep the moss moist if the exposed extremities are to remain green. The easiest method is to soak the basket by sitting the base in a bowl of water. The sphagnum moss acts like a wick and draws water up through the shape. You should also add water as normal in the top of the basket to ensure that the potting mixture remains moist at all times. If the arrangement is growing indoors or in a conservatory, mist spray it daily to keep it looking its best for as long as possible.

In complete contrast, an elegant wirework basket becomes the perfect container for a jasmine's airy trails. Jasmine makes a wonderful basket plant because of its graceful habit and delicate foliage and flower clusters, but it is vigorous and will ultimately need replanting into a large pot or conservatory border. In garden centres, you will often see indoor climbers and lax shrubs trained around hoops. This is just a way of presenting the plant tidily and is not necessary for its cultivation. Before planting it in a hanging basket, gently pull out the wire hoop and carefully untangle the stems. Following on from the spring-flowering jasmine, you will find summer-flowering climbers, such as the passion flower *(Passiflora caerulea)*, Cape leadwort *(Plumbago auriculata)* and black-eyed Susan *(Thunbergia alata)*.

1 This wire basket is actually an egg-holder. The ivy was chosen for the feathery look of its pointed, white-edged leaves.

2 Stuff the head with moist, sphagnum moss. Line the 'body' with a thick layer of moss, leaving a hollow planting centre.

3 Fill the centre with a moisture-retentive, hanging basket potting mix. Work it into the interior space and firm it down gently.

Loose ivy trails will make the tail feathers.

4 Divide up the pots of ivy, separating out the individual cuttings. Plant them in the top of the basket, making a hole for each root clump with your fingers. Arrange them in a circle to ensure even coverage when they are trained.

5 Cut lengths of florist's wire and bend them in half. Cover the moss-filled body with ivy by pinning the trails at intervals. Leave the head uncovered so that the detail is still visible. Hook extra ivy trails through the frame to emphasise the tail feature.

A classic basket

This plain black wire basket, bought from a kitchen shop, was originally intended to hold eggs. But given a black plastic lining, it now makes a good container for plants. Stand it on an outdoor table or picnic bench as a living 'flower arrangement'.

Gazania

Mimulus

Lantana

French marigold

Mimulus

Argyranthemum

6   Attach a handle of fine chain to the basket so that you can hang it up using a butcher's hook. Adjust the position so that it hangs level.

Jasmine in a black wire basket

1   Add a little hanging basket potting mixture to the moss-lined basket. Plant the jasmine, filling in the gaps with more mix.

2   Spread out the stems so they hang over the basket sides. Wind one or two of the longest trails around the handle.

3   To persuade the stems to trail down in the desired position, secure them with long 'pins' pushed through the sphagnum moss.

Jasminum polyanthum

4   Hang the finished basket in a well-lit position. Remove individual flowers as they fade, using a pair of sharp nail scissors.

1 Fit a circle of black plastic inside the base of the basket. This will help to prevent water running straight through later on.

2 Line the base of the basket. This green synthetic material is used like moss but is easier to work with and keeps its colour.

3 Fill the base with potting mix to just below the 'moss'. Firm it lightly down to compress the 'moss' and prevent sinkage later.

4 Hold the wires apart, making a larger gap through which to feed in plants from the outside. Ideally, use small plant 'plugs'.

LOBELIA IN A WIRE BASKET

With a little imagination, all sorts of novel containers can be used for creative plant displays. This basket was originally intended to hold eggs on a kitchen counter, but doubles as a very pretty hanging basket for the garden. You can treat it in much the same way as a traditional wire-sided hanging basket, except that its narrow neck is slightly more difficult to line. The synthetic moss liner holds together in firm wads and is much easier to use in this situation than the real thing. It also keeps its colour all season, unlike real moss which bleaches or browns after exposure to sun. It does not soak up water as well as natural moss, so it is a good idea to mix water-retaining polymer crystals into the potting mix. However, it does hold in the mix rather better. Tease out dense wads of the material, about 1.25cm(0.5in) thick. When compressed by the weight of potting mix, the loose strands form an even layer over the interior of the basket. Since the container is so attractive, accentuate its character by planting it with only one type of plant. Lobelia will trail down, spilling attractively over the wirework and making a cool contrast with the mossy material inside. It will not make such a solid covering that the shape of the container is lost beneath the foliage. The container could be teamed with other wirework containers and garden furniture, or mixed with other planted kitchen containers for a fun-themed display near a back door or in a decorative kitchen garden. Keep it well watered and regularly fed, as dripping will reduce the nutrient levels in the potting mix.

5 Build up a ring of plants, evenly spaced around the edge of the basket. Place them centrally in each section of wirework. Since it is only a small container, one row of plants in the sides will be enough.

6 Tuck more 'moss' closely around the plants. Build up the sides with tight-packed wads of material that will retain potting mix.

7 Make a firm, tidy rim around the neck of the basket. Fill the remaining space with potting mix. Firm down and top up the level.

Lobelia as a feature plant

Lobelia is normally used as a 'filler' between bigger and more striking blooms, but massed together the small flowers create a cloudlike effect that is specially enchanting in hanging baskets. Use it as the mainstay of romantic, feminine, pastel colour schemes.

8 Put more lobelia plants in the neck, as close to the edge as possible. The more plants you can get in, the fuller the final display.

9 Trickle in a little water at a time, so that it soaks thoroughly into the mix instead of running out through the sides.

Right: *Sometimes a very simple display can look as good, if not better, than a large, complicated one. Here, a froth of lilac lobelia makes a dense background for pink, ivy-leaved pelargoniums. This entire basket can be planted using only a small tray of lobelia and three trailing pelargoniums, since the plants quickly spread to create a complete cover.*

10 Hang the basket in a spot out of bright midday sun. Lobelia needs several hours of sunshine outside the hottest parts of the day, but may scorch if conditions are too hot or bright.

11 After several weeks of regular feeding and watering, the basket has almost vanished under clouds of bloom. Either suspend it like a hanging basket or stand it on a garden table.

Above: *Shades of pink lobelia, brachyscome and pelargoniums make a well-filled basket. Part of the effect is created by using different shaped flowers, but hints of purple, mauve and white add depth to the scheme.*

1 Prepare two identical moss-lined wire baskets. Plant a row of busy Lizzies as close as possible to the base of each basket. Use a bucket for support.

2 Tuck moss around each plant to prevent leakage of potting mix. Place a second row of plants about halfway up one of the two baskets, but not too near the top.

3 Fill each basket to the brim with more potting mixture and firm it well down so that the moss settles into the shape of the basket. Add more potting mixture to both baskets if necessary; it is vital that the surface is level afterwards.

A BALL OF BLOOM

When properly planted, normal hanging baskets eventually grow into generous, well-filled shapes. But to make a perfect sphere you need a special kind of container and very neat plants. You can make your own 'ball of bloom' using a pair of identical wire-framed hanging baskets and busy Lizzies. Here we have used two 25cm(10in) baskets and about 20 plants. Since this container holds twice as much potting mix as a traditional single wire basket, it is slower to dry out, and the all-round layer of moss creates better insulation so that the plant roots do not overheat. These are both important factors when growing busy Lizzies, as they prefer cooler, moister conditions than most container plants. This arrangement could hang in semi-shade or in a spot that only receives a few hours of direct sunlight every day. Morning and evening sun is best, since busy Lizzies scorch easily in bright light. A ball of bloom is much heavier than a normal basket, so check that brackets and supporting chains are strong and firmly fixed. This type of container makes a dramatic centrepiece to a container garden scheme. Team it with pyramidal or pillar topiary shapes surrounded by a colourful carpet of plants for a formal look (but avoid duplicating the sphere theme). For a more country garden effect on a patio, team a ball of bloom with a selection of informal containers at ground level, filled with a riotous mixture of flowering plants.

4 Water the potting mix thoroughly; this helps to hold it together and also makes it stick to the moss. If watering causes sinkage, top up the baskets before proceeding to the next step.

5 Place a piece of wood or firm card over the basket planted with just one row of plants and hold it down firmly in place.

6 Invert this basket over the second. Check that the plants are randomly arranged over the surface and adjust if necessary.

7 Make sure that the baskets are perfectly aligned, with one directly over the other. Then prevent the top basket from sliding as you gently pull out the board. An assistant is helpful here.

8 Use plastic-coated wire to secure the two baskets together at several points round the rim, to make a ball shape. Green-coated wire shows up least. Twist the ends tightly with pliers.

9 Hang up the completed basket. To water, carefully trickle water from a can onto the top of the basket; you could tease apart some of the moss to make an opening for easier watering.

10 After just a few weeks, the basket is completely smothered in flower. Keep it well fed and watered all summer and site it out of strong midday sun to keep it looking this good.

Deadhead regularly for best results.

Watering a ball of bloom more easily

Since watering a 'ball of bloom' basket can be difficult, try this technique which, although it makes planting a bit trickier, makes life much easier later on, as water soaks in faster without bouncing back.

1 *Take a plastic pot, 5-9cm (2-3.5in) in diameter. It should be clean and have plenty of drainage holes. Upend it in the very centre of the basket that will form the top of the 'ball'.*

2 *Surround the pot with moss, making sure that it is firmly bedded in place and that the moss makes a good 'seal' round it. Wads of moss are the best material to use for this job.*

3 *Fill all round the edge of the pot with potting mix and press it gently down so there is no sinkage when the basket is overturned later. Once firmly fixed, plant and fill the basket as usual.*

4 *Once planted and in place, the top of the 'ball' has a clear space into which water can be poured quickly and easily. It will be evenly distributed via the drainage holes in the pot.*

Combining a basket with another display

Right: *Coordinating a basket with another container can be very effective. Here, a ball of bloom planted with trailing ivy-leaved pelargoniums makes a good architectural shape to complement a windowbox display featuring the same flower, but used in a much lower key way.*

METAL BUCKETS AND SILVER BASKETS

Shiny metal pails make fun containers, especially for children's gardens, and are easily converted to hanging baskets with a length of silver-coloured chain. You can now buy a wide variety of potted bulbs, in bud or flower, between late winter and early spring. Dwarf varieties are particularly suited to hanging baskets, especially dwarf, multiheaded daffodils, grape hyacinths, chionodoxas, scillas and *Anemone blanda,* all of which flower over a relatively long period. Once flowering has finished, continue to feed and water, maintaining the foliage to allow the bulbs to build up reserves for flowering the following spring.

Planted up, a pair of tiny woven silver baskets would make a lovely gift. One basket on its own is unlikely to make sufficient impact, so try two or more baskets hung at different heights. Be sure to choose correspondingly small plants; the alpine bellflower *(Campanula* sp.) is naturally compact. Campanulas of a suitable size include 'Elizabeth Oliver', *C. muralis* and *C. carpatica.*

1 Put a layer of gravel or small pieces of broken polystyrene trays in the bucket to provide a drainage layer in these sealed containers.

Dividing bulbs

Before dividing bulbs, water them thoroughly a few hours beforehand to help them cope better with the stress.

Right: Tease off as much soil as you can from the daffodil rootball, reducing its size to fit the bucket.

Left: Gently pull apart the rootball, separating individual bulbs for planting in narrow gaps. Take care not to damage too many roots.

2 Add a little soil; use a gritty, free-draining mix if you do not intend to perforate the base. Remove handles for easy planting.

3 Remove some mix from around the roots of the clump of daffodils. Plant the bulbs into the bucket, leaving enough space around the edges for the muscari.

4 Using small clumps or individual muscari bulbs, fill in round the edge of the daffodils. Squeeze in as many bulbs as you can. The flower heads may droop a bit at first, but should re-orientate themselves after a few days.

5 This time, using muscari for the centre, make an outer ring of pale blue-and-white striped chionodoxas. Cover exposed roots or bulbs with potting mix and water to settle the soil. Take care not to overwater.

Campanulas in a silver basket

Here, the delicate, lilac-blue blooms of campanula combine beautifully with the silver of the basket. Dwarf bulbs, such as chionodoxa, scilla, crocus and puschkinia, would also work well in a display like this.

1 To prevent drips, line the basket with transparent plastic. Fold the corners to fit and trim off any excess with scissors.

2 Add gravel or charcoal chippings for drainage. Do not overwater, especially when using drought-tolerant plants.

3 Now plant the campanulas; allow some of the foliage to trail over the basket sides. Fill the gaps between the plants with more potting mixture so that there are no air spaces. Add sufficient water to settle the soil.

4 Suspend the baskets using fine florist's ribbon in a cool, well-lit spot. If they are a gift, add extra ribbon loops to the handles.

Narcissus
'Tête-à-Tête'

Chionodoxa luciliae

Muscari armeniacum
(grape hyacinth)

6 Hang the buckets at head height to appreciate the flowers close up. Pick off individual daffodil flowers as they fade.

Campanula sp.
(alpine bellflower)

143

Assembling a self-watering basket

Self-watering baskets need assembling when new; follow the instructions. Despite their name, they need some attention: check water levels regularly and refill the reservoir as necessary.

1 Feed the wick through the plastic base plate. It draws water up from the reservoir in the basket base and keeps the capillary matting damp.

2 Push the watering tube through the hole in the base plate before adding the potting mix and plants. You should be able to camouflage it.

SELF-WATERING BASKETS

Hanging baskets suffer from one major drawback: they need an awful lot of watering. Size for size, they dry out much faster than containers at ground level, and in hot or breezy weather this can mean daily or twice daily watering. However, there are a few useful techniques that will help to keep them watered. One is to mix water-retaining gel crystals into the soil before planting the basket. (They can be added after planting, if you stir them carefully into the potting mix between the plants, but it is not possible once the container is full of roots.) Another technique is to sink a plastic bottle, with the end cut off, into the middle of the basket where it is hidden by plants. Use this like a funnel to channel water right into the heart of the basket. As an added refinement, leave the screw cap on the bottle and make a couple of pinholes in the neck so that the water leaks out slowly and evenly during the day. (Add a few drops of liquid feed to the bottle, for beneficial 'little and often' feeding.) Alternatively, choose a self-watering hanging basket, which has a built-in water reservoir in the base, into which a 'wick' dangles from the planting space above. Even though they need less attention than other baskets, you cannot afford to neglect them, particularly during spells of very hot weather.

1 Three-quarters fill the basket with potting mix. Lightweight peat or coir kinds are best in baskets. Avoid putting soil in the tube. Do not fill the water reservoir until planting has been completed.

2 Place the taller plants, such as the pelargoniums, between the attachment points for the chains, so that you get an uncluttered view when the basket is hanging up.

3 Use the smaller trailing plants, such as petunia, to fill in the spaces around the front and sides of the basket. They will spill over and soften the straight edge.

4 Use taller flowers with a contrasting shape – these are verbena – to fill any gaps near the back of the display. They will add more colour and a fuller shape.

Pelargonium

Argyranthemum

Verbena

5 Hang the completed basket in a sunny but sheltered spot, making sure that the 'best' side faces front. Top up the reservoir every two to three days as necessary. Deadhead flowers regularly for continuous colour.

Petunia

Channelling water into the potting mixture

Self-watering baskets are easy to use. To prime the system, simply fill the reservoir, water the potting mix, and capillary action will do the rest. Depending on the size of the plants and growing conditions, the reservoir should last two to five days between fills, but check it regularly.

Left: *Self-watering baskets such as this are topped up via a tube that protrudes above the potting mixture, just inside the edge of the container. Fill it by means of a small nozzle on the end of a watering can.*

Right: *Normal hanging baskets that are not self-watering are easier to deal with if you press a 'water well' into the potting mix. Water slowly seeps out through the porous sides, enabling the potting mixture to absorb it slowly.*

Below: *Make a watering funnel by cutting a plastic bottle in half. Remove the stopper. Push the neck into the mix. When filled with water, the soil wedged in the neck prevents the water running out too quickly.*

Above: A purple-and-yellow colour scheme provides a striking theme for a pair of hanging baskets and 'makes' the entrance outside this town house. Hints of other shades keep the combination looking lively.

Planting a gold-themed basket

1 Press a sheet of recycled wool liner into the basket, folding it as necessary. Trim off the excess with sharp scissors.

2 Use soilless potting mix in this 40cm(16in) basket, so that the container does not get too heavy. Offer up a plant to check the depth.

3 Plant yellow-variegated trailing ivy in the top to cover the front and sides of the basket. *Vinca minor* 'Variegata' would also work.

4 Arrange some asteriscus so that the stems hang over the ivy and create a ring of flowers. Deadhead as flowers turn brown.

THEMED DISPLAYS

Containers have to make plenty of impact in a tiny planting area, so a distinct colour scheme often works better than a riotous mixture of colours. This is particularly true of a 'stand-alone' display, such as a single hanging basket or small bowl of plants on a garden table. (Large displays can afford to be more flamboyant as there is more space to play with, and the eye can take in the extra detail.) By limiting yourself to a part of the colour spectrum, it is also possible to establish a mood for a particular part of the garden. Reds, yellows and orange are naturally extrovert colours, perfect for a busy part of the garden; cream and green or blue and silver look cool and sophisticated and pastel colours, such as purple, lilac, mauve or pink have an almost tranquillizing effect, ideal for creating a relaxing atmosphere. The daisylike heads of *Asteriscus maritimus* create a splash of gold at the centre of this basket. It is in fact a rock garden plant, normally sold under the name 'Gold Coin', but with its dense spreading habit, attractive leaves and profusion of flowers, it makes an excellent basket plant, too. Containers planted solely with asteriscus look very effective. The large, vivid purple flower heads of *Verbena* 'Homestead Purple' contrast perfectly with the yellow and gold plants, while the basket sides are camouflaged by a yellow-variegated trailing ivy, another indispensable basket plant. *Erica arborea* 'Albert's Gold' has feathery foliage that adds textural interest as well as colour.

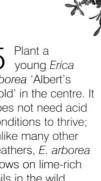

5 Plant a young *Erica arborea* 'Albert's Gold' in the centre. It does not need acid conditions to thrive; unlike many other heathers, *E. arborea* grows on lime-rich soils in the wild.

6 Arrange the purple-flowered verbena at the back, so that some stems intermingle with the asteriscus. Deadhead regularly to encourage further blooms.

7 Fill in any gaps with potting mix and water well. Allow to drain and hang in a sunny spot. Use the correct bracket for this heavy basket.

Verbena 'Homestead Purple'

Erica arborea 'Albert's Gold' (tree heath)

Hedera helix cultivar (variegated ivy)

Asteriscus maritimus syn. *A.* 'Gold Coin'

Making the most of colour

By keeping to a few colours, you can create a huge variety of displays, from cool and sophisticated schemes in understated pots to hot, bright arrangements in coloured containers. Use either different shades of one colour or completely contrasting colours for maximum effect.

Right: *Salmon pink, terracotta and brick-red flowers make a bold display that suits the background brickwork perfectly. The fringe of trailing lobelia prevents the effect looking overdone.*

Below: *Mauve, lilac and purple is a particularly restful combination. The secret of blending a limited number of colours successfully lies in using flowers with different shapes and sizes.*

Left: *Cream-and-green is a classic colour combination. Here, variegated Petasites japonicus makes a strong centrepiece to this unusual hanging basket of foliage and flowering plants.*

Other plants for unusual hanging baskets

As a change from the usual range of bedding plants, look out for other colourful compact and trailing outdoor plants to create novel seasonal hanging basket arrangements. Consider aubretia and arabis for a spring arrangement or *Polygonum affine*, *Erigeron karvinskianus* plus rockery pinks for a summer display in a hot sunny spot. *Campanula* *carpatica*, lithodora and *Geranium cinereum* also provide attractive, long-flowering displays. These are all rock plants, but make good hanging basket displays for a single season's use. After that time, the plants get too big for the basket, so replant them into the garden and recycle the container to make a new display.

1 Line the base of the basket with a circle of black plastic cut from an old bag. Camouflage the edges with sphagnum moss.

2 The lining traps moisture and acts like a small reservoir. Fill the basket with potting mixture and add more moss.

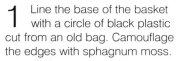

Support the basket on a pot while you work to keep it steady.

3 Separate a pot of rooted ivy cuttings and plant some of them between the wires of the basket. Pack moss around the necks of the plants to prevent drying out and loss of soil.

ELEGANT PASTEL DISPLAYS

In the border, you can enhance the beauty of individual flowering plants with a suitable backdrop of foliage. Here, the same principle has been applied to highlight a mass of viola blooms. This velvet purple variety, with its paler lilac centre, needs to be surrounded by lighter foliage to do it justice; white-variegated plants complement the flowers perfectly. The elegant fuchsia variety 'Sharpitor' used at the back of the basket is unlike most bedding varieties. It has very pale green leaves, edged creamy white, with slender pendant flowers of blush pink, which are most profuse in autumn. As it is frost hardy, you can replant it in the border when you dismantle the display. Variegated ground ivy and real ivy provide a foil at the front. For a brighter overall effect, try lime green and gold-variegated foliage, including the gold-leaved fuchsia variety 'Genii', *Helichrysum* 'Limelight', *Salvia officinalis* 'Icterina', golden feverfew (*Tanacetum parthenium* 'Aureum'), and for trails, golden creeping Jenny and gold-variegated ivy.

4 Soak the remaining plants before adding them to the basket. Add the fuchsia specimen at the back of the basket. Plant the first of the violas, leaving room for the ground ivy.

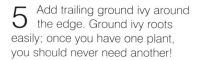

5 Add trailing ground ivy around the edge. Ground ivy roots easily; once you have one plant, you should never need another!

6 Add the remaining violas and fill any gaps with potting mix. The violas will soon settle down. Deadhead them regularly.

A late-season pastel basket

Baskets are traditionally made up in early summer, but that restricts the range of plants available and does not allow for seasonal variation. Hebes and hypericums are two mainstays of the late-season border; compact varieties make good temporary subjects for baskets.

1 Assemble the self-watering basket and stand it in the top of a large pot for stability. Cover the base with potting mix.

2 If the basket tips over when you put in a single plant, counterbalance the weight using a half brick or stone.

7 Keep all the plants well watered and hang the basket in a spot out of the midday sun to keep the arrangement cool.

3 Arrange trailing sedum to hang over the righthand side of the basket and plant variegated hypericum opposite. Fill any gaps with extra sedums. Some white *Begonia semperflorens* make a visual link and bridge the height gap between the front and rear.

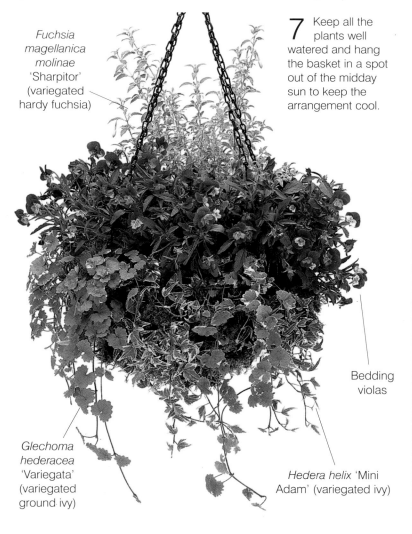

Fuchsia magellanica molinae 'Sharpitor' (variegated hardy fuchsia)

Bedding violas

Glechoma hederacea 'Variegata' (variegated ground ivy)

Hedera helix 'Mini Adam' (variegated ivy)

4 The gentle colours complement the pale basket. Hang it in a well-lit spot, out of the midday sun.

Hebe 'Purple Pixie'

Sedum lineare 'Variegatum'

Begonia semperflorens

Hypericum x *moserianum* 'Tricolor'

A BASKET OF FUCHSIAS

Most people would agree that the ideal way to view fuchsia flowers is when they are growing in a hanging basket. You can really see them in all their glory from below or, best of all, at eye level. For the best effect, restrict each basket to only one variety of fuchsia; if you mix them, they begin to look messy, as different varieties will grow at different rates and flower at different times. Eventually, the whole effect can become untidy. The number of plants that you put in a basket depends very much on the size of the basket. Always plant one in the middle, otherwise you can end up with a hole as the plants begin to grow downwards. The plants still need regular stopping after every two or three pairs of leaves to achieve a longer, but not straggly, look. Choose your varieties with care and you cannot fail to be delighted with the effect that your basket will give, whether it drips with enormous double flowers, or cascades from top to bottom with smaller single flowers. To ensure that the basket flowers continuously for many months, remove dead flowerheads and fruits, and feed it regularly. A slow-release fertiliser is useful if the basket is difficult to reach for liquid feeding. Remember to turn the basket regularly to make sure that it retains a balanced shape as it grows.

1 Choose a peat-based potting medium, which is lightweight, and a suitable cultivar. Use an odd number of plants for best effect.

2 Place a little potting mix in the base of the basket. Position all the plants except one evenly around the edge of the container.

3 Finally add the central plant. This one will prevent a hole appearing at the top of the basket once the plants start to grow.

4 Fill in the gaps between the plants with potting mix, but do not push it down. Add a slow-release fertiliser for easier feeding.

5 Fix the chains so that the plants can grow around them without being damaged. Tie the chains securely to a cane to keep them well above the growing plants.

Above: Fuchsias and lobelia are ideal for a display in light shade. Deadhead the fuchsias after flowering and keep them well-fed and watered.

Best cultivars

Singles: Abigail, Aunty Jinks, Daisy Bell, Hermiena, Jack Shahan, Marinka, President Margaret Slater, Red Spider, Waveney Gem.
Doubles: Applause, Blush O' Dawn, Dancing Flame, Devonshire Dumpling, Frau Hilde Rademacher, Malibu Mist, Pink Galore, Pink Marshmallow, Seventh Heaven, Swingtime, Wilson's Pearls.

Below: This is Lucinda, a semi-double fuchsia that will flower profusely through the summer if properly fed and watered.

Left: Single-flowered fuchsias are delightfully simple; most have four petals. They create elegant displays in baskets.

6 'Wilson's Pearls' has rich, semi-double blooms and dense foliage that totally disguises the basket. It is an ideal basket cultivar.

Pruning a fuchsia hanging basket

The end of the growing season is an ideal time to give fuchsias a rest and to create a plant with a good shape and structure for the following year. Never be afraid to cut back a plant. Baskets and standards will do better the following year if you have cut them back carefully. Shape the plants as you cut until you are happy with the woody structure.

1 Aim to create a sound structure for the following year, but retain a sufficient amount of growth so that any possible die back in the winter will not endanger the final shape of the plant in the following season.

2 Leave the main branches long enough so that they are beginning to hang over the edge, ready for next season. Use sharp secateurs to make clean cuts.

3 You can judge the finished effect and see whether the shape is unbalanced. Label all plants, so that you can identify them when they resume growing.

4 Remove any leaves on the stems. Clear away debris on the surface of the potting mixture to prevent the development of disease during the winter months.

5 Keep the finished basket in a frost-free spot. In areas where the temperature never drops very low, cutting back gives the plant a period of rest.

Raising your own fuchsia plants

Root 5cm(2in)-long cuttings indoors in spring. When well-rooted pot into 9cm(3.5in) pots and nip out the growing tip. Nip out the growing tip again when side shoots are 2.5cm(1in) long. Keep well-watered and feed fortnightly with quarter-strength liquid tomato feed. Do not plant into pots outdoors until after the last frost. In a frost-free greenhouse or conservatory, the container can be planted sooner and grown on under cover until it is safe to move it outside.

A FUCHSIA FLOWER TOWER

Today, the choice of containers for hanging displays is wider than ever. A recent development is a design based on a sturdy plastic bag. Follow the instructions for assembling a container like this; the one shown here has an integral drip tray that prevents splashing and also acts as a small extra water reservoir. Since the aim is to cover the sides as quickly as possible, choose fast-growing trailing plants with a dense branching habit and do not economise on the number of plants you buy. Trailing fuchsias and petunias are good, but also consider solenopsis, nasturtiums, and Swiss balcon pelargoniums. There is no need to buy large plants. Small 'plug' plants (see page 158) are ideal, since their tiny, narrow, pointed rootballs are easy to push in through slits or crosses cut in the sides of the bag. If only larger plants are available, carefully remove loose mix from the base of the rootball and tease out the roots to give a longer narrower shape that is easier to get into the bag. Do not cut or break off roots to fit. And avoid making planting holes any larger than absolutely necessary, as potting mix tends to run out during watering. As with normal hanging baskets, it is a good idea to add water-retaining gel crystals and slow-release fertiliser granules to the potting mix before planting the bag. Check daily and water as often as needed.

1 This hanging 'tower' has plastic sides and a solid drip tray base. Assemble and suspend it and add a layer of potting mix.

2 Cut four or five crosses just above the level of the potting mixture in the base, where you want to put plants. Prepare and plant only one layer at a time, working from the bottom up.

3 Tip small trailing fuchsias out of their pots, remove surplus soil from the roots and squeeze them gently into a narrow column that will fit through the crosses.

4 Gently tuck the roots inside the bag so that they rest on the surface of the potting mix. Tuck the plastic back around the neck of the plant to stop the mix falling out.

5 With the bottom row of plants in place, add another layer of mix. Do this slowly and evenly so that the wrinkles in the sides of the container are stretched out.

6 Cut more crosses halfway up the side walls, staggering them with the lower row of plants. Tuck the new plants in through the sides, in the same way as before.

Alternative planting schemes

The same sort of containers can be used for all kinds of bedding plant schemes; different types can be mixed together in much the same way as you might plant a hanging basket, but for most dramatic displays use all the same type of plant, or even all the same variety.

7 Put in a final row of plants as close as possible to the top of the container. Finish with a large single plant, which could be of a more upright type than the others.

8 Water evenly, so that the mix is moist but is not washed out through the planting holes. The drip tray prevents splashes and stops the tower drying out too fast.

Left: *Here, the same variety of fuchsia has been used throughout the scheme. Although a dozen or more plants have been used to create the display, the effect is of one really outstanding plant.*

9 Keep the tower well watered, regularly fed and in a bright situation, but out of strong midday sun. After about six weeks, the plants will begin to cover the container and come into flower. Deadhead them often.

Right: *Oxalis makes an unusual subject for this tower, but all sorts of plants with plenty of small bright flowers and contrasting dark foliage, especially if strikingly shaped, would work, too.*

Nip out the tips of any shoots that spoil the shape of the display.

Left: *Trailing verbena makes a more traditional display. The dusky pink flowers contrast particularly well with the delicate ferny foliage. Look for plants with similar attributes for alternative schemes.*

153

1   There are various options for lining hanging baskets, many of which use recycled or waste materials, such as this coir matting.

2   Pour in some moisture-retentive hanging basket potting mix. The thick liner also protects plants from drying out.

HANGING BASKETS THAT THRIVE IN A SHADY SPOT

Except for the variegated ivy, all the plants in this main basket come from the herbaceous perennial section of the garden centre. There is no reason why plants from any category – alpine, shrub, herbaceous or houseplant – cannot be used temporarily in a hanging basket, providing they are the right size with an attractive habit and long-lasting colour. More drought-tolerant types are better suited, as it is very difficult to keep baskets constantly moist. Some flowering bedding plants thrive in shade, including fuchsia, impatiens, lobelia and begonia. Team with ivies or gold-leaved foliage plants, such as golden feverfew (*Tanacetum parthenium* 'Aureum'), golden creeping Jenny (*Lysimachia nummularia* 'Aurea') or a gold-leaved hosta. Silver- and grey-leaved plants do not normally tolerate shade, which is why the silver-leaved lamiums, including 'White Nancy' and 'Pink Pewter', make such useful basket plants. Some fernlike dicentras associated with woodland gardening also work well in shade. Here, 'Pearl Drops' makes a wonderful contrast with the golden hosta. Other choices for shady hanging baskets include green, gold and variegated helxine (a houseplant) in a chessboard effect, *Campanula muralis* with sweet woodruff and false strawberry (*Duchesnea indica*), or hardier houseplants such as spider plant, nertera (bead plant), tolmiea and cissus vine.

3   Plant the dicentra, as with all plants, leaving room at the top for watering. 'Pearl Drops' goes on flowering all summer.

4   Add the gold-leaved hosta 'August Moon'. As well as striking foliage, it produces pale pink bellflower spikes in summer.

6   When the basket is full, fill in any gaps with potting mix. Add a thick layer of moist sphagnum moss or fine chipped bark as a water-retaining mulch.

5   Plant ground-covering lamium in the rest of the basket. This one produces a profusion of flowers in early and midsummer. The lamium will grow out, but for instant trails, add rooted cuttings of a gold-variegated *Hedera helix* variety.

Caring for shady baskets

• Turn them round a quarter turn every week so that plants are exposed to light from all directions, otherwise the basket grows over to one side.
• Expect hanging baskets in shade to need a little less watering than those in sun; avoid overwatering, especially when first planted.
• Be particularly fussy about removing dead flower heads and brown or yellow leaves regularly; in shade these may encourage fungal disease, which may spread to plants.
• Feed every two weeks using a high-potash tomato feed; a high-nitrogen feed would encourage lush leafy growth and discourage flowering.
• Avoid mixing shade-loving plants with those that need sunny conditions to thrive.

7 Hang the basket in a shady spot. At the end of the season, transfer the plants to the garden or plant them in a wooden half barrel with dwarf spring bulbs for a woodland effect.

Hosta 'August Moon'

Dicentra 'Pearl Drops' has blue-grey foliage.

Hedera helix cultivar (ivy)

Lamium maculatum 'Pink Pewter', a pale rose-flowered variety.

A self-watering spring basket

In this display, a fresh scheme of yellow and white spring flowers and foliage contrasts with a dark green basket. As it has solid sides, all the planting has to go in the top, so pick at least one plant with long trails to soften the edge. Hang the basket in a lightly shaded, sheltered spot.

1 *Assemble the basket and add a layer of moist potting mix. Try the largest plant for size and adjust the level as necessary.*

2 *Plant two primulas and fill in the gaps left on one side with the variegated euonymus. Add more potting mix as you go.*

3 *Plant two hardy primroses, one on either side of the watering tube. Leave space around the rim for trailing plants.*

4 *Split apart a couple of pots of rooted ivy cuttings and fit them around the edge. Fill any gaps with soil. Water thoroughly.*

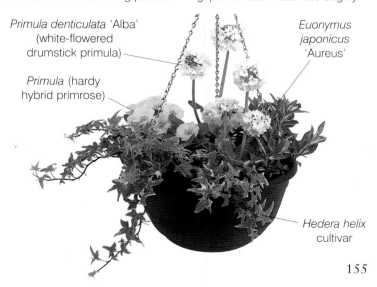

Primula denticulata 'Alba' (white-flowered drumstick primula)

Primula (hardy hybrid primrose)

Euonymus japonicus 'Aureus'

Hedera helix cultivar

155

1 Stand the basket on a bucket for stability. Cut a circle from an old potting mix bag and place it black-side-down in the base of the basket. Fill the plastic circle with potting mixture. Even when the top of the basket is dry, the plant roots should find moisture here.

SUMMER BASKETS

Summer hanging baskets can make an impact without being a blaze of colour. This basket contains an unusual mixture of plants in subtle shades of purple and silver-grey. The deep velvet-purple bedding viola 'Prince Henry' makes a superb contrast with the other flowers and foliage, while *Nemesia fruticans* produces airy flowers all summer long. In the top are the daisylike flowers of *Osteospermum* 'Sunny Lady'. Like all osteospermums, the flowers close in shade, so hang the basket where it will receive sun for most of the day. The foliage ranges from the feathery leaves of *Lotus berthelotii* to the cut leaves of cineraria and the rounded, leathery, purple foliage of *Sedum* 'Bertram Anderson'.

To create a feeling of tranquillity in your garden, consider a combination of white, grey, silver and green foliage. For any monochrome scheme to be truly successful, it is vital to have plenty of textural contrast between different elements. Bear in mind that there is a noticeable variation in the colour of white flowers. Those in the basket are pure white, but the results would not have been so successful if it combined creamy whites and pure whites. Here, the large, solid flower heads of petunia are planted alongside the smaller-flowered busy Lizzie, which is in turn set against white alyssum.

Adding tiny amounts of an entirely different colour will often lift an all-white scheme and make the flowers stand out all the more.

2 Using thick clumps of moist sphagnum moss, line the basket sides. Tuck moss under the edges of the plastic as camouflage. Push bedding violas horizontally through the bars. Pack in as many as will fit to create a full display.

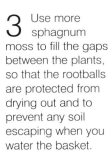

3 Use more sphagnum moss to fill the gaps between the plants, so that the rootballs are protected from drying out and to prevent any soil escaping when you water the basket.

5 Plant nemesias to give height at the back. If the trailing lotus at the front produces orange-red flowers later on, remove them.

4 Add a group of cineraria, tilting one down over the basket sides to soften the edge. Pinch out the tips to keep them compact and bushy. Plant the large sedum to one side, so that the long trailing shoots hang over the edge.

6 Fill in the remaining space at the back of the basket with the osteospermum, and cover all the exposed rootballs with potting mixture. Water the whole display thoroughly and add more soil if gaps appear.

Allow plants to settle in for several days by standing the basket in a shady, sheltered spot.

Osteospermum 'Sunny Lady'

Nemesia fruticans

Sedum 'Bertram Anderson'

Lotus berthelotii (coral gem)

Viola 'Prince Henry'

Senecio cineraria

7 To aid moisture retention, add a thick layer of moist sphagnum moss over the potting mix in the top of the basket.

A classic white arrangement

1 Having lined the basket as before, cover the sides with alyssum, feeding the rootballs horizontally through the wires.

2 Pack moss around the necks of the plants. Angle the busy Lizzie so that it covers the rim of the basket.

3 Plant a pot of the ferny Lotus berthelotii to trail over the edge. Plant petunias into the top and sides of the basket and add a trailing ivy. Squeeze a white-flowered pelargonium into the centre of the basket.

Pelargonium PAC cultivar 'Aphrodite'

Impatiens (busy Lizzie)

Petunia 'Celebrity White'

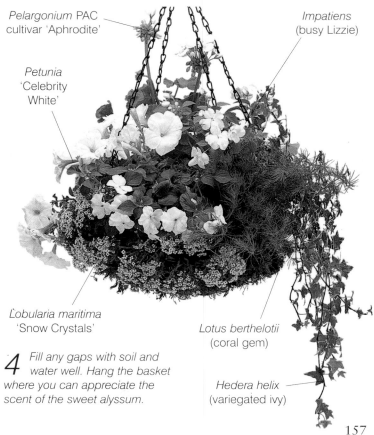

Lobularia maritima 'Snow Crystals'

Lotus berthelotii (coral gem)

Hedera helix (variegated ivy)

4 Fill any gaps with soil and water well. Hang the basket where you can appreciate the scent of the sweet alyssum.

SUMMER PLUGS IN A WIRE HANGING BASKET

Most people plant up hanging baskets in early summer, using good-sized plants that are already in full bloom to make an immediate display. Since all risk of frost is past by then, the containers can safely be put straight out into the garden. But if you have space in a heated greenhouse or conservatory, you can plant the containers much earlier and grow them on under cover. This is a good way to use home-grown seedlings of bedding plants, or rooted cuttings of fuchsias and pelargoniums. However, you can also take advantage of the wide range of 'plug' plants available by mail order, as well as from garden centres from early spring onwards. Later in the season small plants will be harder to find. 'Plugs' are young plants grown in small individual 'cells', rather like multiple egg boxes on a tiny scale. Remove each plantlet from its cell before planting, by pushing the tip of a dibber or pencil carefully up through the base of the cell. Alternatively, stab a tiny fork into the potting mixture to lift out the plantlet. Plugs make planting very simple; root damage is virtually non-existent, as the plugs can simply be pushed into loose potting mix. They are particularly easy to use around the sides of hanging baskets, as they are small enough to fit through the wire sides of traditional baskets.

2 Place a circle of black plastic in the bottom of the basket to act as a water reservoir. Add some potting mixture to hold it in place.

3 Tuck a layer of sphagnum moss under the edge of the plastic. Once the basket is full, you will not notice the plastic at all.

4 Build up the sides with a thick layer of moss. Pack it in tightly to prevent soil escaping when the plants are watered. Add more mix.

5 Gently push the neck of the plant just inside the wire. Pack it with moss and cover the rootball with more mix, filling in any gaps.

6 Plant the ivy, holding the rootball horizontally and feeding the trails through the wires from the inside out. Push the crown against the inside of the basket.

1 Assemble a mixture of flowering and foliage plants, with trailing varieties to cover the basket sides and bushy, upright types for the middle.

Net pots should be left in place during planting, but you must remove solid pots.

7 When the sides are planted up, cover all the exposed rootballs with more mix. Leave space for planting in the top. Add more trailing plants to hang over the top of the basket. Fill in the centre with upright plants; leave room for growth.

8 Cover the surface with a thick layer of moss, Water the basket well and hang it in a light, frost-free place until the plants are established. Once young plants develop a good root system, they quickly fill the basket. Feed regularly to keep them flowering.

Fuchsia 'Beacon' (bush variety)

Verbena 'Blue Cascade'

Fuchsia 'La Campanella' (cascade variety)

Brachyscome multifida

Hedera helix (variegated ivy)

Glechoma hederacea 'Variegata'

Young plants in open-sided pots

Nurseries and garden centres often sell young plants growing in mesh-sided containers, or pots with open, slitted sides. These are designed for the roots to grow through, so do not try to remove the plants from them. Even inexperienced gardeners can deal with young plants without any risk of damaging roots – and be confident of good results.

Above: *Young plants in open-sided pots are often sold in collections, each 'set' holding enough plants for a complete hanging basket. Leave the pots on to avoid root damage.*

Plants in divided trays

Above: *Young plants in the usual divided trays must be removed before planting or the roots cannot get out properly. If you cannot knock the plants out, cut the pot carefully away.*

Alternative planting schemes

A semi-trailing fuchsia such as 'Swingtime' would work well in combination with the trailing *Verbena* 'Sissinghurst' or paler pink 'Silver Anne', both vigorous and with strong mildew resistance. Many hardy annuals, grown in pots and transferred to the basket when large enough, would also give a 'cottage' look. Try *Nasturtium* 'Alaska', with its white-marbled leaves, the pot marigold mix *Calendula* 'Fiesta Gitana' or *Brachyscome iberidifolia* 'Summer Skies', which produces a profusion of blue, purple and white daisies all summer. Several pansies are now available in old-fashioned pastel shades. Try *Viola* 'Watercolours' or 'Romeo and Juliet'.

LATE-SEASON DISPLAYS FOR A COTTAGE GARDEN

This wicker basket has a rustic look, so the planting style is soft and relaxed, just like a traditional cottage garden border. Here, *Campanula carpatica* 'Blue Clips', a hardy alpine bellflower, is teamed with a gold-leaved trailing ivy. Plenty of other hardy herbaceous plants and tender perennials would produce a similar effect, including the dwarf marguerites *(Argyranthemum frutescens* cultivars), and dwarf scabious, *Scabiosa* 'Butterfly Blue' and 'Pink Mist', which flower over a long period.

Wicker baskets are equally suited to an autumnal display. *Thunbergia alata,* commonly known as black-eyed Susan, is very easy to raise from seed in spring and less expensive than buying plants in flower during summer. The stems sometimes become a little congested, so some thinning may be called for to emphasise the elegant trailing habit. Pick up the *Thunbergia* first and carry it around the garden centre so that you can match the flower shade with a pot of bedding dahlias. These remain short and compact, and have a flowering period that extends well into the autumn. Before adding them to the basket, check plants carefully for slugs and earwigs. Like *Thunbergia*, dahlias need regular feeding and must not be allowed to dry out. Take off the dead flower heads as soon as they fade, as they are quite difficult to distinguish from the buds once the petals have fallen.

1 Line the basket to prevent drips if used indoors, and to protect the wicker. To make trimming easier, put some gravel in the base to keep the plastic in place.

2 Add more gravel or bits of broken polystyrene plant trays to create a drainage reservoir to prevent overwatering.

3 For seasonal displays, use a peat-based mix. For alpines or perennials, use a soil-based mix or add coarse grit to a peat mix.

4 Arrange the longest trails of variegated ivy so that they create a rim of greenery that spills out over the basket's dipped edge. Make the composition asymmetric.

5 Fill the centre of the basket with the campanulas. Try not to hide the handle, as this is very much part of the overall design of the arrangement. Fill in any gaps with soil and firm in lightly.

6 Break off chunks of rooted ivy cuttings and fill in any gaps that remain around the edge of the basket. The ivy combines well with the blue bellflower and contrasts with the dark wicker.

Dahlias in a wicker basket

The bronze-purple foliage of Ajuga reptans *'Atropurpurea' makes a striking contrast with the thunbergia. The more upright euphorbia provides a lighter texture altogether and makes an attractive 'filler'.*

1 *Plant a* Thunbergia alata *so that it overhangs one side of the basket. Choose a matching bedding dahlia for the other side.*

2 *Tuck ajuga underneath the dahlia foliage and add some euphorbia between the dahlia and the* Thunbergia alata.

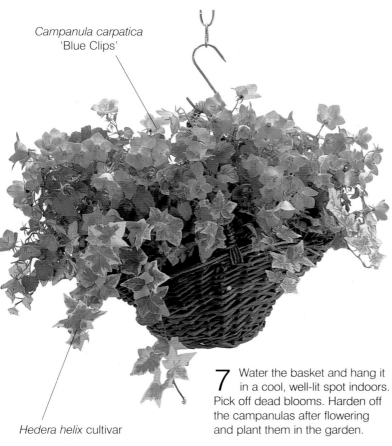

Campanula carpatica 'Blue Clips'

Hedera helix cultivar

7 Water the basket and hang it in a cool, well-lit spot indoors. Pick off dead blooms. Harden off the campanulas after flowering and plant them in the garden.

Euphorbia dulcis 'Chameleon'

Dahlia 'Dahlietta Apricot'

3 *Complete the basket with more ajugas and fill in round the plants with potting mix. Hang the basket out of extreme midday sun, which would bleach the flowers.*

Thunbergia alata (black-eyed Susan)

Ajuga reptans 'Atropurpurea'

1 Six heathers in small pots and a large variegated ivy with long trails will fill a medium-sized hanging basket; this is a self-watering type for low maintenance.

NEAT WINTER BASKETS

The compact shape and free-flowering habit of winter-flowering heathers make them perfect for hanging baskets. Since they are well able to withstand the weather, you need not keep them in particularly sheltered situations, nor do the plants stop flowering or look battered if the weather turns nasty. In the Northern Hemisphere, there is no reason why you should not add ribbons or other decorations to give the container a festive touch for the Christmas period, or even illuminate it with coloured outdoor lights. The secret of success with any winter container is to buy evenly shaped plants just coming into flower at the start of the season and to fill it generously, as plants cannot be expected to grow and hide any gaps at that time of year.

Given a reasonably sheltered sunny spot, it is possible to keep hanging baskets looking good all winter. Choose from the limited range of suitable flowers, particularly 'Universal' pansies and hybrid primroses, backed up by plenty of small evergreens, such as ivy, euonymus, santolina or periwinkle (variegated versions are especially pretty). Use the trailing kinds around the edge of the basket for a fuller, softer effect. In big cities, the microclimate often makes it possible to grow relatively tender plants outdoors in winter; almost hardy indoor plants, such as cyclamen, winter cherry, cineraria and asparagus fern often thrive.

2 Roughly half-fill the basket with potting mixture. If you are using a self-watering basket, do not fill the reservoir until you have finished planting up the basket.

5 Plant the flowering heathers so that the shoots cascade over the edges to create the fullest display without swamping the smaller gold-leaved plants.

3 Knock the ivy out of its pot and plant it – with its stake – so that the top of the rootball is about 1.25cm(0.5in) below the rim of the pot. Firm gently so it stands up straight.

4 Tip out the two gold-leaved heathers and plant them close together at the front of the basket. Their bright foliage complements the variegated markings in the ivy leaves.

6 Using a small hand trowel, scoop a little extra potting mix into any gaps between the rootballs. This prevents the roots drying out, which could make flowers finish early and cause the foliage to turn brown.

7 Cut the ties holding the ivy stems to the cane and untangle the 'trails', so they are all separate, ready to be arranged around the hanging basket.

8 Arrange the ivy trails around the edge of the basket and in the heather. This looks best where the inside of a low basket will be easily visible.

Variegated ivy

Gold-leaved winter heather

Pansies, primroses and ivy

There is no need to buy special hanging baskets for winter displays; reuse summer ones. Excess water can be a problem in winter, so avoid self-watering baskets unless they are to be kept under cover.

1 *If it has a rounded base, sit the basket in an upturned bucket for added stability. Drape the chains over the outside.*

2 *Three-quarters fill the basket with potting mix. The plant rootballs will virtually fill the top 7.5cm(3in) of the basket.*

3 *Put in the plants without disturbing the rootballs. (This ensures that the flowers and buds do not receive a check in growth.)*

4 *Add trailing ivies around the edges; they will partly cover the basket sides and create a fuller, more rounded display.*

Winter-flowering pansies

Cultivated primrose hybrids (*Primula acaulis* hybrids)

5 *Fill any gaps with potting mix, then water well. Check the basket every week to see if it needs watering. Apply a weak liquid feed in mild weather.*

Variegated ivy

1 Cut a circle of plastic from an old potting mixture bag and use it black-side-down to line the base of a wire basket.

2 Add some potting mixture to act as a small reservoir that helps to prevent water from draining away too rapidly.

VIVID WINTER DISPLAYS

A cheerful basket will liven up even the darkest winter day. Here, scarlet primroses really sparkle and their bold yellow centres are accentuated by golden-variegated euonymus. From autumn to early winter, you should find all the necessary ingredients for such baskets at garden centres; many young shrubs in small pots are available at this time. They may seem quite expensive for a seasonal basket, but you can of course plant them out in the garden once the display is over. Instead of golden euonymus, you could try its white-variegated counterpart Emerald Gaiety, evergreen herbs and hebes, such as the pink-flushed 'Red Edge' or silver-leaved *Hebe pinguifolia* 'Pagei'. Although more often associated with summer bedding displays, cineraria is reasonably hardy and it is worth potting up a few plants towards the end of summer. Cut back any long straggly shoots or flower stems to promote bushy new growth and keep them in a sunny spot for later use. You can always find pots of trailing ivy in the houseplant section of garden centres; outdoor ones are rarely so luxuriant. Gradually introduce the ivy to outdoor conditions and temperatures before planting it. Conifer hedge clippings make a good substitute for moss in baskets. The fresh green colouring is especially welcome in winter – it lasts for months without turning brown. Use it thickly to help insulate the basket and prevent the soil from freezing.

3 Build up the conifer lining, tucking the foliage under the edge of the plastic. Weave pieces into each other and through the wire bars.

6 Plant scarlet primroses, tilting one over the edge to show off its flowers. Add another euonymus at the back as a foil for the flowers.

4 Add more potting mix until you reach the point where the first plant is to go in. Offer up the euonymus and adjust the soil level.

5 Place the rootball of the euonymus on the potting mix and feed the stems through the bars. Add a cineraria in the top.

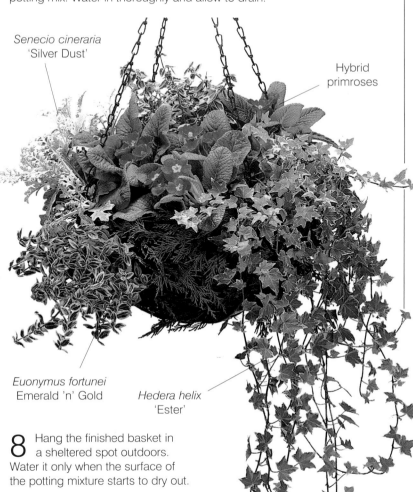

7 Add a well-grown pot of trailing ivy to balance the design. Fill in all the gaps between the plants with potting mix. Water in thoroughly and allow to drain.

Senecio cineraria 'Silver Dust'

Hybrid primroses

Euonymus fortunei Emerald 'n' Gold

Hedera helix 'Ester'

8 Hang the finished basket in a sheltered spot outdoors. Water it only when the surface of the potting mixture starts to dry out.

A winter display in a large container

A delicate combination of foliage and flower suits this classical basket. Its pale blue-green colouring is reminiscent of ice, so the planting is designed to create a frosted effect. You could choose all-white plants, but the graduation of white through to pink is even more effective. Make sure the basket has drainage holes before you plant it up.

1 Broken-up polystyrene seed trays make a lightweight substitute for gravel drainage. Fill the tapering base completely.

2 Add a peat-based mix for these ericaceous plants. Leave room for the largest rootballs and space for watering.

3 Plant the largest element – here Gaultheria mucronata – at the back. Add the heather and then the ornamental cabbages.

4 Fill the centre with pansies of subtly different shades to draw together all the elements of the basket. Fill the gaps with soil.

Gaultheria mucronata 'White Pearl'

Pansy Ultima series 'Pink Shades' F1

Ornamental cabbage

Erica carnea 'Springwood White' (heather)

EYE-CATCHING BASKETS FOR WINTER AND SPRING

1 A simple colour scheme – butter-yellow primroses and a gold chain – picks out the unusual detailing on this delightful wicker basket.

Primroses and pansies bring a welcome splash of colour on dull winter days and a promise of spring to come. The life of primroses can easily be extended, especially if you choose compact plants with many buds still to come and stiff, dark green leaves. Gently tip the plant out of its pot to look at the root system, which should be white and well developed. Avoid plants that are pale and drawn. Overwatering is a common problem, too. It is best to leave watering until the foliage has just started to go limp. Avoid overhead watering, which marks both the foliage and flowers. Provided the basket is protected from the elements, it can be reused many times. After the primroses, you could continue the gold theme with dwarf daffodils or little yellow violas and replace these later on with *Calceolaria* 'Sunshine' or a yellow kalanchoe (flaming Katy).

The most widely sold winter-flowering pansies are the weather-resistant Universal and Ultima series. (Most pansies can be made to flower throughout the year by sowing them at different times, so do not be surprised to see summer bedding varieties on sale in winter; avoid these.) As plants put on little growth until spring, choose bushy specimens with healthy dark green foliage and plenty of flower buds. A basket edged in ivy can be planted up with all kinds of flowering plants, including double daisies, hybrid primroses and even dwarf bulbs, provided the container is deep enough. Keep them in a cool but sheltered place, such as a cold frame, until the bulbs are just starting to show flower buds and then bring them out on display.

2 Line the basket with a circle of plastic cut from a black bag and press the pleated lining into position inside the basket.

3 Carefully trim off any excess plastic until it is just below the rim of the basket so that it will be hidden by the soil.

4 Add a layer of gravel as a drainage reservoir. This helps prevent overwatering, which can cause leaves to turn yellow and rot.

5 Cover the gravel with soil- or peat-based potting mixture and then test the depth by popping in one of the primroses to see the effect.

Hardy primroses

Throughout the winter, garden centres offer trays of colourful primroses for sale. These are normally already in flower, which makes colour scheming easier. Before buying, make sure they are frost hardy. Seed catalogues now offer several weather-resistant varieties, so you can grow your own supply.

166

6 Plant the primroses, arranging the foliage to fit around the handle and drape over the edge. Cut off any leaves that are squashed together at the centre of the arrangement.

Pansies in a wicker basket

Given the protection of a porch, unheated conservatory or sunroom, wicker baskets will not weather and bedding plants are protected from the effects of exposure to cold winds and freezing potting mixtures.

1 To prevent waterlogging in a sealed container, add a layer of pebbles or similar drainage material to a lined wicker basket.

2 Cover the pebbles with potting mix, leaving room for the plants on top. Check the level with a plant and adjust.

7 Fill the gaps in between plants with more potting mixture. Firm the soil gently, making sure that there are no air pockets, as these prevent plant roots from developing. Settle the soil in by watering, but do not overwater.

3 Split up the ivy to make a foliage edging with trails overhanging the basket. Wind some pieces around the handle.

4 Plant the pansies close together, fill in any spaces with potting mix and firm in. Add enough water to settle the soil.

5 Hang the basket by a rope or by a large hook and chain. Water sparingly, allowing the soil surface to dry out slightly between waterings.

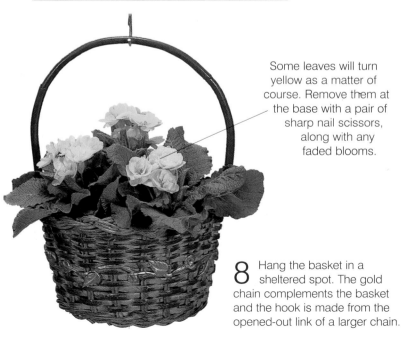

Some leaves will turn yellow as a matter of course. Remove them at the base with a pair of sharp nail scissors, along with any faded blooms.

8 Hang the basket in a sheltered spot. The gold chain complements the basket and the hook is made from the opened-out link of a larger chain.

Pansy Crystal Bowl Series 'Sky Blue' F1

Hedera helix *'Mint Kolibri'*

Pelargoniums and terracotta pots – a timeless combination for the patio.

PART SEVEN

PATIO POTS

The perfect pairing of plants and pots can be the result of much trial and error, but is much easier to achieve once you know what type of plants suit which type of pots, and what colours work well together. Then it is easy to keep inventing new combinations that let you reuse pots over and over again in completely new ways.

1 Cover the drainage hole with a small crock. This frost-resistant, ceramic pot is decorated with an oriental-style design that will match the pansies.

2 Loosely fill the pot with potting mix to within 2.5cm (1in) of the rim. Pack in as many plants as possible; a small pot like this will take four pansies.

PANSIES IN SIMPLE POTS

If you grow your own spring bedding plants from seed, such as wallflowers, stocks, violas and bellis daisies, you could plant up containers in autumn after removing summer annuals. But if left outside, plants must be sheltered from strong wind, and containers protected from freezing solid or becoming waterlogged to prevent roots rotting off. Since they do not start to flower until spring anyway, it is usually much easier to keep plants in their pots over winter. Ideally, store them in an unheated greenhouse or enclosed porch; this way, they take up less room than they would in a big tub or planter. When spring arrives, acclimatise the plants gradually to outdoor conditions by standing them outside on fine days to start with. After a few weeks of 'hardening off', plant them into containers. If the weather is bad, you can even delay planting until they are starting to flower. If you prefer to buy in your plants, there is plenty of choice: forget-me-nots, spring bulbs in individual pots, and pansies are some of the most popular. The temptation is often to plant up the greatest mixture of flowers that will fit into a large container, but as a change, try teaming a prettily patterned pot with flowers that pick out one of the colours from the pot. The result will look lovely on an outdoor window ledge or in the middle of a patio table. Or try standing a row of similar pots along the top of a low wall. Pansies are particularly attractive and are available in a good range of colours, some with delightful 'faces'.

3 Carefully push each plant out of its pot through the hole in the base. You may need to squeeze the rootballs gently in order to fit them into the container.

Four plants are enough to fill a small pot. This one measures 20cm(8in) in diameter.

Choose plants with plenty of flower and buds for an instant effect. Remove any dead blooms.

4 When they are all in place, fill any gaps with potting mix, leaving about 1.25cm(0.5in) between the top of the soil and the rim of the pot for watering.

Above: This crimson spring container display uses the contrasting shapes of snake's head fritillary (*Fritillaria meleagris*), *Erica carnea* and pansy flowers, with dark hebe foliage and a gold conifer.

Remove dead flowerheads and feed plants with a high-potash liquid or soluble feed.

5 If any potting mix has been spilt onto the pot during planting, wipe it off so that the pot is clean. Stand the pot on its matching saucer. Water the pansies in and check the pot regularly; it should not dry out.

Pansies in a metal bucket

Pansies look good in all sorts of simple containers, but you can also adapt all kinds of household items to create unusual 'theme' planters. A metal bucket, for example, would look in keeping next to a well or by a utility room door.

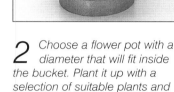

1 Here, an unpainted metal bucket is used as a pot holder. Put a layer of shingle on the base of the bucket to raise up the pot and improve drainage.

2 Choose a flower pot with a diameter that will fit inside the bucket. Plant it up with a selection of suitable plants and stand it on the shingle base.

3 The cheerful little viola 'Jackanapes' was raised by Gertrude Jekyll. Grow plants from cuttings so that they remain true to type; like all pansies, it crosses readily and seedlings are 'mongrels'.

Right: Cream-and-white pansies team beautifully with the variegated foliage of euonymus and hebe. Combined with silver Helichrysum italicum *(one of the hardier kinds)*, the result is a subtle, understated display.

171

HEATHERS IN CONTAINERS

Late summer- and autumn-flowering heathers in containers bridge the gap between summer bedding and the start of the winter-flowering heather season. Good examples include many varieties of *Calluna vulgaris* (ling) and *Erica vagans*. Both need acid conditions, so choose an ericaceous potting mix and team them with other lime-hating plants. Once autumn heathers are over, plant them out in the garden and put winter-flowering heathers into the same pot. (They will not mind the ericaceous mix.) Alternatively, for year-round colour and interest, try substituting some of the late summer and autumn heathers shown here for earlier flowering kinds, particularly those with coloured foliage. They would then act as a permanent backdrop for the evergreens in the centre of the display. The plants used here are a purple-leaved form of leucothoe and a gaultheria with lilac berries, although any acid-loving evergreens would work. A good combination would be *Gaultheria procumbens*, a low creeper with deep green oval leaves and large bright red berries all winter, teamed with a dwarf rhododendron; the latter would flower in late spring, giving an even greater spread of seasonal interest.

1 Cover the drainage hole with a crock, flat stone or 2.5cm(1in) of gravel. Part-fill the pot with ericaceous mix to just below the bottom planting pockets. This glazed container makes a good foil for the flowering plants.

2 Buy heathers in small pots so that the rootballs will fit into the planting pockets. Tip out the plants and push them into the holes. If rootballs are very congested, gently tease out some roots so they can spread out.

3 Add some more potting mixture to cover the roots and bring the level up to the next row of planting pockets. Add the remaining heathers.

4 Plant the top of the container. It is vital to fill up the pot, because plants put in towards the end of the season will not grow much more, but need to make an instant impact.

5 Add two or three trailing ivies around the rim, pulling the trails through the handles and round between the heathers in the side pockets to create an instantly mature finish.

Leucothoe 'Carinella'

Gaultheria mucronata

Hedera helix 'Golden Ester'

Right: The heathers used in this display, reading clockwise from bottom left, are *Calluna vulgaris* 'Glencoe', 'Marleen', 'Alexandra', 'Beoley Gold', *Erica vagans* 'Valerie Proudley', *Calluna vulgaris* 'Dark Beauty', 'Schurig's Sensation' and 'Alexandra'.

6 Stand the pot in a sheltered sunny spot and raise it up on 'pot feet' to aid drainage. Water it regularly. During the spring following planting, start feeding with a liquid feed.

Heathers in a glazed pot

Larger low-level containers, such as tubs and troughs, allow for more expansive winter displays based around heathers. Try combining them with miniature conifers, evergreen shrubs and grasses or alpines.

1 Cover the drainage hole with a 'crock' to contain the potting mix, or use wire gauze, which also keeps out worms.

2 Fill one third of the container with potting mix. Ericaceous mix is not necessary, as winter heathers do not mind a little lime.

3 Position the conifer centrally, so that the top of the rootball is about 1.25cm(0.5in) below the rim of the container.

4 Firm the conifer down gently. Space the heathers evenly around it, squeezing the rootballs slightly to make them fit.

Chamaecyparis thyoides 'Purple Heather'

Heathers clockwise from bottom left: Erica carnea 'Rosalie', E. darleyensis 'Darley Dale', E. carnea 'March Seedling'.

5 Fill the spaces between the heathers with extra potting mix until the container is loosely filled to just below the rim.

Planting crocus

Crocus and colchicums do well in containers. *Crocus speciosus* is a true crocus that flowers in the autumn, a fine free-flowering blue bulb that readily increases. Autumn-flowering bulbs are best planted and then left undisturbed.

The flowering shoot is a tiny protruding tip.

A small dimple with a dark core is the root.

1 A terracotta pan or half-pot is an ideal container for small bulbs. Start by placing a piece of broken pot over the drainage hole.

2 The corms need to be well drained. Put a layer of grit in the base before half-filling the pan with potting mix. Smooth it down.

3 Carefully position the corms about 2.5cm(1in) apart. Make sure that they are the right way up; if in doubt, lay them on their sides.

4 Cover the corms with potting mix almost to the rim. Smooth down gently but firmly and add a sprinkling of grit. Water lightly.

Right: *Crocus medius* is a scarce autumn-flowering species that deserves to be better known. It does well in a sunny, well-drained spot (good for pots or a rock feature). Bright petals contrast with the branching orange stamens.

BULBS WITH STYLE

Bulbs are a great way of adding seasonal touches of style to the garden. Spring species can be used in many innovative ways to brighten up dingy parts of the garden. Place large striking tubs or urns of daffodils under trees or in light woodland to bring colourless areas to life. Team a tub of bulbs and spring bedding with a spring-flowering shrub to make it the centre of attention. Use a row of formal pots all planted with the same kind of crocus to line a path. Or group together a few well-chosen, striking containers planted with bulbs by the front door; include a few hyacinths for their scent. A collection of dwarf bulbs looks brilliant in glazed ceramic pots; choose small pots, each containing about half a dozen bulbs of the same variety, and stage them on tiered shelving on a sheltered patio. This is a great idea for transforming very little material into a superb display. Summer bulbs offer plenty of creative potential, too. Liven up summer shrub borders with huge pots of lilies; scented varieties fill the air with heady perfume. And grow compact patio dahlias in large tubs in a sunny spot. They flower from midsummer into the autumn, filling a gap when many bedding plants are past their best. Even autumn bulbs, such as colchicums and autumn crocus species, provide temporary splashes of colour, well worth adding to your usual seasonal display while they are at their best.

Planting a canna in a pot

1 Choose a pot large enough to take the roots with ease. Part-fill it with potting mix and rest the tuber on the surface, allowing for 5cm(2in) of mix above the tip.

2 Cover the tuber with more potting mix and then fill the pot almost to the rim. Tap the pot down firmly to consolidate the potting mixture.

Above: Spring bulbs associate beautifully with spring bedding to create charming naturalistic container schemes. Here, *Chionodoxa luciliae* 'Blue Giant' is paired with *Arabis* 'Pink Charm' in an old clay pot.

Planting lily bulbs in a clay pot

Lilies are one of the most spectacular and collectable summer-flowering bulbs. Some varieties need lime-free soil, while others do not mind. Although pot-grown plants are available in flower during the summer, lilies are normally bought as dry bulbs in spring.

1 Take a 35.5cm(14in) diameter container (to allow sufficient planting depth) and half-fill it with soil-based potting mixture.

2 Space the lilies an equal distance apart. In pots, you can plant lilies closer together than you would in a garden.

3 Arrange five bulbs around the edge of the pot and one in the centre. Cover the bulbs with potting mix; make sure that they stay upright.

Below: A canna in a pot will not grow as tall as it would in a border. Expect flowers in mid- to late summer.

3 Leave a 2.5cm(1in) gap between the soil surface and the rim of the pot for watering. Water until the soil is evenly wet; allow any surplus to drain away.

4 Once it is in flower, you can stand a pot-grown lily on a patio (but make sure that the pot is in shade) or sink the pot to its rim in a border for instant colour in a vacant spot.

The versatility of grasses

As a group, perennial grasses encompass such an enormous number of species, each with their own distinctive characteristics, that it is not difficult to find grasses for virtually every situation around the garden.

Phalaris arundinacea 'Picta' (gardener's garters)

Hakonechloa macra 'Alboaurea'

Carex comans 'Bronze'

Below: When grown in containers, arching grasses make graceful fountain shapes. Since the seedheads dry naturally on the plant, the effect is very long lasting.

GRASSES IN CONTAINERS

Container planting schemes need not consist solely of bedding plants. One of the most unusual ideas is to use grasses and their larger relatives, such as bamboos. A large container filled with a mixture of contrasting grasses looks particularly striking in a modern setting, where the dramatic shapes really stand out well. It could also be teamed with smaller containers of evergreens, conifers and heathers to make a fuller display. They all go together very well. Ornamental grasses range in height from 15cm(6in) up to 3m(10ft). The real giants, such as the tall bamboos, *Arundo donax* and miscanthus, are best grown in large tubs of their own once they have reached a good size. A row of these makes a good instant screen, which is portable (just) if necessary. But while they are young, they could be used for a year or two in large mixed plantings with other species. Medium-sized grasses suitable for growing on a long-term basis in containers include Bowles' golden grass *(Milium effusum* 'Aureum'), *Carex comans* (an unusual bronze form of sedge which, although not a true grass, does look like one), *Hakonechloa macra* 'Alboaurea' (a graceful, dramatically striped grass with arching gold and green leaves) and *Helictotrichon sempervirens*, which has wide, ribbonlike, steel-blue foliage. Among the smaller grasses are many species of festuca, which have vivid blue foliage.

1 Cover the drainage holes with a crock and half-fill the pot with good-quality potting mix. Put in the largest plant first, placing it up against the side of the pot.

2 Tuck the second largest plant in alongside the first, pushing it well up to leave room for the third. Fill the container well for a display that looks instantly mature.

3 Fit in the last plant, squeezing the rootballs slightly if necessary. Arrange trailing leaves so that they hang over the edge of the pot and are not trapped.

4 Trowel more potting mix between the rootballs and firm it down slightly so that it does not sink when watered. Cover exposed rootballs with more mix.

5 After watering in, move the container to its final position. It will look especially good with potted specimen shrubs, particularly evergreens, or standing on gravel.

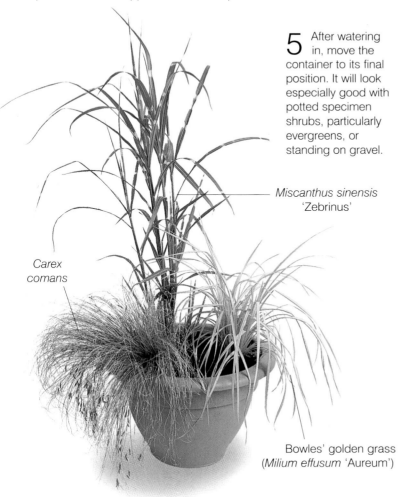

Miscanthus sinensis 'Zebrinus'

Carex comans

Bowles' golden grass (*Milium effusum* 'Aureum')

Grasses in a blue-glazed pot

Grasses and grasslike plants team well with other sunlovers to make an unusual display for a hot spot. Use a colourful reflective container for striking results.

1 Cover the drainage hole with a crock. Roughly half-fill the pot with mix, adding a little sharp sand or gravel to improve drainage if necessary.

2 Put a tall upright species at the back and a looser shaped, more open-textured grass towards the front.

3 Carefully pack the spaces between rootballs with mix. In a small pot it is easy to leave air pockets, so plants dry out.

4 The last plant is a low spreader with evergreen leaves that will hang over the edges of the container.

5 With subtle tones of green and grey, the finished display has a cool elegance that will suit a restful patio setting.

Stipa tenuissima

Ophiopogon jaburan 'Vittatus'

Stachys byzantina 'Silver Carpet'

This container is to be planted with annual flowers, so choose a soilless potting mixture and fill it to just below the rim.

1 Gather together a suitable selection of plants. This is a bright colour scheme of red, yellow and orange. As one is a climber, place a cane in the middle of the tub to support it.

PLASTIC TUBS OF ANNUALS

Large plastic pots make excellent containers for temporary displays of annual colour or for a mixture of flowering annuals, half-hardy perennials and foliage plants in a range of shapes and sizes. Whatever plants you choose, it is a good idea to stick to a basic formula: a large centrepiece – perhaps a climber on a cane, a standard fuchsia or simply a tall, upright plant; various smaller 'filler' flowers for plenty of colour; complementary foliage and either trailing plants or something with large leaves or dangling rosette shapes that will spill over the edges. You can make a traditional display in a wide range of colours, or a more sophisticated one, using just part of the spectrum.

As the plants in the arrangement grow up, remove dead flowerheads regularly to encourage plants to keep flowering. Nip out any shoots that grow out of shape or are very overcrowded. Climbers will certainly need regular attention to stop them getting out of control and smothering their neighbours. They normally grow quickly, so go over them every week or two, tying in the new growth. When it reaches the top of the cane, allow it to bend over and then start winding it back down the pillar of foliage. Tie it into place. This way, new flowering shoots will slowly cover the older parts of the stems that are no longer producing new buds.

2 Plant the centrepiece first – here a climbing black-eyed Susan. Tie it loosely to the cane.

3 Group other plants of the same type next to neighbours that will create a strong contrast.

4 A foliage plant makes a good 'foil' for groups of flowers. This coleus goes very well with the colour scheme of the container.

5 The ornamental cabbage will eventually make a huge rosette shape at the base of the container. By then, the other flowers will have grown quite tall.

6 Water the finished container well. Once the container is filled with roots, water it once or twice a day.

Black-eyed Susan (*Thunbergia alata*)

Argyranthemum frutescens 'Jamaica Primrose'

African marigold, compact type

Ornamental cabbage

French marigold 'Aurora Fire'

Coleus (*Solenostemon*)

Salvia 'Vanguard'

Variations on a summer theme

In this display, the climbing plant is the frost-sensitive purple bell vine (Rhodochiton atrosanguineus). *It is surrounded by* Anisodontea capensis, *a shrubby half-hardy perennial that can be treated rather like a pelargonium, a mauve-and-purple variegated ornamental cabbage,* Viola *'Prince Henry' and* Impatiens *'Accent Lilac'.*

1 Plant the climber alongside the cane. Leave it tied to its existing stick while you plant it to protect the delicate trailing stems.

2 When the roots are planted, untie the plant from the short stick and retie it loosely to the taller cane in the new pot.

3 Arrange the remaining plants around the container. Fill the container well, compressing the rootballs slightly to fit the spaces.

4 Use small plants at the base of larger ones to hide bare stems or too many leaves. Drape a few large leaves over the edge.

5 Water the container well and often. As the roots fill the space, the display will need even more watering and feeding.

1 Choose a pot in proportion to the size of the rose. You can use a clay or plastic pot, but clay looks better. Cover the base of the pot with good-quality, soil-based potting mix.

2 Tip the plant out of its pot. If it does not slide out easily, turn the pot on its side and knock the rim gently against something solid. Support the rootball gently with your fingers to stop it falling apart while you move the plant.

PATIO ROSES

Although climbing and rambler roses can be grown on the patio, up walls and over pergola poles, they must be planted in the ground, in beds of good, deep soil. They will not do well in containers, even large ones, for very long. Only two kinds of roses are really suitable for growing in tubs, namely patio roses and miniature roses. Patio roses are like compact versions of the larger floribundas and hybrid teas, growing to 45-60cm(18-24in) high. Miniature roses are really small – growing to 23-45cm(9-18in) high, according to variety, with densely clustered stems. Choose a well-shaped plant with evenly spaced branches, healthy foliage and plenty of flowerbuds. Use a large container and a good-quality, soil-based potting mixture. It is vital to keep potted roses very well fed and watered, as they are growing in a very limited volume of soil. Daily watering may be needed in summer, even if the pot is a large one. Feed every week from the time growth starts in spring until late summer, using a good-quality liquid or soluble tomato feed or a liquid rose feed. Prune patio roses in the same way as normal bush roses in early spring. Miniature roses do not really need any pruning apart from a light tidy-up in late spring to remove dead twigs. They are not quite as hardy as other types of rose and rather prone to winter damage.

This patio rose is 'Ginger Nut', which grows to 45cm(18in).

3 Stand the plant in the middle of the pot, teasing out any large roots. Fill the gap around the edge of the rootball with a little more potting mixture.

4 Firm the soil down gently, leaving a 2.5cm(1in) gap between the top of the soil and the rim of the pot to allow for watering. Water thoroughly.

5 Stand the pot on a matching saucer, which should be in proportion to the size of the pot. Choose one the same diameter as the top of the pot or very slightly larger. If the potting mix settles after watering, top it up to the correct level.

Patio rose 'Top Marks'. Feed all patio roses weekly with liquid tomato feed.

Left: Patio roses stay naturally compact and flower prolifically all season. They do not need much pruning; just remove any dead twigs in late spring and tidy any straggly stems that spoil the shape.

Right: Like all of the patio roses, 'Pretty Polly' thrives in containers and flowers prolifically all season if kept watered, well fed with half-strength liquid tomato feed, and regularly deadheaded.

Patio rose 'Teeny Weeny'. These small plants bring seasonal colour to a year-round display of evergreens.

Miniature/patio rose 'Gentle Touch'

Pruning patio roses

Prune roses in early spring just before new growth starts. (Leave miniature roses until after the worst frosts; their shoots sometimes die back after cold weather.) Remove dead or weak shoots and thin out congested ones in the middle of the bush to improve the shape. Cut back strong shoots to 10-20cm (4-8in) above the top of the pot, cutting just above a leaf joint. Cut the weaker shoots back further than strong ones to encourage them to become more vigorous.

1 Patio roses may sustain quite a few broken branches. Cut these off, then remove the twiggy growth and any dead material from the middle of the plant.

2 Add a little bonemeal to the top layer of potting mixture to give the rose a good start. A repotted, well-pruned rose should produce plenty of flower.

Patio roses in hanging baskets

Teamed with similarly planted tubs, patio roses in a basket make a complete containerised rose garden, or use them in any sunny spot instead of annuals.

Right: *Patio rose 'Suffolk' makes an eye-catching spectacle, set off brilliantly by the dark walls of the shed. Regular feeding and watering is specially vital, since hanging baskets hold relatively little soil and dry out quickly in the sun.*

Osteospermum flowers only open in bright light, so a sunny spot is essential for a good display. Deadhead regularly to ensure a constant succession of bloom.

1 Select a sufficient number of drought-resistant but non-hardy flowers and herbs to slightly overfill a terracotta pot and arrange them roughly around the container.

TERRACOTTA POTS IN MEDITERRANEAN STYLE

Today, anyone can create a Mediterranean-style patio at home. White walls, simple garden furniture, a vine – perhaps an ornamental one, such as the purple-leaved *Vitis vinifera* 'Purpurea' – and colourful pots of flowers are the basic ingredients. Red pelargoniums are a Mediterranean favourite, and daisy shapes are a good choice; choose blue kingfisher daisy *(Felicia amelloides)*, osteospermum or Swan River daisy (brachyscome). Succulent plants with thick fleshy leaves look at home here, too. Look for Livingstone daisy *(Mesembryanthemum criniflorum)*, lampranthus and portulaca for flowers. Pots of ordinary cacti and succulents can stand outside for the summer for a Mediterranean look. Herbs are also traditional plants of the region. Perennial kinds, such as bay and rosemary, can be grown as specimen plants; pots of bush basil near a patio door are said to keep flies from going indoors. Grow annual climbers up walls and trellis; morning glory *(Ipomoea purpurea)* is very typically Mediterranean.

2 Plant into a peat- or soil-based potting mixture. If the pot is to stand against a wall or in a corner, start by putting the tallest plant at the back of the display.

3 Knock each plant out of its pot, carefully supporting the stem. Gently tease out any large roots coiled around the rootball, but avoid breaking up the rootball.

4 Place taller, upright plants, such as this bay tree, in the centre, with lower-growing and trailing plants around the edge so that they spill out over the sides.

Osteospermum 'Silver Sparkler'

O. 'Pink Whirls'

Bay (Laurus nobilis)

Osteospermum 'Sunny Lady'

Cockscomb (Celosia cristata)

Basil 'Dark Opal'

Ozothamnus microphyllus

Displays for a sunny spot

Traditional Mediterranean-style plants include pelargoniums, evergreen herbs and just about anything with daisy flowers, bright colours or natural drought resistance. All associate beautifully with each other and with terracotta containers in bright sunlight.

Variegated pelargonium

Bedding salvias

Right: *The cheerful red flowers of salvia and pelargonium, together with the reddish tints in the variegated foliage, pick out the red rim of this decorated terracotta pot, creating a simple but pretty display.*

5 Distribute colourful flowers throughout the container. Tuck in small but dense patches of colour to balance up the visual impact of the display. Support the container on pot feet to improve drainage.

Geranium palmatum

Left: *Grow perennial Mediterranean-style plants in individual pots, and then group them together to make summer displays. They can be regularly rearranged to suit what is in flower at the time.*

Festuca glauca

Lavandula stoechas pedunculata

Rhodanthemum hosmariense

Salvia officinalis 'Tricolor'

183

INSTANT COTTAGE GARDEN CONTAINERS

An old cottage – or a newer one with a cottage-style garden – would look at home with a patio paved with old stone slabs, cobbles and gravel, and mock Victorian cast aluminium or rustic hardwood furniture. Containers in a good range of sizes and made of natural-looking materials, such as terracotta flower pots, blend in best. Small pots look good in a row along the edge of garden steps or on top of a low wall; use them to grow drought-resistant sempervivums sedums or red pelargoniums. Larger pots suit single specimen plants of lily, fuchsia, marguerite or perennial herbs. They can bring impact to a dull area or transform an eyesore into a stunning focal point. You could also plant a mixture of cottage garden annuals in big pots; these can stand alone or be grouped together with other plants.

Traditional cottage garden flowers, such as spring bulbs, cultivated wild flowers (such as primroses and violets), wallflowers, pansies and stocks are good for spring colour. They can be planted in spring just as they are coming into flower. A good range is available in small pots at garden centres ready for planting at this time.

1 Choose plenty of different old-fashioned annual flowers and a pair of large matching clay flower pots, one larger than the other.

Cover the drainage holes with crocks. Fill pots with soil- or peat-based mix, not garden soil.

2 Plant the biggest and boldest plant towards the centre back of the pot as a focal point. Use slightly shorter flowers round it.

3 Choose something striking as the centrepiece of the smaller pot, but allow the centrepiece of the biggest pot to dominate.

4 Add more flowers, working forwards from the back of the pots, with the shortest at the front. Contrast the colours and shapes.

Left: Weathered old terracotta teams well with brick. Take care not to clean it so much that the character is lost. This basket-style container holds *Tulipa batalinii* for a simple, cottage-style spring display.

5 The displays in the two pots blend together harmoniously. Keep the plants well fed and watered and deadhead regularly.

Mixed snapdragons

Nicotiana 'Lime Green'

Dwarf sunflower

Argyranthemum foeniculaceum

Snapdragon (*Antirrhinum* 'Coronette Scarlet')

White alyssum

Pelargonium 'Ringo Scarlet'

Lilies in containers

Growing lilies in pots is a useful technique if your garden soil is not suitable for them. Choose large pots, as lilies are vigorous growers and their roots will need plenty of space. Use a rich potting mixture.

1 Select a good-sized pot and place a few pebbles or crocks in the base to prevent the drainage hole becoming blocked.

2 Half-fill the pot with good-quality potting mixture. Be sure to plant lime-hating lilies in an ericaceous mixture.

3 Supporting the roots with both hands, place the plant gently on the potting mix. Space out the other lilies equally.

4 Fill any gaps with potting mixture. Firm it in gently and water the container. Fill any new depressions with more mixture.

'Denia Pixie'

'Buff Pixie'

'Orange Pixie'

5 Lilies need to be watered and fed on a regular basis to flourish. Do not overwater them, but do not let them become dried out, especially by wind.

185

1 Large fibre pots may have several holes around the sides of the base, rather than one large one in the middle, as you find with many other containers. Cover each hole with a 'crock' to keep the potting mixture in.

POTS FOR A SHADY PLACE

Since most of the plants traditionally grown in containers are sunlovers, shady areas can be some of the most difficult to 'decorate' with containers. However, many plants that are suitable for shady gardens grow well in pots. Hydrangeas and clumps of hostas make good specimen plants to grow on their own in large pots. Small plants make more of a show when grouped together in large containers. The plants featured here are moisture lovers, so select a container that retains moisture well and looks at home in moist shady conditions. This fibre pot, made from recycled paper, will biodegrade after a few years in the garden, but is not expensive to buy. Good plants for growing in containers in shade include lady's mantle (*Alchemilla mollis)*, ajuga (ornamental bugle, which has coloured leaves and blue flowers), cultivated celandines, lungwort (pulmonaria, which has silver spotted leaves) and perennial forget-me-not (brunnera). Finding bedding plants that do well in shady sites is more difficult; most kinds need direct sunlight for at least half the day to perform well. However fuchsias, busy Lizzie (impatiens) and *Begonia semperflorens* will thrive, but choose plants that are already in bloom when you put them in, or they may take a long time to start flowering. In winter and early spring, the choice of flowers for shady containers is very limited. However, coloured primroses, violets and early varieties of miniature narcissi (such as 'February Gold') are ideal as they flower in shady conditions.

2 Fill the pot to within 5cm(2in) of its rim with a soil-based mixture. This will suit the perennials to be planted here, as they will remain in the pot for several years, and its weight keeps the pot stable.

3 Choose the plants and, leaving them in their pots for the time being, arrange them together in the container while you decide which ones look best next to each other.

4 Plant the foliage plant first – here a hardy fern – and add the flowering plants next. Knock each one carefully out of its pot and plant it without breaking up the ball of roots.

5 Tuck a few trailing plants, such as the ivies used here, around the sides. Alternative edging plants for shade include ajuga (bugle) and *Alchemilla mollis* (lady's mantle).

6 Fill any gaps with potting mix to leave the surface level. The plants should now be growing at the same depth as they were when planted in their original pots.

Making the most of a shady spot

Make a few flowers go further by mixing them with plenty of brightly variegated ivy (such as 'Goldheart', which has a gold splash on each leaf) or combining a similar type of euonymus, such as Blondy, with spring flowers. At any time of year, use water features such as fountains (with ferns or soleirolia instead of normal waterside plants) and light-coloured planters, especially those with shiny glazed surfaces, to reflect light and help make more of shady corners.

Above: Hardy ferns and hostas are fashionable and collectable plants for a shady spot. They associate together very well and thrive in containers. Keep the plants moist at all times.

7 To finish off, twist the ivy trails together to form a definite edge. Hold the ends in place with paper-covered wire 'twist ties'.

Hardy fern
(*Dryopteris filix-mas* 'Crispa Cristata')

Drumstick primula
(*Primula denticulata*)

Primrose
(*Primula vulgaris*)

Ivy (*Hedera helix*)

Viola labradorica

Handsome hostas

Hostas are fashionable and very decorative herbaceous plants, grown mainly for their handsome foliage. They are well known as plants for moist, shady conditions and look particularly striking in glazed ceramic pots as part of an Oriental-style feature. Once planted, avoid disturbing hostas until the clumps are very large and really need dividing.

1 *Growing hostas in pots makes it easier to protect them from slug and snail damage. Partly fill the container with a soil-based potting mixture.*

2 *Tip the plant out of its pot without breaking up the rootball. Transfer it to an oriental-style ceramic pot, keeping it as central as possible.*

3 *Fill in around the edge of the rootball with more potting mix. Leave a gap of about 1.25cm (0.5in) between the soil and the rim of the pot for watering.*

4 *Water well in. Hostas need moist conditions, and though usually recommended for shade, they will grow in sun if they are wet enough.*

FESTIVE WINTER TUBS

Festive holly and ivy foliage forms the basis of this winter container display, backed up by traditional berries and evergreen foliage, plus an ornamental cabbage, which makes a long-lasting alternative to winter flowers. If you cannot find a standard holly, you could remove all but one of the stems of a poorly shaped bush to convert it into an instant standard. Alternatively, use a bushy holly with fewer surrounding plants. For a formal entrance, make a pair of matching pots and place one on either side of a porch. For a less formal look, team a single container with smaller but matching pots of evergreens, winter-flowering heathers and early spring bulbs. Keep winter displays in a well-sheltered spot, with containers raised up on pot feet and in as much light as possible. Even plants that normally prefer partial shade will thrive in better light during the dull winter days. Check containers regularly, even in winter, to see if they need watering; normal rainfall may not be able to get through dense foliage and into the potting mix. Feed during mild spells in spring. Pick off discoloured leaves and generally tidy up container displays every week.

A mixed display

If planting a mixed display, be sure to choose evergreens with contrasting leaf shapes, textures and colours for a varied effect. Combine plants with prickly leaves, variegation, flowers and/or berries if possible, and include a mixture of tall, bushy and trailing plants. Evergreens and conifers that grow too big for permanent use in a container can be planted out in the garden later.

1 Remove plants from their pots before planting them. 'Golden King', the standard holly, is a female that bears red berries if there is a male holly nearby.

A soil-based potting mix is the most suitable one for winter arrangements, as its greater weight gives it added stability. It also provides better drainage than peat-based potting mixes.

2 Cover the drainage hole with a crock and part-fill the pot with potting mixture, but leave enough room for the plant roots.

3 Stand the holly in the centre; add the golden tree heather at the base to soften the upright line of the trunk. Firm in gently.

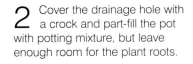

4 Plant gaultheria and flowering heather at the front of the display and the taller ornamental cabbage at the back. Add the trailing ivy, so that it curls round the sides of the pot.

5 Fill any gaps with potting mix. Stand the display on pot feet, say by a front door. Water well in and check weekly to make sure it does not dry out. No feeding will be needed until spring.

Seasonal interest

Make the most of plants with good winter effects, such as small conifers, evergreen grasses and sedges, winter-flowering heathers, variegated ivies and euonymus, and berried gaultheria or skimmia to create colourful, miniature seasonal cameo displays such as these.

Right: A pot with skimmia, conifer, gaultheria, sedge and euonymus is suitable for a reasonably exposed spot, so long as it has good drainage.

Below: A container with purple ornamental cabbage, winter-flowering pansies and golden thyme needs more shelter; if it is too cold, the pansies will stop flowering and the cabbage runs to seed.

Ilex x altaclerensis 'Golden King'

Erica arborea 'Albert's Gold'

Ornamental cabbage

Gaultheria procumbens

Hedera helix 'Sagittifolia' has long, narrow, arrowhead-shaped leaves.

Calluna vulgaris 'Alexandra'

The frilly leaves of this ornamental cabbage are particularly attractive.

Compact chamaecyparis are ideal for containers.

Right: The vivid red berries of Skimmia japonica reevesiana add bright points of colour to a winter patio display that features conifers, grasses, heathers and winter-flowering pansies in a shallow bowl.

Planting bamboo in a pot

1 Put a crock over the drainage hole in the base of the pot to stop the potting mix running out when you water the container.

2 Add 2.5cm(1in) of coarse grit or fine gravel for drainage and to prevent soil from trickling out through the drainage hole.

3 Add a handful or two of potting mix, so that the roots of the bamboo do not lie directly on the grit when it is planted.

4 Knock the plant out of its pot. If it is difficult to dislodge, tap the side of the pot firmly onto a hard surface to loosen it.

ORIENTAL-STYLE POTS

Exotic plants and containers are easy to obtain and by teaming them together you can create some very interesting effects. Oriental pots are specially attractive. They are frost-resistant and available in a wide range of sizes and designs, often with matching saucers. To continue the oriental theme, you could plant them with a trimmed conifer, flowering quince (chaenomeles) or Japanese maple (acer) – one per pot – to give a suggestion of bonsai trees. Another good choice would be bamboo. Despite the huge size to which some species grow, bamboos make first-class container plants. Choose any of the normal varieties found in garden centres, such as the *Pseudosasa (Arundinaria) japonica* shown here. All the above plants are woody perennials and if they are to remain in the container permanently, use a soil-based planting mix. Choose a pot and plant in proportion to each other. A large plant and pot can look good on their own or try a collection of three or five smaller ones of different sizes to make a group. For an oriental-looking background, stand the pot on a patch of raked gravel or on a raised platform with trelliswork behind it. Pots are easy to rearrange if you want to change the scheme later on. All the suggested plants grow relatively slowly and can be planted in the garden or repotted when they outgrow their tubs.

5 Sit the plant in the middle of its pot. The top of the rootball should come to about 2.5cm(1in) below the rim of the pot. If not, lift it out and either add or remove soil to bring it to the correct level.

6 Fill the gap between the rootball and the sides of the container with more of the same potting mixture and firm it in very lightly to make sure that the pot is completely filled.

7 Move the pot to its final position, sit it on the saucer and water the plant in well. If the soil level sinks, top up the pot and water it lightly.

Making an oriental display

1 Place crocks over the holes in the bottom of each pot, then partly fill them all with a good-quality, soil-based potting mixture.

2 Knock the plants out of their pots, teasing out some of the largest roots if necessary. Lift each plant into a suitably sized pot.

3 Put the plants in position. Spread 2.5cm(1in) of gravel over the area around them, ideally over soil or over concrete or some other hard surface. Add a group of large pebbles or cobble-stones. Press them lightly down so they stay put without appearing to sink.

Miscanthus sinensis 'Zebrinus'

Cryptomeria japonica 'Spiralis'

Picea glauca 'Alberta Globe'

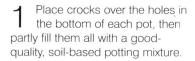

Oriental-style plants

Bending a ginkgo's horizontal shoots over and tying them in place creates an instant oriental look. Try tipping the tree to see if you can get a better bonsai shape by inclining the stem at an angle. Remove the ties after a year.

Ginkgo biloba (maidenhair tree)

Acer palmatum 'Atropurpureum'

Hebe 'Green Globe'

Aim for a range of foliage shapes and textures. Rhododendrons add a touch of colour.

Fargesia (Arundinaria) murieliae

Rhododendron yakushimanum 'Vintage Rose'

Cryptomeria japonica 'Elegans'

A shallow pot with sempervivums

Low, clump-forming alpines, such as sempervivums, look good in a small shallow container. Choose hardy but drought-resistant kinds, as the container will dry out faster than a large, deep sink garden.

1 Place a curved crock over the drainage hole, then part fill the dish with a gritty potting mix made of equal parts of grit, soil and peat or coir potting mixes. Place a small rock in the centre.

2 Sempervivums, with their neat, geometric shapes and interesting colours and textures, are particularly suited to this rather symmetrical style of planting.

3 Tip the plants out of their pots, and tuck in as many as will fit between the rock and the edge of the container. An odd number of plants always looks best.

4 Fill the gaps between adjacent rootballs with more of the same potting mix and tap the pot with both hands to settle the mix. Top up the mix if it sinks slightly. Water each pot well.

Recognise drought-proof alpines by their thick, fleshy, waxy coated, succulent leaves.

ALPINES IN TERRACOTTA

When you buy alpine plants from a nursery, the pots seem to accentuate the fascinating shapes and textures of the plants. Different varieties form domed shapes, mossy 'buns', ground-hugging mats, silver-crusted rosettes or craggy mounds. There is no need to lose this appealing aspect by planting them out; most alpines can be cultivated in pots for years. Do not leave plants in their nursery pots for long; despite being small, they need to be able to put their roots out into fresh soil. Repot them into larger pots using a well-drained gritty mix. A collection of alpines in matching terracotta pots, grouped together, makes a great display. Stand them in a row on a ledge, arrange them on staging or shelves or stand them along the edge of steps. Even a small collection can transform a tiny space into a miniature garden. Alternatively, use pots to extend an existing alpine feature, say by grouping a few pots around a stone birdbath planted with trailing alpines; stand them along the edge of a low wall or perhaps around a raised bed. Potted alpines look particularly good on gravel, which also makes them easier to look after as surplus water can drain away quickly. If pots are standing on paving, raise them up slightly or check that the paving slopes gently so water can run away.

A large pot of alpines

Drought-lovers that will spill down over the sides look best in bigger pots. Choose pots of the same colour when planning a group; new terracotta pots look very bright when used with old, weathered ones.

1 Cover the drainage hole with a crock and add alpine potting mixture to within 5cm(2in) of the pot rim. Tip the plants out of their nursery pots before planting.

2 Position the alpines so that adjacent rootballs almost touch. Fill the gaps with more mix, tap down on a hard surface to consolidate, top up, then water.

A single alpine specimen in a small pot

Smaller pots look best with one type of plant rather than a mixture, which could look rather 'bitty'. Choose a plant with a more open shape for a change of emphasis. Clean old pots before reusing them.

1 A crock in the base will stop soil escaping, while allowing excess water to drain out. Half-fill the pot with an alpine potting mix.

2 To give the impression of an 'instant' large specimen plant, group three smaller ones tightly together in the centre of the pot.

Putting it all together

For an effective display, team three (or five) matching containers of different sizes, each with its own separate alpine planting theme. Here we have used flowering, dumpy and spreading plants.

Right: *Finish off with a layer of fine grit, ideally matching the colour of the rock. It looks decorative and lifts the lower leaves up off the potting mixture. This helps to prevent alpines rotting off at the neck, a common problem, especially in winter when it is cold and damp.*

Below: *With succulent, drought-tolerant alpines, these pots can be left for up to a week between waterings, even in summer. Most alpines need regular watering, however, just like bedding plants.*

3 Firm the plants in gently and interweave the stems slightly so that they look more like a single plant. Alternatively, plant five rooted cuttings into the same pot.

Orostachys spinosa

Rosularia platyphylla

Sedum 'Silver Moon'

Erodium trifolium

Sedum spathulifolium 'Cape Blanco'

Sedum spurium 'Fuldaglut'

Sedum anacampseros

Sedum lydium

Sempervivum marmoreum

Sempervivum montanum stiriacum

Sempervivum 'Kramers Spinrad'

Sempervivum 'Pekinese'

Sempervivum arachnoideum 'Minor'

1 Part-fill a shallow terracotta pan with potting mixture and sink the jagged broken base of a pot about half that diameter into the centre. Leave most of its rim above the rim of the outer container.

GIVING DAMAGED CLAY POTS A NEW LEASE OF LIFE

Broken clay pots of all sizes can be recycled in many exciting and creative ways, however major or minor the damage. Curved pieces of pot, including those with the entire base still complete and only jagged bits of sides remaining, look stunning 'planted' into the middle of a larger circular container. The tips protrude above the potting mix rather like the tips of icebergs, setting off rock plants to perfection. Meanwhile, the submerged pieces actually help to keep plant roots cool and moist in hot summer weather, as they are porous and so hold moisture. Alternatively, you could use a series of pots in diminishing sizes with jagged rims, partly filled with potting mixture and then 'stacked' in much the same way as the strawberry tower on page 320. Instead of strawberries, plant a 'cracked' tower with alpines or other small drought-proof plants, which look more natural given a craggy setting. They will also be able to cope better with the drier conditions that result; water that would normally be retained by the rim of an unbroken pot runs out of cracked ones. Large pots that only have a chunk missing from the rim can be used in several ways. Either lay them on their side, with the damaged side uppermost, and plant the opening with alpines. Or take advantage of the unusual shape to build a matching plant display, teaming upright, bushy and trailing or spreading varieties. Given a large container, capable of holding a reasonable volume of potting mix despite the damage, choose plants that are reasonably tolerant of extreme conditions. Most fairly drought-tolerant annuals and half-hardy perennials, including pelargoniums, osteospermums, gazanias, felicias, mesembryanthemums and portulacas, would make good subjects.

2 Arrange more curved pieces in a flower pattern in the centre, with others inside and outside. Leave a gap of at least 2.5cm(1in) between the pieces.

3 Add more potting mix, filling the gaps between the curving pieces so they become planting pockets. Lift some pieces of pot slightly before firming in place.

4 The centre of the concentric rings should end up quite a bit higher than the rim of the container. Plant a lewisia into the centre; it enjoys sharp drainage.

5 Tuck a few small curved shards around the lewisia to exaggerate its rosettelike shape and to lift the leaves so that they do not rot in wet weather.

6 Plant more small alpines that need similar growing conditions – full sun and good drainage – into the planting pockets around the container. Leave room to see the pattern made by the shards.

194

7 Use compact trailing alpines close to the edge of the container. These will sprawl loosely over the sides and add to the effect of plants cascading down from the raised centre of the display without swamping it.

8 Finish off by spooning fine gravel around the plants and pieces of pot as a continuous carpet. Tuck some of the gravel under the leaves of the alpines to improve drainage and prevent neck rot in wet weather.

9 Place the display on a sunny patio, on a wall or add it to a collection of alpines and drought-proof shrubs, such as whipcord hebes, in matching containers.

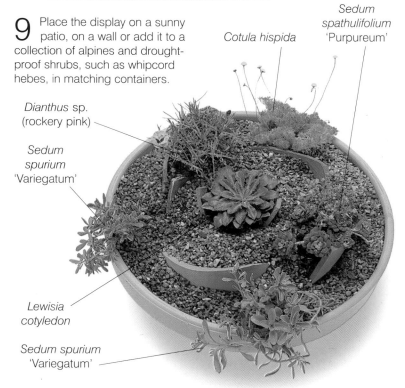

Sedum spathulifolium 'Purpureum'

Cotula hispida

Dianthus sp. (rockery pink)

Sedum spurium 'Variegatum'

Lewisia cotyledon

Sedum spurium 'Variegatum'

Gazanias in a pot with a broken rim

There is no need to throw away a pot with a broken rim; instead, plant a banked display to take advantage of its unusual shape and create a dramatic cascade of flowers that tumble forwards out of the container.

1 Fill the pot with potting mix to the level of the break and bank up the mix towards the back of the pot. Plant a tall, upright gazania variety at the back.

2 Plant successively shorter, bushier varieties of gazania, in toning colours, in the centre of the pot. Face them forwards for a graduated effect. Fill the pot well.

Gazanias enjoy a very sunny position; in fact, the flowers will close up when the sun goes in.

3 Use trailing varieties and lighter colours at the very front, to make the most of the sloping shape of the display.

4 Stand the display in a sunny spot, ideally where it will be viewed from the front. Deadhead the gazanias regularly to keep them flowering; do not overwater.

1 Part-fill a large terracotta half-pot with free-draining potting mixture. Use a trowel to sink a large clay shard across the middle of it, leaving the top half showing.

2 Press in a similar but shorter shard alongside, parallel with the first and about 2.5cm(1in) away from it. Firm the mix lightly to hold the two pieces roughly in place.

3 Fill the gap between the shards with more mix, up to the top of both pieces and well above the level of mix in the pot. Firm gently; top up if necessary.

4 Tip a small sempervivum out of its pot. Make a small hole in the mix between the two shards and put in the plant, firming the mix between both ends of the shards.

5 Tuck a shorter piece of broken clay pot into the front of the container, parallel with the first two pieces. Press this in so that it is roughly halfway in height between the two large pieces and the rim of the pot.

CREATIVE DISPLAYS WITH BROKEN CLAY POTS

If you use clay pots, it is inevitable that from time to time a few will break. Rough handling or accidental knocks can cause anything from total shattering to odd-shaped pieces breaking off, usually from the top. Frost commonly causes clay pots to crack from top to bottom, producing long straight shards. However, with a little imagination, broken pots and pieces of shard can be recycled to make novel displays of their own. Investigate all sorts of possibilities before finally rejecting damaged pots. They can be used on their side, partly sunk into a gravel path. Broken pieces of pot can be used curved side up instead of rockery stone or on edge placed close together to suggest the natural strata of slate. Small bits of smashed pot could even be used as a top-dressing round plants instead of gravel. If you do not have any broken pots of your own, look in garden centres; they may let you have damaged pots cheaply or even give away bags of broken pieces. Old broken pots are often hidden away behind hedges at nurseries, and proprietors may be glad to get rid of them, especially if you are buying plants. The natural rocky feel and small soil capacity of recycled broken pots make them ideal homes for small, slow-growing, compact alpine plants. Houseleeks (sempervivum), many of the smaller sedums, such as *S. spathulifolium*, and lewisias are ideal partners. But do not overdo the planting; allow the interesting craggy shapes to be seen as part of the display, not like a mistake you are trying to hide.

6 Space out a few more small sempervivums in between the shards so that you can still see the pattern made by the pieces and to allow room for the plants to grow.

7 Add a final shard at the back of the display, filling up part of the large remaining gap. Again this should be parallel and slightly lower than the two central pieces.

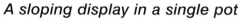

8 Put in one last plant, tucking it between the last piece of shard and the back of the pot. Allow the plant to rest on the side of the pot where its offsets will later dangle down over the edge.

9 Scatter a light topdressing of grit over the surface of the potting mix. Tuck it under the rosettes of foliage to provide extra drainage and to stop the plants rotting in wet weather.

Sempervivum 'IWO'

Sempervivum 'Lentezon'

Sempervivum 'San Ferdin'

Sempervivum 'Heliotrop'

Sempervivum 'Starion'

10 The finished pan has the look of a natural rocky outcrop. Stand it in a sunny spot on a wall, or by the side of garden steps, or use it as a novel outdoor table centrepiece

Sempervivum 'Purdy'

A sloping display in a single pot

A pot that has virtually broken in half from top to bottom makes a good shallow pan for drought-resistant alpines, when laid on its side. Here, sedum and sempervivum make a good combination.

1 Arrange the pot on its side and bank up potting mix to form a slope from front to back. Tip a large houseleek out of its pot and plant it in the deeper mix at the back of the container.

2 Plant a low, spreading sedum on its side in the shallow mix in front of the sempervivum, so that the stems and flowers spill out towards the lip of the pot.

3 Use a narrow-bladed trowel to tuck more mix between the plant rootballs and the sides of the container. The more mix you can get in the better.

Sempervivum cultivar

Sedum floriferum 'Weihenstephaner Gold'

4 To prevent it rolling, bed the finished container into loose soil or, better still, gravel (which is more decorative). Set the back of the pot slightly deeper so that water does not run straight out.

197

A vibrant display of agave and nasturtium in a stylish glazed container.

PART EIGHT

PATIO DISPLAYS

Given the range of both plants and containers now available, there is no excuse for boring displays. Try out unusual materials, explore new themes and bring imaginative and creative ideas to life. Adapt the latest indoor decorating styles for garden use and you can become a garden trendsetter rather than a follower.

BULBS IN CONTAINERS

With daffodils, tulips and hyacinths in containers, a patio can be a riot of colour from early spring onwards. Dry bulbs are on sale in garden centres in autumn. Choose compact varieties. Buy daffodils as soon as they are available and plant them straightaway, as they start rooting earlier than many spring bulbs. The bulbs should be plump and healthy, without cuts, bruises or mouldy bits; the biggest bulbs will bear the most flowers. You can plant containers entirely with one kind of bulb, but if you want to mix them, choose bulbs that flower at roughly the same time. When it comes to planting, normal peat- or soil-based potting mixture is fine. After planting, stand the containers outdoors in a cool, shady spot protected from heavy rain. When the first shoots appear, move the containers to the patio. While the bulbs are flowering, feed them weekly with general-purpose liquid feed. When they are over, tip them out and plant them in the garden. Buy new bulbs for the following year's container displays, as they will flower better than the old ones.

Potting hyacinths

1 Half-fill 9cm(3.5in) pots with potting mix. Gently press a single bulb into the centre of each pot.

2 Fill the pot to the rim, covering the bulb, then tap it down on a hard surface to consolidate the potting mix.

Below: As hyacinths come into flower, bring them inside or plunge them into containers.

3 Moisten the potting mix well. Allow the surplus to drain away. Put the pot in a cool, dry and protected place.

1 If your container does not have drainage holes, you should drill some. It is vital that containers that will be standing outdoors in winter can drain freely.

2 Place 2.5-5cm(1-2in) of coarse gravel over the base to aid drainage. Bulbs can easily rot if the potting mix is too wet.

3 Add 2.5-5cm(1-2in) of potting mix. It may not be possible to plant bulbs in pots with twice their own depth of potting mix.

4 Press each daffodil bulb into the mix, giving it a half turn so that the base makes good contact with the soil. Bulbs should not touch each other or the tub.

5 Cover the bulbs with enough mix to leave the tips on show so you can see where they are when you plant the next layer.

6 Gently press in *Anemone blanda* corms between the tips of the lower layer of bulbs. Cover these corms with more mix.

Planting tulips in a container

Tulips need well-drained soil and a warm sheltered spot. If these do not prevail in your garden, try growing them in containers.

1 Remove the dead, brown, outer skins from the bulbs. This helps them to root well and removes any disease spores.

7 Dot another layer of *Anemone blanda* over the surface, about 2.5cm(1in)above the last. Fill the tub to the rim with potting mixture.

8 Leave the potting mixture roughly level on top. Take care not to knock over the bulbs, as they are still quite unstable.

2 Put a layer of coarse gravel and potting mixture in the trough as before. Press the tulip bulbs lightly down into the soil in groups of five.

3 Arrange the bulbs with small gaps between each group. You can then tuck forget-me-not plants in between the bulbs early next spring.

Right: Daffodils will do best in the sun, but they tolerate light shade. *Anemone blanda* grows to 15cm (6in). Blue is popular, but mixed colours are usually available.

Below: This cross section shows the layers of bulbs, with 'Golden Harvest' daffodils below and *A. blanda* 'Blue Shade' above.

Below: These bulbs have been cleaned of their dead, outer skins. The planting depth shown is fine for this trough. They are bulbs of 'Red Riding Hood' (shown right).

4 Cover the bulbs with potting mix. Fill the container with more mixture to within 1.25cm (0.5in) of the rim. Water evenly.

INSTANT BULB DISPLAYS

The cheapest way to create a good display of flowering daffodils, hyacinths and tulips, etc., throughout spring is to plant dry, dormant bulbs in autumn. However, you can still have a superb, instant display by buying bulbs that are growing in pots. These are available from early spring until the plants are in flower. Team them with double daisies, polyanthus and violas that are also sold in flower at this time to transform tubs and windowboxes. Although this is more expensive than buying dry bulbs, creating displays instantly from growing bulbs has much to recommend it. Since the bulbs are in bud when you buy them, it is possible to select plants at the same stage so that they all open together – ideal for containers. And since it is possible to judge the colour of the blooms, even from quite tight flower buds, you can choose bulb plants that will match with other spring bedding to create harmonious, colour-coordinated schemes. Best of all, each bloom will be in perfect condition, since you will only buy the best. However, there are a few pitfalls to avoid. Bulb plants that are sold in bud or flower in spring will almost certainly have been grown in greenhouses during the winter, so harden them off for a week or more by standing them outside during the day and moving them under cover at night. Choose a sheltered spot and avoid planting during cold spells. Do not disturb the roots of growing bulbs; instead plunge the entire pot to the rim in soil.

Left: Team pots of bulbs and other spring bedding for a striking seasonal display. Containers should have something in common – perhaps all terracotta and with matching colour-schemed plantings as here.

1 Choose a trough deep enough to take the bulbs without damaging the roots. Cover the drainage holes with crocks.

2 Half-fill the trough with potting mixture, completely covering the crocks. Use either a soil- or peat-based potting mixture.

3 Bulbs need not be knocked out of their pots; simply plunge the complete pot to the rim inside the trough. You may need to compress the rootballs slightly to make them fit in; in this case gently tip the plants out of their pots first.

4 Pack in as many plants as possible to create a really full display. By choosing plants in flower, you ensure that they are all at the same stage and looking their best.

5 Use tall daffodils towards the centre and back, and shorter, chunkier flowers such as hyacinths to add 'weight' near the centre of the group for a pleasing effect.

6 Buy short spring bedding plants, such as polyanthus, just as they come into flower. Tuck them at the front and sides. In a trough, a roughly symmetrical design looks best, so repeat the same flowers at both ends of the display.

7 Trickle more potting mix into any spaces between the plants. Water well. Lift out any plants that finish flowering early and replace them.

Daffodils

Hyacinths

Tulips

Primulas

A spring display in a plastic cauldron

Inexpensive containers are ideal for brilliant spring displays; the secret is to pack them with plants. Spring bulbs and bedding plants just coming into bloom will not have time to make much more growth, so they must create immediate impact. Choose plants at roughly the same flowering stage, and with varying heights and shapes.

1 *Part-fill the container with potting mix and knock plants out of their pots. Avoid breaking up the rootballs or the plants may wilt and fade rapidly.*

2 *If the container will be seen from the front, plant the tallest flowers at the back with shorter kinds in front. This hides foliage and gives a fuller display.*

3 *Complete the display with a low spreading plant such as this winter-flowering heather at the front to soften the hard line created by the container rim.*

4 *Leaving plants grouped together instead of splitting them up randomly throughout the display creates a stronger effect. Their foliage sets off each clump.*

203

1 Use curved pieces of clay pot as crocks to cover the drainage holes in the bottom of the container; these prevent soil from running out but allow excess water to drain away freely.

2 Almost fill the sink with equal parts of lime-free gritty sand, soil-based mix, and coir, coarse peat or sterilised leafmould.

PLANTING UP A SINK GARDEN WITH ALPINES

Few people have room for conventional rockeries; they are expensive and hard work. There is also growing concern about the removal of rock from natural habitats for use in gardens. The most practical alternative, especially where space or funds are limited, is to grow alpine plants in containers. This way it is possible to avoid using any natural rock at all, as the hard surface of the container provides a suitable backdrop. The traditional container for alpines was an old-fashioned butler's sink, but you can adapt 'modern' china sinks by covering them with hypertufa, or create a sink entirely from hypertufa (page 44). Sink-type containers must have drainage holes in the bottom. Most alpines will thrive in a free-draining mixture with some organic matter to hold moisture. You may need to prepare this at home, as suitable mixes are normally only sold by specialist alpine plant nurseries. More moisture-loving plants, such as tiny alpine primulas, dodecatheon, ramonda, etc., are happy in a mixture of equal parts soil- and peat-based potting mix. Be sure to group plants that will happily share similar growing conditions. Most alpines will thrive in a situation where they get direct sun for at least half the day, although very drought-tolerant, sunloving kinds such as sedum and sempervivum need a very sunny spot. Few alpines are happy in shade; go for ramonda, haberlea and dwarf ferns. Water sink gardens in dry weather, and feed plants occasionally in spring and summer with weak tomato feed.

3 Decide on the arrangement and start from the centre. Tip each plant out of its pot and use a small trowel to scoop out a hole.

4 Using mixed colours, arrange the plants so that clump-forming or upright types alternate with mound or spreading shapes.

5 Nestle plants into the corners so the sink has a well-filled but natural look. Make sure a few plants trail over to soften the sides.

6 Tuck in a few small pieces of stone as you work. These add contours, trap condensation in hot weather and help keep roots cool.

7 Use plants with long flowering seasons and some, such as mossy saxifrages, that make good background foliage when not in bloom. Mix plants with contrasting shapes and textures.

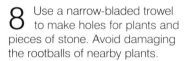

8 Use a narrow-bladed trowel to make holes for plants and pieces of stone. Avoid damaging the rootballs of nearby plants.

9 Drape sprawling plants over pieces of stone to set them off. Lifting leaves and stems clear of the soil also prevents rotting.

Summer colour

The vast majority of well-known alpines, such as saxifrages and dwarf bulbs, are spring flowering. To keep containers such as sink gardens looking good for a longer season, it is vital to include some later colour as well. Good plants for summer flowers include small species of phlox, erodium, geranium, sedum and dianthus, plus rhodohypoxis. All alpines growing in containers need watering regularly during prolonged dry spells; even they can be killed by drought. And since plants will be growing in the same container for several years, apply weak liquid feeds several times during the summer months.

10 When all the plants and rocks are in place, spread a generous mulch of gravel or granite chippings over the whole surface.

Above: *Summer flowering phlox and dianthus spilling over the side of this sink garden coincide with the last of the saxifrages to create a display that always has something in flower but never looks garish.*

11 The sink garden looks good straight away, but will improve as plants blend together and spill over the sides. Water well and raise up on bricks for extra drainage.

Barbarea vulgaris 'Variegata'

Aquilegia flabellata pumila

Phlox 'Chattahoochee'

Aubretia 'Greencourt Purple'

Saxifraga x arendsii 'Ingeborg'

Primula auricula

Aubretia 'Red Carpet'

Aubretia 'Wanda'

Rhodanthemum hosmariense

Armeria juniperifolia x maritima

Aubretia 'Aureovariegata'

Ranunculus montana 'Molten Lava'

Trifolium repens purpurascens

Saxifraga moschata 'Cloth of Gold'

ALPINES IN TUFA

Tufa is a very soft type of limestone that forms underwater in some locations. It is popular with alpine plant growers as its unique honeycomb structure (imagine fossilised sponge) provides secure foundations and fast drainage for choice plants, which are planted into small, specially made holes in the rock with very little soil round the roots. Tufa is usually sold by weight at alpine nurseries, but well-weathered pieces attract a premium. Small or slow-growing alpines are the best choice for growing in tufa; if grown in a conventional rock garden, they would easily be swamped by bigger plants. Silvery saxifrages, shrubby helichrysums, androsace and alpine gypsophila are all good examples. Although it is a type of limestone, tufa can be used for growing plants that normally hate lime and it is a brilliant way of growing notoriously difficult plants. Plant small plants into tufa at the start of the growing season, in spring, so that their roots can begin to grow straight out into it. Keep the tufa moist by dripping water over it; it soon soaks in. If you stand a piece of damp tufa in a large container as here, it will draw up its own moisture by capillary action. After a time moss, lichens and possibly self-sown alpine plants will appear on the surface. This helps the rock to look weathered; hasten the process by laying a new chunk of tufa on damp earth in a shady bed for several months before use, or watering it occasionally with diluted liquid feed.

2 Drill or chisel out a few holes 2.5cm(1in) wide and 5-7.5cm (2-3in) deep. Leave space between them or the rock will break.

3 Scoop out powdered tufa to leave a clear planting hole. Tufa is naturally soft, so set the speed to slow if using a power drill.

4 Put a little soil in the planting hole, knock plants out of their pots and squeeze roots gently into a tubular shape to fit into the hole.

5 Firm the plant in gently, so that the 'neck' is level with the mouth of the hole. If not, remove the plant and enlarge the hole.

1 Fill a trough with gritty potting mix, and sit a craggy, weathered piece of tufa rock firmly into the top. Pick a small selection of compact, slow-growing drought-tolerant alpines.

6 Put several more plants around the rock, drilling into existing hollows where possible for a more natural look. Let the rock predominate.

7 Add extra plants round the base of the rock, planting into gaps between the rock and the edge of the trough. Bushier plants create a good background to the rock, but they still need to be drought tolerant.

8 A 1.25cm(0.5in) layer of grit shows the plants off well, helps to make a visual link between rock and container and assists good drainage around the necks of the plants. Choose a colour that goes with the rock.

9 Water all the plants well in and trickle water into the planting holes in the tufa. Raise the finished trough up on bricks to improve drainage, and water in dry spells.

Ozothamnus (Helichrysum) selago 'Minor'

Saxifraga 'Edith'

Androsace sarmentosa watkinsii

Saxifraga cinerea

Eriogonum brevicaule var. *nanum*

Saxifraga 'Penelope'

Saxifraga 'Tumbling Waters'

Lewisia 'George Henley'

Growing alpines from seed

In the wild, many alpines grow naturally from seeds lodged in crevices in rocks. Tufa allows you to recreate this effect in the garden. You can sprinkle alpine seeds with a little soil into crevices in tufa. Alternatively, sow seeds in pots of seed sowing mixture and transplant later on.

Above: *The Cheddar pink,* Dianthus gratianopolitanus, *a compact plant with scented, pale pink single flowers, grows well in all sorts of dry environments.*

Left: *In summer,* Polygala calcarea *'Lillet', a small creeping evergreen shrub, is covered in curious butterfly-shaped flowers. The plants are quite short lived.*

Below: *Cushion plants look good on tufa, as their shapes contrast so well with the craggy rock all around them; this is a pink form of* Anthemis montana, *a compact mountain daisy.*

207

1 Cover the drainage holes in the base of the container with crocks to stop the soil trickling out. Any surplus water can still escape.

2 Put a 2.5-5cm(1-2in) layer of coarse gravel over the base to assist drainage and to prevent the crocks becoming clogged.

ALPINES IN HYPERTUFA

Any plants that will grow in normal containers will also grow in hypertufa, but stone or hypertufa containers are mostly used for rock plants. All sorts of alpines, dwarf bulbs and drought-tolerant small shrubs are suitable, as long as you only group together plants that share similar soil conditions and cultural requirements. Plants that need particularly well-drained potting mix, such as encrusted saxifrages, armerias, erodiums, sedums, sempervivums and lewisias, do best in a mixture of 1 part grit to 4 parts soil-based potting mix. Less fussy rock plants, such as arabis, aubretia, diascia, small hardy cranesbills, such as *Geranium lancastriense,* and most campanulas, are quite happy in soil-based potting mix on its own. Gentians can be grown in containers, but need relatively moisture-retentive soil, as they dislike drying out; a half-and-half mixture of peat and soil-based potting mixes with a little added grit would be best. (Check plant care labels with gentians, as some varieties only grow in lime-free soil.) They also like partial shade. In a very shady spot, fill the container with the peat/soil mix and plant ramonda and haberlea, or primula species and small hardy ferns, such as *Adiantum pedatum,* the bird's foot fern, and *Adiantum venustum,* the hardy maidenhair fern. They all need rather damper conditions than normal alpines; the soil should never quite dry out. Larger shrubby rock plants for stone or fake stone containers include helianthemum, cistus and hebes: the whipcord hebes have dramatic string-like foliage, although others have more striking flowers.

3 For growing alpines in this container, add 1 part of coarse grit to 4 parts of soil-based potting mixture.

4 To create an authentic alpine look, embed a craggy chunk of tufa rock in the centre of the container as though it were a natural outcrop.

6 Choose alpines that need the same soil and conditions. Flowering kinds and those with hillocky shapes and coloured foliage make interesting combinations.

5 This trough has a small hole where an air pocket was left in the mixture. It can be enlarged if necessary and makes a side planting hole for a sedum, pushed carefully through from outside.

7 Evergreen plants look interesting in winter, when many alpines die down to ground level. In time, they creep over the sides of the trough and up the tufa chunk.

8 Topdress the finished surface with coarse grit, such as granite chippings. It helps to improve surface drainage and prevents alpines rotting at the neck.

9 The planted container already begins to look like real stone. You can spray the sides with dilute liquid feed to encourage mosses and lichens to grow.

Sedum spurium 'Variegatum'

Campanula muralis

Rhodohypoxis 'Fred Broome'

Saxifraga correovensis

Sempervivum hybrid

Sedum lydium

Erodium 'Natasha'

Hebe in a hypertufa pot

If you have made too much hypertufa mixture for the trough, why not try covering an ordinary flowerpot? Planting a Hebe franciscana *in the pot, as shown here, teams well with the rock plants in the trough. Once you have planted the hypertufa pot, you can spray the sides with a diluted houseplant feed so that moss and lichen develop to make it look old.*

1 Start by soaking the flowerpot in water. This is particularly important if you are using a brand new container.

2 Wearing gloves, press handfuls of the hypertufa all over the surface and stand the pot in a sheltered place to dry.

3 Cover the inside rim of the pot so that, when planted, the original surface is not visible. It dries to a stonelike colour.

4 The coarse sand and peat in the mixture will give the pot a rough stonelike texture. The *Hebe franciscana* shown here teams well with the rock plants in the trough.

209

1 Fill the tub with a suitable potting mixture and make a hole in the centre large enough for the rootball to fit with ease, allowing about 5cm(2in) of soil below the roots.

A CLIMBING DISPLAY OF FRAGRANT HONEYSUCKLE

Honeysuckles are universal favourites and there are many different species and cultivars to choose from. They can be grown in hedgerows, up trees, as pillars or as specimens in a tub with a trellis support. They are energetic stem climbers, have spectacular flowers and can fill the evening air with evocative scents. So which do you choose? There is a good chance that your native honeysuckle will perform the best in your area, but honeysuckle species such as *Lonicera periclymenum* or *L. etrusca* are very reliable, adaptable and free-flowering. Other good performers include *L.* x *heckrottii* 'Gold Flame' and the favourite, 'Graham Thomas' featured here. Honeysuckles can contribute to many yellow and green themes in the garden, whether they are grown in pots or not. You might consider Japanese honeysuckle, *Lonicera japonica* 'Aureoreticulata', or the yellow trumpet honeysuckle *L. sempervirens* f. *sulphurea*. In hotter areas with a typical Mediterranean climate, the Burmese honeysuckle, *Lonicera hildebrandiana*, can look staggering with its 18cm(7in)-long yellow-orange giant flowers. This powerful climber is ideal for growing on pergolas, where it will relish the sunny conditions. Keep honeysuckles in tubs very well watered and feed regularly in the growing season.

4 Use soft string to tie individual climbing stems to the trellis, taking care not to damage any of the delicate stems. Tie the knots loosely.

5 Also use string to tie the cane to the trellis. Again, take care not to crush or damage the climbing stems of the honeysuckle.

2 Tap the nursery plant out of its pot, together with its cane, and place the rootball into the hole without losing too much of the soil adhering to the roots. Firm in well.

3 Add more potting mixture around the plant. Distribute the mix evenly in the box and level it off to within 5cm(2in) of the top of the pot to allow space for watering.

Honeysuckles in tubs

Stand honeysuckle in a tub in cool shade, but where the tops can grow out into sunlight. In a sunny situation, surround the tub with pots of plants to cast shade, or place large stones over the surface of the mix. Water often. Add slow-release fertiliser in spring, and water with diluted liquid tomato feed every few weeks in summer. Refresh the surface potting mixture each spring.

Above: Lonicera x heckrottii 'Gold Flame' has heavily scented flowers from mid- to late summer. The top leaves look as if the stems grow right through them.

Left: The early Dutch honeysuckle, Lonicera periclymenum 'Belgica', flowers in late spring/early summer and again in late summer and autumn. Team it with containers of patio roses or clematis.

Climbing potato vine

The flowers and foliage of climbing potatoes make exciting subjects for pots. They twine with their stems, but tie them to a trellis for added support. Choose a fairly large tub and buy a well-grown nursery plant such as Solanum jasminoides. The white form, Solanum jasminoides 'Album', featured below can grow to 6m(20ft). Site climbing potatoes out of direct draughts, in a spot where they receive plenty of sun. Soak the potted plant in water and allow it to drain before planting.

1 Lower the plant, with its cane, into soil-based potting mix so that the stem is covered by about 5cm(2in) of soil. Firm the plant in with your knuckles.

2 Having firmed down round the edges of the climber, top up the tub with more mix to within 5cm(2in) of the top of the pot. Firm down lightly once more.

Lonicera periclymenum 'Graham Thomas'

6 Give the honeysuckle a generous watering to ensure that it gets off to a good start. Water it every day for the first ten days so that it becomes well established, and do not allow it to dry out after that.

3 Cut off some of the nursery ties, especially if they are restricting plant growth, but take care as you release the plant. Separate the climbing stems.

4 Attach the stems to the trellis with twist ties and water the plant in. Water it every day for the first ten days and do not allow it to dry out after that.

CLEMATIS IN CONTAINERS

A good way of growing climbers is on a framework that stands in the pot itself. Of the annual climbers, canary creeper *(Tropaeolum peregrinum)*, cup-and-saucer vine *(Cobaea scandens)*, morning glory (ipomoea), Chilean glory vine (eccremocarpus) and sweet peas are all good choices. But if you want a climber that can be left in the same container for several years, a clematis is ideal. All climbers in pots need frequent watering and generous feeding. Start two weeks after planting in the tub, using a liquid or soluble tomato feed to encourage flowering. After a few weeks, alternate this with a general-purpose feed. Although most annual climbers are real sunlovers, clematis prefer cool conditions at the roots. In a sunny spot, stand other containers around them so that their foliage shades the soil and the base of the plant. Prune clematis in pots as if they were growing in the garden; pruning strategies vary from one variety to another, so keep the instructions that come on the plant label. After three years, tip the plant carefully out of its pot in early spring before it starts growing, carefully shake off the old soil and repot the clematis back into the same tub or one that is a size larger, using fresh potting mix.

Suitable cultivars

Hundreds of clematis cultivars are available from specialist growers; most garden centres stock a fairly good range of the most popular varieties. These are some of the best for growing in containers.

'Bees Jubilee'
'Comtesse de Bouchaud'
'Edith'
'H.F. Young'
'Hagley Hybrid'
'Horn of Plenty'
'Lady Londesborough'
'Lady Northcliffe'
'Lasurstern'
'Miss Bateman'
'Mrs. N. Thompson'
'Nelly Moser'
'Souvenir de Capitaine'
'Thuilleaux'

Above: Planted correctly, a clematis will quickly establish and provide a colourful display. This is 'Lady Northcliffe'.

1 Carefully remove the clematis from its pot, with the cane still supporting the stem. Ease the clematis and cane into the tub.

2 Add potting mix to within 5cm (2in) of the top of the tub; firm down. About 5cm(2in) of the stem should be covered with mix.

3 Remove the cane. Set up the trellis as instructed, working the legs of the obelisk into the tub without disturbing the plant rootball.

4 Space the stems around the support. Tie them in loosely to prevent them becoming trapped in between the trellis panels.

6 As a finishing touch to the feature, put the white cap in place over the tapered ends of the wood. This secures the panels into a pyramid shape.

Clematis in pots around the garden

Stand a large tub of clematis at the base of a wall and let the plant climb up trellis or netting. Or place it on a patio and encourage the stems to grow over pergola poles. Provide extra grip by tacking wire netting tightly round the upright timbers. Or just stand tubs containing plant supports anywhere round the garden to act as focal points.

Right: *Grow clematis with an evergreen plant in a large pot for a year-round display. The shrub acts as a living support for the climber, which needs no other support.*

5 Ease in the final support and water the tub well. If the soil sinks or the obelisk tips to one side, add more soil, adjust the obelisk and rewet the soil.

Left: *Clematis can be grown into a dome shape by training it over a framework of wire netting or twigs. This complements a formal container such as a classical urn.*

Below: *Stand a tub of clematis at the base of a wall with an existing climber trained out over it, and the clematis will cling to the framework of stems.*

Clematis 'Hagley Hybrid'. Tie in new growth regularly to maintain a good shape, and remove dead flowers.

7 Water the tub profusely every day to ensure that the clematis becomes well established. Do not let it dry out at any stage. Most clematis prefer a coolish spot where the roots are in shade but the tops can grow into sunlight.

SIMPLE WICKER BASKETS

One specially attractive way of using baskets is to create a colourful, informal display of country garden flowers. For this to work well, follow a few simple guidelines. Choose plants with enough height; the tallest plant should be about one-and-a-half times the height of your container. Use plenty of plants for a well-filled display that looks good right away. If you choose a limited colour scheme, as here, it is vital to include two or three shades of the same colour, otherwise the finished arrangement will lack depth. It also needs plenty of contrasting shapes and textures, both of flowers and foliage, to make up for the lack of different colours. The secret of working with baskets is to keep the display simple but striking, in keeping with the container. Baskets are summer containers; even when painted or varnished, they soon deteriorate outside in cold wet weather. So make the most of them in summer and bring them inside to use with indoor plants or to repaint at the end of the season.

1 Loosely line a wicker basket with black plastic and make a few holes in the bottom. Place 5cm (2in) of clean gravel into the base.

2 Part-fill the basket with good-quality potting mixture. Leave the top of the plastic liner rolled over the top of the basket for now.

3 Put the tallest plants – here lythrum - at the centre-back of the display in order to create a graduated effect. This allows all the plants to be seen properly.

4 Use a mix of flower shapes; contrast spires of astilbe with the chunkier, flat-topped shapes of verbena. Contrast is important in displays that use mainly one colour.

5 As a focal point, add the strongest, most concentrated colour low down at the front. This phygelius has flowers that hang down slightly over the basket edge.

6 Finally, add a penstemon. The combination of flower shapes and textures add variety to the display and make the most of a limited colour scheme.

7 Top up with potting mixture, then roll the liner over to make a firm edge and tuck it just inside the rim of the basket.

8 A chipped bark mulch looks decorative, teams well with the natural cane basket and helps to keep plant roots cool and moist.

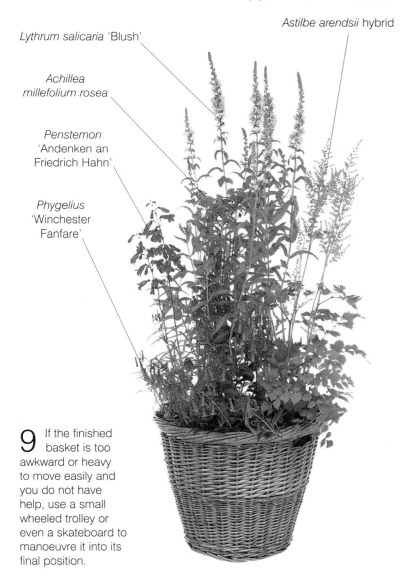

Astilbe arendsii hybrid

Lythrum salicaria 'Blush'

Achillea millefolium .rosea

Penstemon 'Andenken an Friedrich Hahn'

Phygelius 'Winchester Fanfare'

9 If the finished basket is too awkward or heavy to move easily and you do not have help, use a small wheeled trolley or even a skateboard to manoeuvre it into its final position.

Plain and simple

Old wicker baskets can be given a new lease of life by painting them (see page 43). A small basket looks best housing a single striking specimen instead of a mixture of plants. Team the plant carefully with the basket colour. Here, the phygelius has leaves of a very similar silvery green to the eau-de-nil of the container.

1 Push a black plastic liner well down into the base of the container. Gather up surplus plastic to keep it out of the way.

2 Spread an even layer of washed gravel in the base. Roll down the top of the liner inside the basket or cut it off.

The plant should be at least as tall as the container for a balanced display.

3 Lift a suitable plant into the basket. Choose a well-grown specimen in a large pot, and leave it in the pot. The display is then easy to change.

4 Phygelius is a long-flowering plant, so this display will grow bigger and keep blooming all summer and into early autumn if well watered, fed and dead-headed. Do not allow it to dry out.

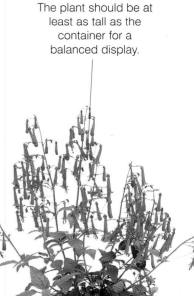

1 Line the basket with black plastic. Simply fit it into the basket and cut away the surplus plastic, leaving a 5cm(2in) rim.

2 Add potting mix, making sure the corners are well filled but leaving room for plants. The plastic liner will settle into the basket.

3 Firm the mix lightly to settle it into the container. Roll the top of the plastic over and tuck it under the rim of the basket out of sight.

4 Twine a trailing plant (here *Convolvulus sabatius*) around the handle; the stems will be safe while you put in the other plants.

A SUMMER DISPLAY IN A BLUE WICKER BASKET

Baskets make good containers; both new and secondhand ones can be used out of doors for several years, but first treat them with varnish to prevent fading and help the wickerwork to resist the damp. (They will eventually start to deteriorate, but this can be delayed by retreating them every year before use.) Clear varnish is fine for a natural rustic look, but for a more stylish effect try a varnish containing a wood-stain, as we have done here. When using a strongly coloured container such as this, you need to give much more consideration to the choice of plants than when using a neutral or terracotta colour, which goes with virtually anything. Decide on a look that either contrasts directly with the colour of the container – orange is the 'opposite' colour to blue – or opt for a harmonising scheme, as shown here. The secret of success in this case is to use a variety of shapes. Choose flowers of roughly the same shade as the container, but in a wide range of contrasting shapes and textures; go for large funnels, trumpets and daisies, and masses of small foamy sprays. This ensures that each flower stands out as an individual, otherwise a one-colour scheme could easily look dull and uninteresting. Even though there is not room for many plants, take advantage of every dimension by choosing a climber and a trailer, as well as bushy plants. Baskets make lovely 'country garden-style' containers, so avoid a symmetrical arrangement and aim instead for a loose, informal planting scheme that reflects the way plants grow naturally in a garden.

The convolvulus flowers will reorientate themselves after a few days

5 Plant one large, bushy flowering plant on each side of the basket handle for the best effect; this one is the kingfisher daisy (*Felicia amelloides*), which is covered with attractive blue daisy flowers all summer.

6 Plant *Solenopsis axillaris* on the other side of the handle. Its star-shaped flowers contrast well with the funnels of the convolvulus and the daisy shapes beyond. Choose a good bushy plant.

7 Choose a low trailing plant for the front of the basket. This one is *Bacopa* 'Pink Domino', which, despite its name, is closer to lilac in colour. It teams perfectly with the rest of the colour scheme.

Alternative planting schemes

Baskets have a pleasing natural style that goes well with country flowers, such as daisies and their relatives. This is why gazanias and argyranthemums suit them so well. For baskets with handles, the sort of flowers sometimes used for cutting create a 'still-life' effect, almost as if the flowers were waiting to be brought indoors for arranging. Avoid adopting a formal look or 'smart' city flowers.

Right: *A mixture of pink flowers in various shapes give this well-filled basket its air of country charm; they include drooping fuchsias, flaring petunia trumpets and snapdragons (antirrhinums).*

8 Finish off by tucking in a compact ageratum to fill the last gap at the front of the basket. The fluffy flowers add another textural contrast, and the shape keeps the display informal and cottagey.

Left: *This pale pink basket is almost hidden under a flourishing display of busy Lizzies in all shades of pink, punctuated by occasional colchicums.*

Convolvulus sabatius

Felicia amelloides (kingfisher daisy)

9 The completed basket looks pleasantly full; water it thoroughly and stand or hang it in a sheltered situation. All the plants chosen enjoy sun, and both felicia and convolvulus flowers close up in shade.

Sutera 'Pink Domino'

Solenopsis axillaris (Laurentia axillaris)

Ageratum

Above: *Sunflowers echo the pale yellow of this basket, but shades of deeper yellow and orange predominate. A touch of magenta creates a lively contrast.*

Summer displays

Trailing fuchsia

Petunia

Ageratum

Below: Trailing fuchsias add elegant arching sprays of bloom to ageratum and petunias, whose large flowers provide a focal point in the heart of this display.

PLASTIC CAULDRONS

One of the things that makes container gardening fun is the way you can keep finding new combinations of pots and plants that work well together. Try out new kinds of plants that you find in garden centres and do not always go for the same species, colour schemes or style. And experiment with different kinds of containers – even ones that perhaps look a little unlikely to start with. There is no need to spend a fortune. Cheap plastic containers can be made to look sensational, given the right sort of plants, and secondhand 'finds' in junk shops or rummage sales can be given a new lease of life with an unusual paint effect or simply by cleaning them up. If you cannot take an existing container to the nursery with you, try to find something similar in the shop and stand your selection of plants next to it to see how they look. Also look at the striking ready-planted containers that many garden centres set up; they are often a source of fresh inspiration. If you grow your own plants from seed, you can judge the effect of various flowers and containers by cutting pictures from magazines and catalogues. That way, you can have all the fun of planning summer displays in midwinter, in good time to send off your seed order.

Making the most of containers

• Hide cheap, unexciting or damaged containers with plenty of trailing plants around the edge.
• Make plants the focal point, not the container.
• Plants stand out best in neutral containers – black, terracotta, cream or green.
• Use a large variety of plant material of varying shapes and sizes.
• Go for bright colourful displays, not subtle shades.
• Instead of mixing plants randomly, group them together for impact.
• Check all plants need the same growing conditions.
• Fill tubs well so they look good from the start.

1 The secret of success when pairing plants and containers is to put everything together in a group before buying, so you can gauge the final effect.

2 Almost fill the container to the rim with potting mixture and knock each plant in turn out of its pot. Avoid breaking the rootball.

3 Position the largest and most striking plant in the centre of the container and fit the others around it in the remaining space.

4 Group different shaped flowers next to each other, with the palest species towards the front to add depth to the display.

5 Tuck spare soil into the gaps between rootballs. When all the plants are in place, add 1.25cm (0.5in) of soil over the surface.

French marigolds

French marigolds

Mimulus

Pelargonium

Calceolaria

Striped single French marigolds

Mini-outdoor 'Carnival' chrysanthemums

A winter display

A cauldron makes an effective container for all kinds of year-round displays. Instead of standing it on the ground, try hanging it up or stand it on a table or a brick plinth, especially if it is filled with trailing plants.

Right: A simple group of primroses makes a striking winter or early spring display; if deadheaded, it will flower for several months. Keep the container just moist and in light shade.

Left: Alternatively, use a few primroses with a background of foliage plants, such as euonymus and a small conifer, plus a winter-flowering heather (this sort is happy in normal potting mixture).

A spring display

Double bellis daisies, arabis, violas, primroses, heather and a hyacinth make up this arrangement.

Right: These plants are available in flower as spring bedding for instant displays. After the flowers are over, plant them in the garden for the following year.

219

1 Place 2.5cm(1in) of washed gravel or crocks into the urn for drainage. It already has small holes to allow water to run out.

2 Fill the urn to within 5cm(2in) of the rim with good-quality potting mix. Leave the mix loose and fluffy for planting.

3 Plant bushy, medium-upright verbenas into the centre of the urn. Separate each plant from the others without damaging the roots.

AN URN AS A FOCAL POINT

Paint effects can transform an inexpensive plastic urn into a container that earns its place as a focal point in the garden (see page 46). When planting up a container such as this, choose a simple but striking scheme. Here, we have picked out two different types of plants: bushy, upright verbena and trailing annual dianthus, both of which have a classic look. They are planted in a simple but formal geometric scheme. This is best kept low and compact, in much the same way as the Victorian carpet bedding schemes on which this design is loosely based. The classic pastel colour scheme looks even more striking because the deeper shade of the dianthus echoes the stronger tints in the verbenas. You could create similarly effective schemes with a combination of mauve and purple, green and white, or pink and cream. Since plastic containers are very lightweight, it is essential to weight the base of the urn well down with gravel or crocks. These not only permit excess water to drain freely out of the bottom of the planter, but also prevent the container from rocking about in windy weather. Avoid top-heavy planting schemes, which could render the urn unstable.

4 Continue planting thickly; it does not matter if rootballs of adjacent plants touch. The more plants you can get in the better.

5 Plant compact, bushy, trailing plants around the edge. These annual dianthus pick out the strongest colour from the verbenas.

6 Make a complete ring of dianthus around the edge. Fit in as many plants as possible so the effect looks generous right from the start and provides instant impact.

Effective colour-themed plant combinations

Experiment to discover the best colour schemes for flowers to use with coloured containers. It is much harder to coordinate plants with coloured tubs than with plain, neutral colours. Verdigris urns, for example, look best planted with silver and white, plus hints of blue. Alternatively, try dark greeny blue. This is not an easy colour to find in flowers, but available plentifully in the foliage of, for example, hosta leaves. Combine it with touches of white or silver. Do not just pick any plants with flowers of the right colour; aim for a mixture of strong shapes that work well together, so that each flower stands out from its background.

Select toning colours for highly decorated containers. If you use contrasting colours, such as blue flowers for a yellow container, choose pale shades of each so that the effect is not overpowering, Include hints of the container colour in the plant display to 'link' the two.

White: lobelia, petunia, fuchsia
Pink: ageratum and *Erigeron* 'Profusion'
Blue: anagallis and pansies.
Purple: brachyscome, browallia
Lilac: ageratum and double-flowered lobelia 'Kathleen Mallard'
Bronze-green: apricot nasturtiums and *Bupleurum griffithii* 'Green Gold'.

7 The finished display looks classically elegant, yet has cost very little to create; the 'stone' paint effects combined with formal planting have transformed a cheap plastic container into something special.

Verbena

Dianthus

A late-season display

1 Roughly fill the urn with potting mixture and begin planting from the back, starting with the tallest kinds.

2 As this is only a temporary display, use a mixture of whatever plants look good together and are the right size.

3 Ornamental cabbages make a good focal point. Lean them over at an angle (even over the side of the urn) for impact.

4 Tuck trailing ivy around the front to soften the edge. Ivy frames the focal point, drawing the eye to the heart of the display.

5 Choose plants with colours that tone well together. They should provide a variety of shape and texture and peak at the same time. Try a mix of shrubs, perennials, trailers and bedding.

Gaultheria mucronata

Sedum spectabile

Winter-flowering heather

Ornamental cabbage

Variegated ivies

1 Cover each drainage hole with a clay crock to prevent soil being washed out during watering.

TERRACOTTA TROUGHS

Patterned terracotta troughs can turn a few inexpensive plants into a designer display; the art lies in choosing plants that suit the background textures and/or colours. Use the same techniques as you would use when choosing fabrics or clothing to go together. And although painted terracotta may seem rather unconventional, an effect like this is easy to achieve (page 53). As an alternative colourway, try a mint-green base coat sponged over lightly with white to give a mottled effect and fill the trough with soft apricot tuberous begonias, fuchsias and busy Lizzies in shades of pink, peach and white, all with a foil of white-variegated foliage. A rich powder-blue would suit the strong orange and lemon shades in a pot marigold mix such as *Calendula* 'Fiesta Gitana', or mixed nasturtiums such as 'Alaska'. Alternatively, use a mid purple-blue as a base coat and add touches of crimson, blue and white paint diluted with water to the relief pattern. Plant with deep purple, velvet red and light lavender-blue flowers and silver foliage. For example, at the back you might use *Salvia farinacea* 'Victoria' and in the foreground crimson-red verbena and deep purple petunia, interplanted with silver cut-leaved cineraria and red trailing lobelia. Highly ornate terracotta troughs are perfect for a period setting; modern-looking bedding varieties could spoil the illusion of age, so look for muted shades of pansy, verbena and nicotiana. And do not forget the many herbs, small-flowered bedding violas, *Erigeron karvinskianus* 'Profusion', marguerites, heliotrope and scented-leaved pelargoniums.

2 A layer of gravel for drainage is important if a terracotta container has been lined with plastic to prevent moisture loss.

3 Use a peat-based mix for bedding, soil-based for long-term planting, and a soil-based seed/cuttings mix for nasturtiums.

4 Pick a shade of impatiens that complements the painted container. Here, busy Lizzies are teamed with white-variegated ivy.

Impatiens F1 hybrid

Hedera helix cultivar

6 This pastel display is perfect for shady walls. Other summer plants include begonias, bedding fuchsias, violas and *Lamium maculatum* 'White Nancy'.

5 Use the deep pink busy Lizzie to fill in the gaps at the back, then work in more mix around each of the plants to cover the rootballs.

1 Position the purple-leaved sedum in one corner so that the foliage drapes over the side of the trough. Next, plant the blue-grey echeveria hybrid.

2 Tuck the silvery sedum under the echeveria where it can fill out gradually. Add the second echeveria, again at the front.

3 Finally add one or two pots of variegated *Sedum lineare*. This grows more quickly, so pinch it out regularly.

Echeveria hybrid

Echeveria hybrid

Sedum spathulifolium 'Cape Blanco'

Sedum lineare 'Variegatum'

Sedum spurium 'Purple Carpet'

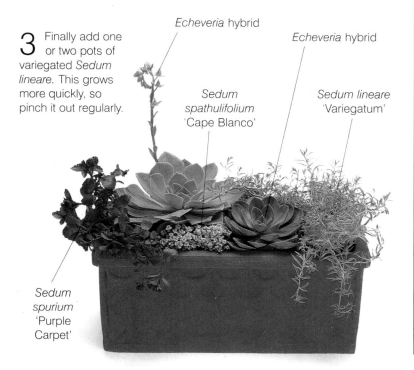

Teaming plants with patterned containers

Containers with raised patterns on their sides look best planted simply, with evergreens, a light curtain of trailing plants, or unfussy flowers. Coloured decorations are more limiting; select plants that pick out one of the minor colours from the pattern for a well-coordinated look.

Above: A pastel display of salvia, thyme, brachyscome and osteospermum is set off perfectly by the yellow paintwork of the terracotta trough. It demonstrates how simple it is to achieve a match between container and plants.

Above: Here, the yellow eye of the violas echoes the Iris bucharica. They make an unfussy display for this ornamental trough against a background of variegated lamium.

Below: A row of Peperomia caperata *growing close together in a trough would complement a group of flowering plants or look good on a shady shelf.*

CHIMNEY POTS AND FLUE LINERS AS CONTAINERS

Chimney pots, both old and new, make a striking display when used in groups of varying styles and height. When planting a tall container of this sort, it is better to find a plastic plant pot (or bucket) large enough to lodge in the top. If you fill the chimney itself with soil, it will become too dry and compacted to support a healthy plant – and also immovable. Look at your chimney pot both ways up before deciding how to use it; many, especially the tall ones, are a better shape upside-down and more effective planted this way, because being wider at the base, they will hold a larger pot. The height of the chimney will dictate the type of plants to grow in it; the tallest ones look better with plants that flow out and down, such as ivy or trailing pelargoniums. There are also plenty of tender perennials to choose from. Short, stubby little pots look equally good with erect, bushy or trailing plants, such as phormium, grasses, hosta and helianthemum. It is often a great help to be able to raise a group of plants in, or at the back of, the flower bed for those times when there is a gap in the flowering succession, or to keep it going when it is past its best. With their narrow, straight lines, the tall chimney pots are excellent used in this way.

Flue liners make perfectly acceptable alternatives to chimney pots. They are available in a buff or terracotta colour and may be round or square. Because they are open-ended, the roots of plants put into them can grow into the earth beneath. At 23cm(9in) or 30cm(12in) in diameter, flue liners are large enough to accommodate the most vigorous species. Find old chimney pots in architectural salvage yards and antique shops, especially those dealing in garden antiques. New chimney pots and flue liners are available from builders merchants.

1 In this instance, the chimney pot has been reversed. Choose a flowerpot with a suitable diameter to lodge inside the rim.

2 Put a few broken crocks in the bottom of the flowerpot to improve drainage, and add potting mixture until it is two-thirds full.

3 Place the first plant well over to one side of the pot, so that it leans outwards. Cover the roots with a small amount of potting mix.

3 Gently separate the roots and then place the plant in the pot. Water it in, fill up with potting mix and water again.

A hosta in a short chimney pot

1 Because this pot is just 12in (30cm) high - it does not need to be lined with a flowerpot before you start planting it up.

2 Two-thirds fill the pot with a good-quality potting mixture. A soil-based mix would be ideal for planting up hostas.

4 Position the remaining plants around the pot in the same way. Generously fill the spaces between them with potting mixture, firm down and water well.

Golden *Helichrysum petiolare* (at front) will spread out and down to balance the cerise *Pelargonium* 'Knaufs Bonfire' and salmon-pink *Pelargonium* Rokoko.

Osteospermum 'Sunny Girl', 'Sunny Boy' and 'Langtrees'

Pelargonium 'Mars'

Hosta fortunei aureomarginata

Above: Chimney pots make ideal plant holders used together or individually for height and emphasis.

Creeping Jenny *Lysimachia nummularia* 'Aurea'. Keep it out of strong sun and wind.

Herbs in flue liners

Some herbs are rampantly invasive and need to be sited very carefully away from the rest of the garden and out of the prevailing wind. Try containing them in pots on a bed of shingle, where the seedlings can be easily hoed away. Flue liners make excellent containers. Arrange them at varying heights, sinking some deeper into the ground than others. Put those herbs that enjoy moist conditions in the lower ones.

1 Settle the base into the ground and fill it two-thirds full with good-quality garden soil. Do not use potting mixture.

2 Put in the plant and water it. Top up the soil until it is 5cm (2in) below the rim of the liner to retain moisture when watered.

3 With the plants in separate liners, you can cater for their individual watering needs. Do not let the chives dry out.

Purple sage has attractive foliage and spikes of blue flowers in early summer.

Flat-leaved parsley has a better flavour than the curly-leaved variety.

Chives – lavender-pink flowers in early summer.

1 Choose a roomy half barrel and loosely fit a large black liner into the bottom, leaving the surplus plastic rolled back round the top. Almost fill the barrel with potting mixture and firm down gently.

EVERGREENS FOR SHADE

Many kinds of evergreens make good plants for shady spots, and are specially valuable as they provide all-year-round interest. Because of this, they need not be replaced regularly, like bedding plants. The same plants can be left in their containers for up to three years or until they become overcrowded, whichever is sooner. The trick is to grow them in good-quality, soil-based potting mix and refresh it each spring by removing the top 2.5-5cm(1-2in) layer and replacing it. Remember to keep plants well fed during the growing season, using a good-quality brand of liquid feed that contains trace elements as well as the major nutrients, nitrogen, potash and phosphate. There is a wide choice of suitable plants. Evergreen perennials are good for creating mixed displays, with a variety of interesting leaf shapes and textures. Plants such as bergenia, *Euphorbia robbiae*, *Iris foetidissima* and hardy ferns such as asplenium have naturally strong shapes that work well in a group. (But watch out, as not all hardy ferns are evergreen.) Shade-loving shrubs with good foliage, especially those with variegated or gold leaves, and those that produce seasonal flowers are specially worthwhile. Skimmia, aucuba, trimmed box, bamboo, choisya (especially the gold-leaved form) and euonymus are all very good choices. In this way, each plant has enough room for its true shape to develop normally. Container growing artificially 'dwarfs' shrubs by restricting their roots, but even so it pays to choose naturally compact varieties, as they make dense bushy growth. These kinds will not need pruning or reshaping in the way that evergreen plants with a larger or more open habit would.

2 Trim away the excess plastic, leaving a 5cm(2in) overlap – enough to tidy the edge and, if the mix sinks later, to protect the tub.

3 Roll the edge of the liner over and tuck it between the mix and the side of the container, so it is about 2.5cm(1in) below the rim.

4 Begin by planting the biggest, most striking plant near the back of the display. This hardy evergreen fern is *Asplenium scolopendrium*, the hart's tongue fern.

5 Team this with a plant such as bergenia, whose huge, saucer-shaped leaves will cover plenty of the potting mixture and mask the edges of the tub. In winter, the foliage of this variety turns an attractive purple.

6 Finally tuck in a smaller plant. This *Gaultheria procumbens* is an evergreen with red berries in the autumn and winter. In spring, it has clusters of bell-shaped white flowers among dark green leaves.

Specimen plants

All kinds of evergreens make good specimen plants. Camellias, pieris and rhododendrons do well in half barrels filled with ericaceous mix; replace the top layer of mix each spring and feed with a product containing sequestered iron to keep the plants healthy. Plants with striking leaves such as fatsia, the dramatic shapes of bamboo and the bright foliage colour of *Choisya ternata* 'Sundance' are all good subjects for tubs in shade. Or choose trimmed box, which does well in shade, even in situations that only receive an hour of sunlight per day.

Bergenia cordifolia 'Purpurea'

Asplenium scolopendrium

Gaultheria procumbens

7 The finished display will grow slowly during the season. Stand it in light shade. Container displays in shady spots need much less watering than containers in a bright, sunny situation.

Evergreen shrubs for shade

Compact, shade-loving evergreen shrubs are ideal for containers, as they need little attention and do not dry out quickly. During the summer months, water them every few days and feed every one to two weeks.

1 Line a wooden tub with black plastic. Make a small hole in the bottom to coincide with the drainage hole in the base of the container. Part-fill with potting mix.

2 Knock the choisya out of its pot. If roots are tightly coiled round the inside of the pot, gently tease out a few of them. Place the plant centrally in the tub.

3 Trowel more potting mixture around the rootball, inclining the plant slightly if necessary. Fill the tub to within 2.5cm(1in) of the rim and firm the mix in gently.

4 Roll down the spare plastic to make a collar inside the rim of the pot. This prevents damp mix touching the wooden container.

5 Move the plant to its final position and give it a thorough watering. Turn the tub occasionally so that the shrub grows evenly all round, otherwise it will lean towards the light.

227

1 A compact evergreen shrub, ivies and winter-flowering annuals make a colourful display. Put a crock over the drainage hole of the pot.

2 Fill a large container to just below the rim with any good-quality soil-based potting mix. If a container looks top-heavy, place a house brick in the base before filling it with the potting mixture for added stability.

Choosing plants

Choose only the best plants for containers. They should have plenty of buds and healthy leaves. Anticipate problems if the soil is bone dry or plants seem neglected. Well cared for plants in bud with a few flowers just open and fresh green foliage are best. Before planting, remove dead flowers or yellow leaves.

WINTER DISPLAYS

All the plants suggested for winter hanging baskets are equally suitable for containers. Being closer to ground level, tubs suffer less from the weather, so you can grow a wider range of plants, including winter-flowering heathers, Christmas rose *(Helleborus niger)*, early spring bulbs and any of the early spring bedding plants. It is also possible to use taller plants, such as evergreen shrubs, as the centrepiece of a floral display; variegated or coloured kinds, such as euonymus and *Choisya ternata* 'Sundance', whipcord *Hebe* 'James Stirling' or dwarf conifers, are good. Plants bought straight from a garden centre are ideal. Shrubs can remain in their new containers for a couple of years, but will fairly quickly fill them with root, preventing new bedding plants being put in to replace those that are over. So unless the plant is to become a solo specimen, repot it with new flowers into a larger container each autumn, or plant it out into the garden in spring. Stand winter tubs in a fairly sheltered sunny spot and raise the base up on 'pot feet' or bricks so that excess water can drain away. Team winter-flowering tubs with year-round containers planted with standard bay trees, topiary trimmed box, or ivies trained round topiary frames. And as winter flowers 'go over', remove them and replace them with spring bulbs or bedding, sinking the pots to their rims in the same place, to keep the display looking fresh.

3 First, put the largest plant in the centre of the tub. Keep the rootball intact, as space will be short and there are several other plants to put in.

4 A large ivy trailing over the tub softens the straight edges and helps the evergreen to blend in with the arrangement.

5 Fit in as many flowering plants as possible. They will not grow any more, so the finished result must provide the full impact.

6 Pull out strands of ivy for a wispy effect. Site the display in a prominent position. Water well. Apply a weak feed in mild weather.

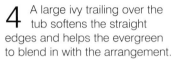

Skimmia japonica 'Rubella'

Cultivated primrose hybrids

Variegated ivy

Alternative planting schemes

Below: *Evergreen shrubs provide a weather-resistant winter display. Choose a mixture of good foliage, berries and attractive flowers.*

Variegated euonymus

Ophiopogon planiscapus 'Nigrescens'

Viburnum tinus 'French White'

Juniperus chinensis 'Expansa Variegata'

Osmanthus heterophyllus 'Variegatus'

Variegated ivy

Dwarf variegated chamaecyparis

Solanum pseudocapsicum

Erica carnea hybrid

Gaultheria procumbens

Euonymus fortunei Emerald Gaiety

Right: *This display will provide colour and interest all winter in a mild city centre garden or a protected porch.*

229

THE PATIO YEAR

Keep a patio looking good all year by growing a wide range of plants. Using evergreens as the backbone of your displays, add seasonal highlights in the form of spring, summer and winter bedding throughout the year. And as an inexpensive alternative to replacing long-term plants or containers, regroup plants regularly to make new arrangements.

SPRING

Even though it may be too cold to sit outside in spring, the patio is still visible from indoors and a colourful display is very welcome at the end of a long winter. Good plants for spring displays include bulbs – daffodils, hyacinths, tulips, etc., – and polyanthus, wallflowers, forget-me-nots, stocks and double bellis daisies. In mild areas, you can plant these out in autumn after removing summer annuals. But if you wait until spring, you may find a wider range of plants and as they have not had to weather the winter outside, they will probably be in better shape than those

planted out in autumn. Harden them off in a cold frame or start off by standing them outside during the day and bringing them in at night for a week or so before planting. Choose plants that are still in tight bud to give them a bit of time to adjust to the conditions before the flowers open. Add a few evergreens – ivies and small conifers – as temporary background plants to set off a container of flowers. To create new displays fast, simply stand them, still in their original pots, into containers and pack round with moss or old potting mix.

Above: Bellis daisies make a pretty seasonal display in a wooden tub, set off by a top-dressing of oyster shells. These were traditionally used to edge cottage garden paths.

Above: Containers of mixed spring bulbs, such as these ranunculus, narcissi and tulips, brighten up groups of foliage shrubs and add splashes of colour to dull corners.

Right: Add pots of bulbs to a group of spring-flowering shrubs and evergreens. This technique makes the most of plants some distance away from the house.

SUMMER

In summer, bedding plants, summer-flowering bulbs, patio roses, dwarf shrubs, herbs and perennials all contribute to a riot of colour. You can choose a traditional mixture of colours or, for a more sophisticated effect, a scheme based on one or two colours. Use colour with care; decide whether you prefer a strongly contrasting effect or a gentle harmonising one. Bright colours stand out best against a contrasting background. In containers you can achieve these effects by teaming bright flowers with coloured foliage plants, such as coleus and purple-leaved basil. For a harmonious effect, use similar coloured flowers and foliage together – blue, purple and mauve or shades of pink and red. Colour can also create an atmosphere. A 'hot' scheme of red, yellow and orange looks tropical and busy, while cool green and white or blue and mauve are still and relaxing. Play with colour to make a small patio look bigger. Red and yellow plants in the foreground give the impression that they are close to you. Mauves and misty purples at the other end of the patio give the impression of distance. By grading colours from hot to cool across the patio, you can create the sensation of space. Heighten this effect by making the patio narrower at the far end.

Above: Petunias are very reliable summer bedding plants, as they are smothered in flower all season, but they do need deadheading.

AUTUMN

Patios can easily lose their impact in autumn as summer annuals come to an end. To maintain the display, raise or buy a late crop of annuals for midsummer planting. By late midsummer, they will be coming into bloom and be ready to replace any annuals that have flowered themselves out by then. Alternatively, winter-flowering pansies are available in garden centres, already in bloom, throughout autumn, so you can replant summer containers then for an instant display. Another plan is to cultivate containers of autumn-flowering perennials, such as schizostylis, phygelius (Cape figwort) and miniature pompon dahlias, which team up perfectly for a late-season display.

Above: *Cape heath (Erica gracilis) flowers in autumn and teams well with evergreens and late pansies. Never allow potgrown heathers to dry out.*

WINTER

Small evergreen shrubs with variegated, silver or aromatic foliage, such as euonymus, santolina and rosemary, together with ivies, make the backbone of most winter displays in tubs, windowboxes and hanging baskets. Add long-lasting berries

of skimmia (also good for winter buds, depending on variety) and flowers of winter jasmine. Use young plants bought from garden centres and give them a season's use in containers before planting them out in the garden. For flowers, add winter heathers or, in mild spells, winter-flowering pansies. Polyanthus, wallflowers, double daisies and spring bulbs turn late winter into early spring, and lead on colourfully to the start of the summer bedding season.

Below: *Winter containers of evergreens, berrying shrubs and winter-flowering heathers (Erica carnea cultivars) make long-lasting, weather-resistant displays.*

Above: To make the most of the profusion of summer flowers, bank displays up on tiered staging. This way, each plant can be seen as an individual instead of looking crowded, and they all have room to grow and look their best.

Left: Pelargoniums are very versatile and suitable for every kind of container, including hanging baskets. One reason for their great popularity is their toughness. Plants enjoy strong direct sun and do not mind if the potting mix dries out occasionally.

A completed peacock attended by fledgling box topiaries in terracotta pots.

PART NINE
TRAINING AND TOPIARY

Growing climbers over shaped frames is a smart way of creating potted topiary quickly but cheaply. You can raise all the popular shapes and even invent some of your own. Trimming also turns potentially large shrubs into happy container subjects and adds a variety of shapes, styles and heights to a potted plant collection.

Training a cone

1 Transfer a suitable plant to a large ornamental container. This fast-growing shrub is *Lonicera nitida* 'Baggesen's Gold'.

2 Sit the plant in the centre of the pot. Fill in round the root-ball with potting mix. Firm in gently and water well before proceeding.

3 Gather the stems loosely and fit the frame over the top. With all the stems inside, press the cone gently into the mix until it is stable.

4 Tuck any stray shoots behind the wires. This thickens up the shape and ensures that protruding stems will not be snipped off.

5 Working all round the plant, secure strong upright stems to the frame with ties. This makes the shape more solid right away.

6 Snip off any protruding straggly shoots. Remove the very tips of thin straight shoots to encourage them to branch out.

CLASSIC TOPIARY SHAPES

Classic topiary shapes include domes, pillars and spirals, right through to more fanciful shapes, such as peacocks and teapots. On a smaller scale, any of the free-standing forms and many other currently fashionable shapes such as teddy bears, are suitable for growing in pots. Topiary specimens are traditionally created from box, yew and bay, which are ideal due to their evergreen foliage, dense bushy nature, slow growth and ability to withstand tight clipping. For quicker results, try euonymus and lonicera. The foundation of all the shapes is a frame to which the plant's main stems are secured. Frames can be made of wire, wire netting or timber and can be bought preformed or you can make your own, which allows you to create more individual designs. Where a chunky pillar is topped by a crown or peacock, only the decorative device on top needs a framework. This is held up by a post driven into the pot through the foliage, which hides it from view. Potted topiary takes several years to train, but is very satisfying to create, and the saving in cost compared to that of buying ready-trained plants is immense. Use potted topiary to decorate a low-maintenance front garden, as an effective year-round display on a patio, or as focal points anywhere round the garden. They particularly suit formal features such as herb gardens, but look brilliant tucked into a flower bed, where they contrast startlingly with flowers in formal beds, herbaceous borders and even simple cottage garden borders.

7 Already the shape of the cone is emerging from the original untidy bush. Work your way round the plant, lightly 'tipping'. Cut close to the framework at this stage.

8 *Lonicera nitida* soon fills out the frame. When horizontal side shoots start to make the outline look rather shaggy, the plant is ready for its final shaping.

10 At the top, tie the string firmly to the frame. Snip off any protruding stems, leaving the cone with a neatly pointed tip.

11 Sheep shears are ideal for trimming off any stems that stick out from the sides of the cone, leaving the sides tidy.

9 Tie a string to the base of the frame. Sweep the stems up with one hand and bind them in place with the other. Do not cut them off; they fill out the shape.

The finished cone has taken less than three months to complete. It will need clipping every few weeks from spring to autumn.

Training a sphere

1 Set the circular base of the sphere framework into the bottom of the pot. Add sufficient potting mix to cover the frame base and the bottom of the pot.

2 Knock the plant out of its pot. Tip the frame slightly so that you can fit the plant underneath it and sit the rootball close to the middle of the pot.

3 Still tipping the frame, gently push the stems inside the shape. Young stems are flexible, but it is easiest to arrange a few at a time. Spread them well out.

4 Straighten the frame and hold it firmly in place while filling the pot with potting mix. Firm gently round the rootball and water well; top up if the mix sinks.

5 Divide the main stems into four evenly spaced groups. Push them gently out towards the edges of the shape. Secure the stems to the frame with plant ties.

Euonymus Emerald 'n' Gold

6 Keep well fed and watered and tie in new growth. Once the sphere is solid with foliage, finger prune to keep the shape tidy.

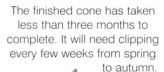

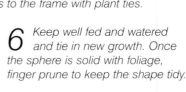

1 Start with a strong, rooted box cutting. Nip off the growing tips of the shoots using forefinger and thumbnail in a pincer movement. Repeat when the side shoots are 2.5cm(1in) long.

SHAPING BOX AND BAY

Box and bay are popular topiary subjects. If you are starting from scratch with box, use *Buxus sempervirens* and not the miniature cultivar 'Suffruticosa'. To shape existing bushes, choose a plant that already suggests a simple shape, such as a bun or sphere, and exaggerate it by regular light clipping. For more complicated shapes, start with a very small plant or, better still, rooted cuttings. Take these from established box plants during late spring and summer. Snip 7.5cm(3in) pieces from the tips of the shoots and remove the lower leaves. Push them to two-thirds their length into pots or trays of seed mix and keep them moist and shady. When rooted – after six to eight weeks – pot each cutting into a 10cm(4in) pot and pinch out the growing tips to make it bushy. Nip out the tips of subsequent side shoots so that the young plant is bushy from the base. Then start training.

Unlike box, bay has large leaves, so it is not clipped, but pruned with secateurs, or even 'finger-pruned' by nipping out the very tips of the shoots while they are tiny to encourage branching. The large leaves also make bay unsuitable for training into very detailed shapes, such as spirals or peacocks, as it is not possible to achieve such a neat outline as with a small-leaved subject. Move a potted tree under cover during spells of cold, windy weather in winter, which might otherwise cause the ends of the branches to die back, or the evergreen foliage to be browned and spoiled.

2 Use secateurs to nip back the tips of the next crop of side shoots. Each time new growth reaches 5cm(2in) long, shorten it.

3 Regular pruning makes the plant bushier. At the same time, you can roughly form the basic outline of the required shape.

6 Frequent clipping is important while the shape is being formed. By 'stopping' side shoots, growth is kept bushy and dense.

4 Do not worry too much at this stage if the results are not very precise. The important thing is to have plenty of side shoots growing out in all directions.

5 As the first pot becomes filled with roots, move the plant into a larger pot with fresh potting mix to keep it growing well. Continue clipping regularly using small shears instead of secateurs.

7 When it reaches the required size, clip back the box to the previous outline each time. By then, clipping three of four times a year should be enough.

8 Trim the tips of the young shoots back just enough to encourage branching, which gives a dense, leafy shape, while allowing the shape to grow in size.

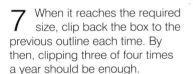

9 It is possible to create a good box ball about 23cm(9in) across by this method in three years. Clip it two or three times a year to retain the shape and size.

Right: A large trained evergreen in a container is a useful way of filling a gap in a display. The formal shape makes a striking contrast with an informal arrangement of plants – a technique much used in cottage gardens.

Training a bay tree

Bay trees are traditionally trained into ornamental shapes, such as standard 'lollipops' or cones. They are often grown in terracotta pots by a doorway or on a patio or used to decorate a formal herb garden.

1 Slip a tripod of canes over the tree. Encircle it with an adjustable wire hoop to help you achieve an even conical shape.

2 Using secateurs, neatly snip away any shoots that extend beyond the conical outline. Move the wire hoop as you work.

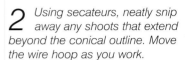

3 Pinch out the tips of young shoots growing towards the edges of the desired shape. Bay leaves are quite large and would be spoiled if they were cut in half.

4 The end result is a smartly trimmed tree. Do not expect a totally smooth outline as you would get with a small-leaved plant that has been clipped.

237

TRIMMING A CONIFER

Some conifers are traditional subjects for bonsai, notably Japanese white pine, larch and mountain pine, though junipers, cryptomeria, cedars and others are sometimes used. These are coaxed to resemble ancient and stunted trees by a combination of trimming, wiring and root pruning over many years. 'Proper' bonsai requires a great deal of knowledge, care and attention, but with a little trimming, it is possible to accentuate the natural characteristics of virtually any conifer or create interesting shapes of your own. Naturally dwarf types that can be grown in pots are the most convenient to work on, but you can also trim larger conifers growing in the open garden. (However, if you make a mess of it, the result cannot be kept out of sight until the effect of the bad haircut 'grows out'.) To start with, find a plant that is already growing into an interesting shape – perhaps a lopsided specimen at a garden centre or one of the varieties that typically grows into an uneven shape. Trimming can mean thinning out cluttered growth to reveal the true shape of the plant, or altering the entire shape of the plant. Dense-packed conifers with tiny leaves, such as some of the chamaecyparis, can also be given topiary shapes – domes, spirals or peacock shapes – small-scale versions of the type of trimming done using the traditional yew. However, for a reasonable-looking result, do not stray too far from the basic framework shape of the plant, and try to finish up with a plant whose 'visual' weight is evenly balanced from one side of the trunk to the other. If you are not happy with the result, simply wait for the plant to grow and then have another try.

1 Choose a frost-proof terracotta pot of oriental design to underline the bonsai feel. Cover the drainage hole with a flat stone or crock and part fill with soil-based potting mix.

2 Select a naturally 'craggy' plant and plant it in the centre of the container. It need not be upright - sometimes a slight lean accentuates a natural feature.

3 Water the plant well in to settle the potting mix around the roots. If the mixture sinks, fill in with a little extra mix and water as before.

4 Look closely at the natural shape of the plant and plan what you want to alter before cutting. Use sharp scissors, secateurs or bonsai trimming shears, and do a little at a time.

5 Clip away small sections of foliage to accentuate that part of the shape you want to exaggerate. Stop, stand back and look at the result after removing each piece to see the effect.

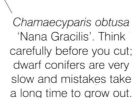

Chamaecyparis obtusa 'Nana Gracilis'. Think carefully before you cut; dwarf conifers are very slow and mistakes take a long time to grow out.

6 To help you decide whether to remove a section of foliage or not, try 'blanking' it out with a piece of card. This is safer than cutting it off and then wishing you hadn't!

7 The shape emerges gradually. Take your time; meditation is all part of the art. The shape of this plant looks rather like a peacock – it could easily end up as one.

8 Continue to thin out until you are happy with what is left. Avoid getting carried away; it is easy enough to take off a bit more later.

9 The finished plant retains the attractive lacy texture and billowing shape of the original, but now it can all be seen more clearly.

Most conifers put on much of their year's growth in one big spurt in late spring, so this is the time to retrim to keep the shape neat.

SUITABLE PLANTS

Chamaecyparis obtusa
'Lycopodioides'
C.o. 'Tetragona Aurea'
C. pisifera 'Boulevard'
Gingko biloba
Ilex crenata
Thuja occidentalis
'Pygmaea'

Maintaining and developing the shape

New growth at the top means the plant has lost its shape.

1 A year later, the plant has made new growth. Let the plant revert to its unpruned state or trim to keep the shape defined.

2 Tidy up round the base by removing cluttered shoots, leaving a clean shape here; also remove any lower brown leaves.

3 Snip off shoots that spoil the shape; cut them back just beyond overlapping foliage so that cuts are hidden by leaves.

4 By pruning just after the late spring flush, the shape is assured for another year. Meantime, the plant will thicken out.

Creating a standard fuchsia

1 Choose a cutting with a straight stem and, if possible, three leaves at each node. Insert a stick into the potting mixture and prepare to tie the cutting to it.

2 Gently bring the cutting close to the stick. Use a soft tie to avoid damaging the tender growth. Keep the stem as straight as you can; it is very supple at this stage.

3 Carefully break off any side shoots that appear in the axil of the leaves by gently bending them to one side. Retain the top five sets of leaves; they will form the head of the plant.

4 When the young standard has reached the required height, remove the growing tip, but not the large leaves on the main stem.

5 Now the remaining five side shoots will grow. Leave them to produce two or three pairs of leaves. Pinch out the growing tips.

GROWING STANDARDS

Standard plants are like small lollipop-shaped trees. In pots, they add height and temporary colour to a container display without taking up much room, and are particularly striking used as focal points in geometric garden features such as knot gardens. Fuchsias are the plants most often trained as standards, though many other plants also look very effective when trained in this way. These include argyranthemum, datura, lantana, ribes, pelargonium, syringa species, such as *S. patula,* evergreen ceanothus and weigela. Given a strong stake to support the stem, wisteria, honeysuckle and clematis can be trained as standards, too. Using the same technique for all of them, you can normally produce a fair specimen in a year. The best kind of plants to use are shrubby ones, as woody stems are essential to give the standard strength. A naturally upright habit is helpful, as it makes it easier to get a straight, upright main stem. You can use bushier plants and even climbers; they just need more tying up to keep them straight. In winter, you need to protect the roots from freezing and tender plants have to go inside.

6 As the bushy head starts to form, remove the large leaves on the main stem, which has become quite woody at this stage.

7 Gently break off any side shoots, otherwise they are wasting the plant's energy. Take care not to damage the main stem.

Slow growers

If a fuchsia is not growing, gently scrape off a little bark with your fingernail. If it is green underneath, it means that the plant is alive. If it is brown, scrape another area of bark, as the plant may have died back a little. If it is still alive, it will need some extra nurturing to stimulate it into life.

If a small standard fuchsia does not grow from the top, trim off the top and grow it as a tall bush instead.

Above: Spray the wood with tepid water daily to soften the bark and stimulate the plant.

Below: If a standard is slow to grow, lay it down so the sap can reach the top more easily.

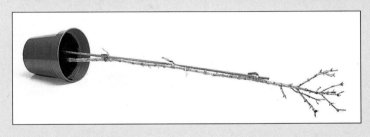

'Royal Velvet' is a fine old double-flowered cultivar. Other doubles suitable for growing as standards include 'Annabel', 'Brookwood Belle', 'Cotton Candy', 'Dancing Flame', 'Happy Wedding Day', King's Ransom', 'Natasha Sinton', 'Paula Jane' and 'Swingtime'.

Right: The weight of the large double flowers of 'Royal Velvet' give it an almost weeping shape. This type of growth may need tying to a central cane for extra support.

Pruning a standard fuchsia

As you cut back, try to visualise the final shape. By careful cutting, you should be able to create a woody structure at least as good as the current year's growth. Careful trimming should produce an even better woody shape that will pay dividends the following growing season.

1 At the end of the season, leaves turn yellow and there is a clear lack of flower. This is the time to give the plant a rest and prune it back.

2 The aim of pruning is to produce a good, woody shape and structure for the new growth. Use sharp secateurs.

3 Work your way around the plant to create a well-balanced shape. Be cautious; you can always cut off more later.

4 As you prune, the woody structure becomes clearer. Take this opportunity to make a lopsided plant more symmetrical.

5 Remove all the leaves left on the wood, otherwise you may encounter problems with fungal infections, such as botrytis.

6 Now there is a good framework for new growth in the following season. Any leakage of sap will stop and is not harmful.

241

CREATING AN IVY SPIRAL

Traditional topiary takes years to perfect, but for quicker results try 'instant' topiary, made by training ivy round a light framework of wire or willow. Preformed wire topiary frames – usually two-dimensional animal shapes – are sold in garden centres or you can create your own hoops and spirals by bending stiff fencing wire into shape. Make more complicated shapes, such as teddy bears, from wire netting. Plant several climbers in a large tub all round the shape and peg out the stems to ensure complete coverage. Ivy is the usual subject for instant topiary; small-leaved forms are best for modest-sized topiaries; experiment with the many variegated or gold forms, and also the arrowhead-shaped *Hedera* 'Sagittifolia' cultivars.

For even greater variety, experiment with other evergreen climbers: *Euonymus fortunei* varieties such as Blondy or Emerald 'n' Gold can be trained in this way although they are not normally regarded as climbers. For a bigger topiary, use larger climbers, such as *Jasminum nudiflorum*. Grow it on the same frame as a strong-growing ivy for an interesting effect, or choose the variegated evergreen honeysuckle, *Lonicera japonica* 'Aureoreticulata'. For a scented topiary, grow *Trachelospermum jasminoides* or *T.j.* 'Variegatum', both of which have fragrant white flowers in summer, as well as evergreen foliage. Do not overlook plants that need greenhouse protection in winter, such as passion flower, plumbago and bougainvillea, all of which make good flowering topiary shapes for summer patios.

1 Push a spiral training frame into a large pot, plant two climbing ivies and twist the stems up round the frame. You can sometimes buy ivy 'topiary' at this stage.

2 By the time the ivies reach the top, side shoots lower down start to make the shape 'fuzzy'. The topiary will need trimming three to four times a year to keep it neat.

3 Twist in all the overhanging stems around the base. Avoid cutting them off while the topiary is young, as they help to thicken the shape. Tie in place if necessary.

4 Working up, twist wayward stems firmly round the frame to keep the shape defined. Use long new shoots to 'bind' existing stems close to the framework.

5 Hold stems in place with plant ties – as many as you need to achieve a tight shape. Do not worry about the appearance; ties soon disappear under the foliage.

Training climbers round a hoop

Large climbers in pots are best dealt with by training their long stems around hoops of wire. Not only does this keep them tidy, it also encourages better flowering, since when more of the stem is horizontal, flower buds can develop along the length instead of just at the tips.

6 At the apex, twist the top stems together before winding them round the tip of the spiral. This creates a neater finish with more leaves and less visible stems.

1 To train climbers such as this passion flower around a framework, unravel the tangled stems and insert the frame into the pot.

2 Secure the stems to the frame with plant ties or wire clips. Clips reopen easily, so you can add extra stems as you work.

7 Secure the top of the ivy firmly in place. This is particularly important, because if it comes adrift, the rest of the plant will slacken on the frame and the topiary will 'relax' out of shape.

Regularly tie in new growth to keep the shape neat.

8 About 20 minutes work restores a fuzzy topiary shape to mint condition. Repeat the process at the start of the growing season (late spring) and thereafter at regular intervals two or three times every summer.

3 As the plant grows, fix new stems into place until the framework is thickly covered with foliage. As the pot fills up with roots (around midsummer) the plant will begin to flower.

Branch pruning

Here we see how to carry out simple pruning where a small to medium-sized branch needs to be removed. Always use very sharp tools, ideally sterilised by immersing them in methylated spirits for a few minutes.

1 If you do not have any proper bonsai tools, use sharp bypass secateurs. Make sure that the non-cutting blade is furthest from the trunk as you cut.

2 If you have special branch pruners, use them to finish off the cut close to the trunk. It will heal more neatly if you create a slight hollow in the exposed wood.

3 Clean up the edges of the wound with a very sharp knife. Ragged edges heal unevenly and are likely to harbour fungal spores that may later infect the whole tree.

4 Seal the wound thoroughly, especially around the edges. If you do not have any bonsai sealant, mix a little olive oil with grafting wax or modelling clay.

Shaping with wire

Wiring is the most fundamental process in bonsai training, allowing the accurate positioning of branches and shoots. Follow these simple steps.

BASIC BONSAI TECHNIQUES

A healthy young bonsai – say up to ten years old – in a small pot will pack its container with roots within one season, so it will need to be root pruned each year. Older trees, especially conifers, tend to grow more slowly, taking perhaps up to five years to fill the pot. However, it takes time for problems associated with root confinement to take effect, and you can miss a year every so often without putting your tree at risk. The ideal time for root pruning is just as the roots begin to grow in spring. Although it is possible to repot at any time during the dormant season, the longer the wounds wait before they can regenerate, the more they are at risk of further damage from frost and fungal attack. After repotting, wait two weeks before heavy pruning, and delay feeding for four to six weeks, or until new growth has been established.

Wiring involves coiling wire of a suitable gauge around a branch or shoot and manoeuvring the two into the desired position. After a period of growth, the branch will be set in position and you can remove the wire. Conifers, especially junipers, may take several years to set, during which time you may need to remove and reapply the wire several times to avoid damaging the bark. Some deciduous species may set in a matter of weeks. The principle of wiring is simple, but the skill takes a little time to acquire. Practice wiring on a twig or branch from a garden shrub, similar to your chosen bonsai. See how thick the wire needs to be and how far the branch will bend without breaking. Remove the wire with bonsai wire cutters; although it seems wasteful, do not reuse the wire, as it will be kinked and difficult to manipulate.

1 For your first try, use fairly thick wire – this is easier to handle. Always hold the wired part of the branch firmly with one hand and coil the wire with the other.

2 When you bend the branch, do it gradually. Spread your hands, so that you hold as much of the branch as possible and use both thumbs as leverage points.

3 When wiring long branches, reduce the thickness of the wire as the branch diameter decreases. Overlap the different thicknesses by two or three turns.

Maintenance pruning

Each year your bonsai will throw out new shoots from the buds created in the leaf axils during the previous growing season. In established bonsai, this annual growth will need to be cut back during the dormant season to allow the next season's growth room to extend before outgrowing the design. These steps show how to carry out winter pruning of a tree with opposite leaves, in this example a Japanese maple.

1 During the previous growing season this maple produced a few long shoots. The first step is to cut them back to a short shoot, or spur.

2 Every few years you will find it necessary to prune away older growth to prevent the branches getting overcrowded and to maintain neat foliage pads.

3 Finally, cut back all spurs to one or two buds. You may have to look quite closely to see the buds because they can be minute. Look carefully at the base of each spur.

When to prune

Winter prune late in the season, before the buds swell but after the worst weather is over. Newly pruned bonsai will suffer in very late frost, however, so if necessary prune once the buds are fattening; the setback will only be slight.

4 After a good prune, the branch looks rather naked, but remember that every remaining bud will generate a new shoot next season, producing an ever more compact twig structure.

Repotting and root pruning

In the wild, a tree extends its roots each growing season. As it matures, some older roots die back to be replaced by new ones. In a pot, you have to reproduce this cycle artificially to keep the bonsai healthy.

1 *After two years, the healthy roots of this medium-sized trident maple are filling the pot, and need to be pruned.*

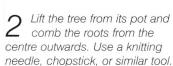

2 *Lift the tree from its pot and comb the roots from the centre outwards. Use a knitting needle, chopstick, or similar tool.*

3 *Trim the roots back so that the remaining root mass does not quite fill the original pot. Use a sharp pair of scissors.*

4 *Trim the roots underneath, or the tree will rise in its pot as it grows. Prune thick roots back to encourage compact growth.*

5 *Nestle the tree into a mound of soil. Place it off-centre for best visual effect, with the surface of the root mass just below the rim.*

6 *Pull the wire ties down over the root mass and twist until the tree does not rock. Cushion the bark with rubber foam pieces.*

7 *Fill the spaces with fresh soil. The soil is much easier to apply if it is virtually dry, because it runs freely and does not compact as you work it into the empty spaces.*

BONSAI EASY PROJECTS

Nowadays, most bonsai are created by reducing larger plants or by growing branches onto preformed trunks. However, there is still a very important place for growing bonsai straight from seed. It helps you to learn about the growth patterns of each species and makes you more aware of the structure of the trees. But most importantly, by growing bonsai from seed you can create an almost perfect little tree on a very small scale. Being able to display a tiny, unblemished and well-formed bonsai that you grew from seed is a most satisfying and rewarding achievement.

Having pricked out a seedling, let it grow unchecked for the rest of the season, as it is vital to have an established root system before you begin training. The following year, during late spring or early summer, or as soon as the new growth has hardened off, you can make the first pruning cut, retaining just three or four tiny spurs. This forces the seedling to produce side branches and is the most drastic pruning you will ever need to do. Once the new branches have grown a little, carry out the initial wiring. Plant the fledgling bonsai in a shallow but oversized container at the beginning of its third growing season. From now on, year after year, the continuing process of painstakingly wiring new shoots into position and regularly pinching out growing tips will gradually produce an incredibly realistic branch structure bearing a crop of tiny leaves. Do not hurry the process. Remember that you are 'building' the final shape of the tree, much as nature does. The longer you take to achieve the final shape, the better the result will be.

These rooted beech cuttings were intended for hedging. Other hedging stock includes hawthorn, privet and field maple. Such raw material is relatively cheap.

1 These beech cuttings are not particularly inspiring at first sight, but their different thicknesses and lines are just right for creating a group.

2 Prepare each cutting in turn. Cut away the long roots with sharp scissors, leaving as many fine feeder roots as possible. These will nourish the young tree.

3 Work a sticky mixture of equal parts of clay and fine peat between the roots and mould it into a ball. Do this for each of the cuttings featured in the group.

4 The clay balls keep the trees in position while they are being arranged in the pot. Start with the tallest tree, just off-centre, and place the two next tallest ones either side.

5 When the arrangement is complete, add soil between the clay balls covering the root masses. Dry soil is easier to apply as it does not stick to the wet clay.

6 Complete by 'landscaping' the soil surface with different kinds of moss and grit. Water the pot and moss first, and avoid pressing the moss down too hard.

Creating a bonsai cotoneaster

This cotoneaster has strong branches growing in all directions. Tilting it to one side shows its potential as a cascade-style bonsai.

1 Cut back to the lowest pair of heavy branches. This will make the trunk begin its cascade very close to the base.

2 Bend the trunk as sharply as possible, reflecting the tortuous conditions suffered by natural trees in the mountains.

3 The branches should cascade in the same way as the trunk, with similar curves but on a smaller scale. Note how the sparse branches in the stunted crown also cascade, giving unity to the design. Once the tree is planted in a proper cascade pot, final adjustments can be made to the branches. It will grow away well, especially at the top and bottom.

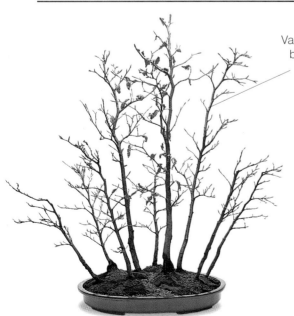

Varying the spaces between the trees produces a more natural effect.

7 The new beech group planting is already pleasing to the eye. Note how the trees at the edges of the group have been pruned so that each apex sweeps outwards.

A juniper bonsai

This sequence features a two-year-old cutting of Juniperus squamata 'Meyeri'. Its compact foliage allows it to be formed into an almost instant bonsai subject. Deciduous species need two or three years.

1 *Clear all the foliage and small shoots from the trunk, leaving the larger branches. Try to avoid leaving opposite branches.*

2 *Do not let the size of the original plant dictate the size of the bonsai. Cut off one of the twin leaders and shorten the other.*

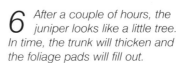

3 *With the trunk and wire held together, begin to coil. Hold close to where you are coiling and move your hand as you progress.*

4 *Grasp as much of the trunk as possible to spread the pressure and bend it into the desired shapes and curves.*

5 *Bend the branches down, ensuring there are a few at the back. Bend close to the trunk. Clear any growth facing down.*

6 *After a couple of hours, the juniper looks like a little tree. In time, the trunk will thicken and the foliage pads will fill out.*

247

A BONSAI GALLERY

The main aim of bonsai is to create a treelike form in miniature. This can be anything from a precise replica of a classic parkland beech to the image of a gnarled and weather-beaten mountain-top juniper, which can be almost abstract in its design. In nature, there is an infinite variety of tree shapes and these are imitated in bonsai. Over the centuries, the Japanese have devised a number of general classifications, each having its own aesthetic rules. These govern the shape, angle and proportion of the trunk, number of trunks and location of the branches, etc. The literati (called in Japanese bunjingi) style, for example, is reminiscent of ancient pines that tend to shed their lower branches as they age. The focal point of the design is the trunk, which should be full of character. In rocky terrain, the scarce soil is constantly being eroded, exposing the rocks and the roots of the trees growing amongst them. The root-over-rock (sekijôju) style depicts such a tree, whose roots cling to any rocks beneath them as they thicken. Clump (kabudachi) describes any odd number of trunks in a variety of sizes, all growing on the same roots. This may be created from suckers arising naturally from the roots. The group (yose-ue) style incorporates any number of trunks, from seven upwards.

Left: This mountain pine in a classic cascade style represents the shape a tree takes on when growing over the edge of a cliff or mountain side. The lowest shoot should be lower than the base of the pot.

Below: The gnarled trunk, spreading limbs and partially visible roots of this upright-style Japanese maple duplicate an aged tree growing naturally in the wild.

Below: Being small, this award-winning field maple bonsai needs regular leaf pruning to reduce the scale of the leaves.

This is an example of the root-over-rock style of bonsai.

Above: In summer, this clump-style Japanese maple needs constant attention. You may need to pinch out the shoots almost every day. Regular leaf pruning produces tiny foliage more in scale with the size of the tree.

Right: Japanese white pine is a popular bonsai subject, here trained in a slanting style that mirrors the way trees develop when grown in exposed areas, leaning away from the wind. This fine tree is 53cm (21in) high and 30 years old.

Flowers and berries on bonsai trees

Many suitable bonsai species also produce flowers and fruit. Cherry, flowering cherry, rhododendron and chaenomeles are traditional favourites, but winter jasmine (Jasminum nudiflorum), pomegranate and cotoneaster all make good 'dual-purpose' bonsai subjects.

Above: A stunning azalea with bicoloured flowers. Rhododendron indicum *(Satsuki)* and R. Obtusum Group *(Kurume)* are the most popular.

Right: Pyracantha make very attractive bonsai, especially when the feminine beauty of the flowers and fruit is contrasted with the more masculine styles, such as cascade or this root-over-rock.

A conservatory can be an oasis of peace surrounded by foliage and flowering plants.

PART TEN
CONSERVATORY CONTAINERS

Container gardening under glass is the only way to grow plants that are too tender to grow outdoors and too big to grow indoors as houseplants. A conservatory can be a tropical garden, a Victorian-style garden room, a glassed-in patio or an extra living room. Suit it to your lifestyle and decorate it with plants.

SUNNY CONSERVATORIES

For many people, the whole reason for having a conservatory is to create a suntrap for enjoying the outdoors indoors. The sunniest side of the house seems the obvious place to site it, but in summer the conservatory heats up quickly and soon become too hot for plants – and sometimes even people – especially if it is inadequately ventilated. Extra ventilators, circulator fans and blinds all help, but it can still be difficult to find plants that thrive. In this situation, there are two possibilities. One is to use the conservatory for plants only between autumn and early summer, then move them to a sheltered patio for the summer. Most conservatory plants will be quite happy with this arrangement, but do not treat orchids or other tropical plants in this way. Removed plants will not dry out so fast, and pests will be less of a problem. The second alternative is to grow plants that are happy in hot, dry conditions. Those with aromatic, silver or felty leaves, and thick or waxy leaves are natural candidates. Zonal pelargoniums, scented-leaved pelargoniums, cacti and shrubby salvias, such as *Salvia grahamii,* are ideal. Sunloving garden flowers, such as osteospermum, gazania, arctotis and mesembryanthemum (all native to hot dry places) will be happy. Bougainvillea also thrives in dry heat, and like pelargoniums, needs a cool, dry winter rest below 10°C(50°F) in order to flower well the following year. Compact forms can be grown in hanging baskets and are sometimes sold as trimmed shapes, including pyramids and standards. For something more unusual, try *Brahea armata*, an unusual palm species with soft blue foliage, or *Washingtonia filifera*, which has shredding edges to the large fanlike leaves.

Left: *Agave attenuata*, the tulip-leaved agave, has a bold architectural shape and suits terracotta pots. In time it reaches 90cm (36in) across, and has soft leaves with a spike at each tip.

Bougainvillea

Oleander (All parts of the plant are toxic.)

Left: Bottlebrush, *Callistemon citrinus*, has bright, bristly flowers in summer. When they are over, the rows of knobbly seed capsules remain and are quite decorative in their own right. It requires no pruning

Scented-leaved *Pelargonium* 'Jessel's Unique'

Right: *Agave salmiana ferox* lives up to its name, with a display of ferocious spines. It makes a striking, slow-growing plant for a hot bright conservatory, and puts up with any amount of heat.

Below: Stripy *Yucca gloriosa* 'Variegata' is virtually hardy, so it would not mind an unheated conservatory in winter. It can reach 120cm(48in) tall, but a pot tends to dwarf it. Good in terracotta.

SUITABLE PLANTS

Architectural plants for a sunny conservatory kept at 10°C(50°F) in winter (but shade from strong midday sun in summer).

Acacia dealbata, *A. pravissima*, *Agapanthus africanus*, Agave, *Albizia julibrissin* (silk tree), Aloe, *Cassia corymbosa*, *Chamaerops humilis* (dwarf fan palm), Cordyline, *Cycas revoluta* (sago palm), Heliotrope, *Lavandula dentata*, *L. multifida*, *Musa ensete* (banana), Oleander, *Pittosporum tobira*, Plumbago, Standard trained olive tree, *Strelitzia reginae* (bird-of-paradise flower), *Tibouchina urvilleana*, *Tweedia caerulea*, Yucca

Cacti and succulents

Cacti and succulents are the most reliable plants for a sunny conservatory if you are busy, as they tolerate some neglect. However, they grow best if well ventilated and watered twice weekly during the summer.

Right: *Grow cacti in a variety of terracotta pots and bowls, and group them together to create a dramatic display. They associate well with chunks of natural rock, pebbles, gravel and driftwood.*

Cereus peruvianus monstrosus

Mixed bowl of cacti and aloe

Kalanchoe 'Multi'

Mammillaria elongata 'Cristata'

Echeveria hybrid

Euphorbia trigona

Above: *Unlike cacti, succulents do not tolerate strong direct sun, so do not stand them next to the glass in bright sunny conditions, and shade them lightly in very sunny weather. Water freely in summer.*

Echeveria gibbum

253

SHADY CONSERVATORIES

Sometimes there is no alternative but to site a conservatory on the shady side of the house. However, it may still receive quite good indirect light, and this can be increased by painting the interior walls cream or white and using a light-coloured, ideally shiny, floor covering to reflect back all the available light. A small water feature, such as a shallow pond or small fountain, will also increase light reflection. If light levels are roughly equivalent to those inside the house and the conservatory can be well heated in winter, then indoor plants will have virtually perfect conditions. If there is little or no heating, consider the sort of planting schemes popular in Victorian times, using hardy or nearly hardy shade-loving foliage plants. You could create a fernery with unusual forms of fern from specialist nurseries, displaying them in terracotta pots or landscaping them into raised beds edged with logs. Ivies are also very collectable, and include bizarrely twisted and variegated forms that can be trained over wire shapes to make potted topiary specimens (see page 242). Or grow a mixed collection of ferns and ivies with other shade-loving plants such as aspidistra, spotted laurel (aucuba) and fatshedera, with soleirolia (helxine) – the silver and gold versions – and hosta. The latter do well in pots in a cool shady conservatory and are easier to protect from slugs. Add shade-loving flowering plants such as potted hydrangeas plus, in summer, fuchsias and busy Lizzie. Look for unusual, exotic kinds, such as 'Congo Cockatoo' (*Impatiens niamniamensis*) and species fuchsias, with their long, trumpet-shaped and unusually coloured flowers. Trailing interest can be provided by kangaroo vine and grape ivy, two of the tougher, more cold-resistant houseplants, and spider plant (chlorophytum).

SUITABLE POTPLANTS

Asparagus meyeri,
Camellia,
Campanula isophylla
Cineraria, Cyclamen,
Dicksonia antarctica
(tree fern), *Duchesnea indica* (false strawberry),
Euonymus, Indoor azalea,
Lily-of-the-valley,
Miniature rose,
Oxalis triangularis,
Pot chrysanthemum,
Primroses and polyanthus,
Primula obconica and
P. malacoides,
Spring bulbs

Left: A wide range of indoor plants are happy in a shady conservatory; here ladder ferns, yucca, ivies, soleirolia and asparagus ferns provide a backdrop of foliage for seasonal flowers, azalea and peace lily (spathiphyllum).

Below: Some shade-loving foliage plants and ivies are hardy enough to survive in a conservatory without any winter heating at all.

Aspidistra variegata (cast-iron plant). A compact form with spotty foliage.

Fatshedera lizei (a cross between *Fatsia* and *Hedera*)

Soleirolia soleirolii

Hedera helix (ivy)

Foliage begonia species occur in a huge range of leaf patterns.

Begonias are shade-tolerant and easy to grow.

Group several foliage begonias together to create a high-profile display.

Unusual plants for shade

Many unusual and collectors' plants that need a warm humid shady environment make fascinating conservatory displays, but need heating to room temperature in winter – and no cold draughts. Mix them with other plants to create a varied display, not a botanical collection.

Left: *The 'Congo Cockatoo'* (Impatiens niamniamensis) *is a most unusual relative of busy Lizzie, with bizarre large, red-and-yellow beaklike blooms. However, they soon become untidy, so take cuttings often to replace old plants.*

Above: *Begonia rex* and other foliage begonias look exotic and enjoy warm, humid, shady conservatory conditions. This group, in attractive oriental wicker containers, makes a superb cameo to stand on a table.

Left: This fine, genuine Victorian conservatory was set up for plants rather than people. It has decorative cast-iron staging topped with gravel. The grilles in the floor cover heating pipes.

Below: *Gesneriads are a very collectable group of plants, which include scarce species found at specialist nurseries, as well as the popular streptocarpus, which is available in many colours.*

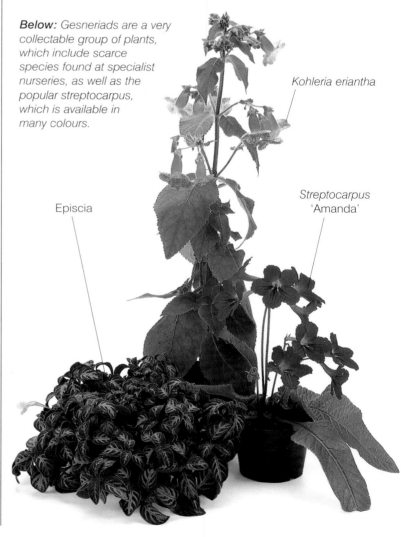

Kohleria eriantha

Streptocarpus 'Amanda'

Episcia

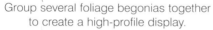

1 A wooden tub suits a mainly foliage display. Loosely line the tub with black plastic, rolling the excess down over the rim. Half-fill the container with potting mix.

2 Trim away the spare plastic, leaving an edge that can be folded over and tucked in round the tub to make a neat finish. It will soon be hidden by plants.

3 The main feature is to be a large, variegated *Fatsia japonica*, which is not quite as hardy as the plain green form. Tip it out of its pot and set it in position.

COLD CONSERVATORIES

Even a totally unheated conservatory offers plenty of scope for year-round colour and interest. For maximum colour, use two sets of plants, one each for summer and winter displays. In summer, choose fragile or warmth-loving annuals, such as grandiflora petunias, rhodochiton and ipomoea, and discard them in autumn. Add half-hardy perennials, such as laurentia, pelargoniums and argyranthemum. Overwinter these as cuttings in the conservatory until frost threatens and then move them to a window indoors. For winter displays, go for evergreen shrubs with striking foliage, such as whipcord hebes, *Choisya* 'Sundance', fatsia, ivies and phormium. Slightly tender shrubs, such as pittosporum and olearia, will appreciate the protection of cold glass in winter. Add early spring-flowering outdoor plants, such as the Christmas rose *(Helleborus niger)* and camellias. Although these plants are themselves perfectly hardy, the flowers can be spoilt by bad weather as they open. By growing them indoors you see them at their best and they flower several weeks earlier than outdoors. Grow them in large pots outdoors from late spring to mid-autumn, then bring them inside for the winter. You can also use arrangements of near-hardy houseplants with seasonal flowers or winter bedding for extra colour, in autumn, winter and early spring.

4 To make room for other plants and to create a more pleasing display, tip the fatsia slightly over to one side. Fill in round the rootball with more mix and firm in gently.

5 Remove the kalanchoe from its pot and plant it. The foliage is the same shade as the deeper green of the fatsia's variegation and the red flowers tone in with the tub.

6 Add the last plant – a spider plant. Place it so that the arching foliage drapes elegantly over the side of the pot for a fuller effect. Arrange the fatsia leaves so they frame the other plants.

A cream-and-green arrangement

7 Use a small, narrow-bladed trowel to ease some more potting mix carefully into any gaps between the rootballs of the plants. Gently firm it down and give the arrangement a thorough watering.

1 *Half-fill the container with potting mix. Plant a plain green* Fatsia japonica, *inclined at a very slight angle, towards the back and firm it in gently.*

2 *Add a frilly edged cream-and-green ornamental cabbage (these do well in an unheated conservatory). Place it at the very base of the fatsia.*

3 *Add an upright, deep green euonymus at the back, and cream/green variegated trailing foliage plants at the front to hang down over the sides of the tub.*

Fatsia japonica (variegated)

Kalanchoe blossfeldiana (flaming Katy)

Fatsia japonica

Euonymus

Ornamental cabbage

Soleirolia soleirolii 'Variegata'

8 The finished display will look good for several years before the plants outgrow their space. When the kalanchoe finishes flowering, you could replace it with another seasonal plant.

Chlorophytum comosum (spider plant)

4 *The finished container will not need much water in winter, although the potting mix should never dry out. It does not need bright light or direct sun; it will be happy in a shady corner.*

Ivy

FOLIAGE PLANTS

Foliage plants provide a good all-year-round conservatory display; use them on their own or make them the backdrop to an ever-changing tapestry of flowering plants. Since foliage plants tolerate shadier conditions than flowering kinds, they are ideal for a conservatory that has to be built on the sunless side of the house; choose ferns for the shadiest places. Large-leaved plants, such as palms, monstera and philodendron, are the perfect way to create a rich, tropical-looking landscape. Grow a few large, impressive specimens with pots of smaller, coloured-leaved plants, such as maranta, calathea, solenostemon (coleus) and begonia, to fill in fine detail. All these plants associate well with tropical flowering plants such as anthurium and orchids. This type of display needs light shade, constant heat and high humidity to succeed; it is no good turning the heat down in winter, as tropical plants such as these need a minimum of 16-19°C(60-66°F).

In a cooler conservatory, use near-hardy plants, such as aspidistra, ivies, *Oxalis triangularis*, fatsia and fatshedera, with the various asparagus ferns to create the leafy look; use chlorophytum (the spider plant) or rhoicissus in hanging containers and make tabletop displays of small plants, such as tolmiea and *Saxifraga stolonifera* (mother-of-thousands), grouped together for added impact. Or use a mixture of gold, green and variegated soleirolia (also called helxine) in a pretty container. The soft tree fern, *Dicksonia antarctica*, makes a stunning specimen plant for a conservatory that is only heated enough to keep out frost in winter.

Above: The sago palm *(Cycas revoluta)* is exceptionally slow-growing, with dramatic curved comb-shaped leaves, so stiff they appear unreal. Do not overwater; shade the plant from strong sun, and keep it at 10°C(50°F) in winter.

Growing conditions

Temperature
Summer max: 30°C(86°F)
Winter min: 5°C(40°F)

Humidity
Reasonable levels in summer; lower in winter

Light/Shade
Good light; shade plants from strong direct sun

Watering/Spraying
Water well in summer; less in winter

Feeding
Use liquid feed in summer; not in winter

Left: The ferny foliage of *Asparagus meyeri* teams well with terracotta, and this is a particularly novel way of growing it. Plants are nearly hardy, so a frost-free conservatory is fine.

Left: *Pedilanthus tithymaloides* 'Variegatus' (Jacob's ladder) has extraordinary stems that, coupled with its striking coloured foliage, make it an unusual and eye-catching plant. Avoid strong direct sun, which may scorch it.

Left: The variegated form of Swiss cheese plant, *Monstera deliciosa* 'Variegata', makes a dramatic specimen to grow up a moss-covered pole. Give it a large container in a shady spot in a warm conservatory.

Trailing foliage plants

Trailing plants with especially striking foliage or unusual shapes make a good year-round backdrop to more easily changed flowering plants elsewhere. However, do not neglect to feed and water them.

Right: *Tradescantia zebrina* (wandering Jew) is a colourful trailing plant that does best grown in a hanging container. Water generously in summer but less in winter, when the plants rest. Keep at a minimum of 7°C (45°F) at that time.

Above: *Swedish ivy,* Plectranthus oertendahlii, *occurs in various colours, although variegated forms are most often seen. It tolerates a wide range of conditions.*

Left: *Sedum morganianum (burro's tail) is a succulent that occasionally has a few flowers. It does not exist in the wild; the original plant was bought at a market stall in Mexico.*

Below: Although hardy outdoors, when grown under cover, *Fatsia japonica* has even bigger leaves that remain in perfect condition.

Right: *The rabbit's foot fern (Davallia canariensis) has delicate foliage. In time, the container is almost surrounded by furry stems that cling round the outside. Keep shaded and humid.*

FLOWERING PLANTS

A conservatory has to meet the needs of both people and plants. It can be used as an indoor patio, a garden dining room or as a plant room – and often ends up being a bit of each. When buying plants, take into account the way the room is mainly used and consider the size, habit and growing requirements of the plants (especially winter temperatures). If the main use is for sitting in the sun, use plants as you would on an outdoor patio, with climbers trained up trellis on the walls, a few specimen plants in large pots, flowering plants grouped in planters between the furniture and hanging containers overhead. If is not heated, or only kept frost-free in winter, then it is best to grow near-hardy permanent plants and add seasonal, tender, flowering plants in summer. The conservatory is a good place to 'store' plants such as citrus in winter that stand outside on the patio in summer. If dining is the main use, keep to compact plants in pots, perhaps on shelves on the wall. When a dining room/conservatory is in use all year round, it will be heated to room temperatures and be shaded by blinds in summer, making it suitable for plants such as orchids and tropical houseplants. You could add a large, spectacular, tropical climber such as allamanda or *Medinilla magnifica* on one wall or out over the roof, but be prepared for a certain amount of falling leaves, insects and debris in your eating area. Most true conservatory plants need a minimum winter temperature of around 7-10°C(45-50°F), so ensure adequate heating – an electric greenhouse heater is ideal.

Columnea 'Sanne'

Above: Columnea make waterfalls of red/orange flowers. They need humid air but not too much water at the roots, especially in winter.

Left: Gloxinia are superb plants for a slightly shady spot with moist air. They flower all summer and autumn, then die back to a tuber and rest until the following year.

Allamanda cathartica, a large climber, needs humidity, warmth and plenty of light.

Lantana 'Radiation'. Lantanas are prone to whitefly. Stand plants outdoors for a few weeks in summer.

Plumbago auriculata, a rather floppy, sprawling shrub, is usually trained against a wall or, while a small plant, on a wire shape.

Growing conditions

Temperature
Summer max: 30°C(86°F)
Winter min: 5°C(40°F)

Humidity
Reasonable levels in
summer; lower in winter

Light/Shade
Good light; shade plants
from strong direct sun

Watering/Spraying
Water well in summer;
less in winter

Feeding
Use liquid feed in summer;
not in winter

Above: *Passiflora citrina* is a new
introduction from the pine woods
of Honduras, where hummingbirds
pollinate the pale yellow blooms.

The bell-shaped flowers of
abutilons come in a range of
bright colours. Given enough
light, plants bloom almost all year.

Tibouchina urvilleana is
ideal for a large free-
standing container.

Coping with large plants

*To stop potentially large conservatory shrubs getting out of hand, grow
them in pots to restrict the roots and train them as standards, which
take up much less space than bushes. Form the basic shape as for a
standard fuchsia, then finger prune as required to keep the head neat.*

Solanum rantonnetii

Left: Solanum rantonnetii *is a
very tender plant that left to grow
naturally would make a weak
sprawling shrub. However, it
makes a good standard in a
container and is used as a wall
plant in Mediterranean gardens.*

Displaying flowering plants

*A plant room can be equipped
with tiered benching, shelves
and large beds (or space for
large pots) for showy conservatory
shrubs such as tibouchina,
abutilon or* Strelitzia reginae, *the
bird-of-paradise flower. This way,
you can fit lots of plants into a
tight space without overcrowding
and create maximum impact.*

Right: *Seasonal flowering plants,
such as cineraria and calceolaria,
are available in autumn; they are
ideal for a cool or cold
conservatory, and being annuals,
are thrown away after flowering.*

1 As this is a ready-lined container, add some gravel for drainage. Expanded clay pellets for use in gravel trays are also suitable.

HOUSEPLANT BASKETS

Hanging baskets are not only decorative outdoors; you can also use them to create unusual displays in a conservatory. This is a good way to grow trailing indoor plants, such as asparagus fern, that sprawl untidily when planted in normal pots and are difficult to accommodate. You can make up mixed displays, as here, or use a basket to grow a single specimen plant. Both trailing and climbing plants can be grown successfully in this way. When choosing plants for particular places or certain containers, consider their natural habit. Some plants, such as *Hoya bella* and *Scirpus cernuus*, are actually compact, bushy plants with a floppy habit. They could be grown in a normal pot, but are only seen at their best when allowed to hang down freely. If the conservatory is in a very bright spot, fix blinds or apply shading paint to prevent the plants from scorching. Try to prevent the temperature from rising above 30°C(86°F) by providing plenty of ventilation and, if possible, using an electric fan to circulate cool air around the plants.

2 Add a layer of potting mixture. Make sure that the plants have been given a thorough soaking beforehand. Try the largest plant in the trug for size to gauge the depth of potting mixture that will be required.

5 Lift the foliage so that you can fit the creeping figs underneath the impatiens. Fill the gaps around the rootballs with more potting mix as you work, so that there are no air gaps.

3 Place the first of the two busy Lizzies in the basket, turning it so that the stems fit round the handle. If the basket is to be viewed from one side only, you can tilt the plant to give a fuller effect.

4 Fill the middle of the basket with the other impatiens. Arrange the plants so that they are off-centre, with some stems overhanging the edge of the trug. This results in a more natural look.

Ficus pumila (creeping fig)

New Guinea hybrid impatiens (busy Lizzie)

Ferns in an oriental basket

1 Add gravel to provide a layer of drainage in the base of the container. This basket is ready lined and has no drainage holes. It will suit the fern foliage perfectly.

2 Cover the gravel with peat-based potting mix. Offer up a plant to check the depth and make sure that there will be sufficient space at the top for watering.

3 Soak the plant rootballs and plant three *Pteris* ferns, adjusting their position so that the foliage fills the basket and works in comfortably around the handle.

4 Fill any gaps with more mix and firm in. Water to settle the soil. Ferns like a constantly moist but not wet soil, so take care not to overwater this sealed container.

Pteris cretica albolineata (variegated table fern)

5 Suspend the basket using natural coloured twine or raffia to blend in with the other materials. To keep the plants looking good, remove brown or damaged fronds at the base with nail scissors.

A mixed houseplant display

This display features houseplants that thrive in a conservatory. The container has an integral drip tray that prevents splashes on the floor when watering and acts as a small water reservoir for the plants.

1 Fill the container with potting mix to within 5cm (2in) of the rim. Choose a soil-free mixture, as it is lightweight.

2 Group the plants around the container to create an interesting scheme. Choose foliage plants with trailing stems and a variety of leaf shapes and colours for contrast.

Tolmiea menziesii

Kalanchoe blossfeldiana

Asparagus sprengeri

Ficus pumila 'Variegata'

Chlorophytum comosum 'Vittatum'

TRAILING HOUSEPLANTS

Some plants, such as spider plant (chlorophytum) and mother-of-thousands *(Saxifraga sarmentosa)*, cascade by means of 'pups' at the end of runners. Though common, it is unusual to see well-grown specimens, and in hanging containers they are displayed at their best. Many fast-growing trailing plants need a long drop to house them. *Hoya carnosa* and stephanotis, for example, are in fact, weak climbers that in the wild would scramble up through other plants. They can also be trained around the container and even up the supporting chains to create a much neater feature. Otherwise, train them out over trellis or round support frames in a normal pot. Tie the stems in regularly. Good climbers/trailers for a sunny situation include trailing succulents, such as ceropegia, as well as hoya, columnea, dipladenia and stephanotis. Most other trailing houseplants need shelter from strong direct sun, while foliage plants, such as ficus, chlorophytum, epipremnum and trailing philodendron must have indirect light only, otherwise the leaves will scorch.

Above: The long, trailing stems of *Epipremnum aureum* (devil's ivy) are best displayed in a hanging container. Plants need humid, still air; keep roots moist in summer, but drier in winter to avoid brown spots on the leaves.

Left: *Peperomia scandens* 'Variegata' is a pretty trailing species. Grow the plants in light shade, wait until the potting mix is starting to get dry before watering, and keep them at 13°C(55°F) in winter.

Right: *Campanula poscharskyana* is hardy and suitable for a totally unheated conservatory. It makes a fast-growing spreading shape, covered in attractive flowers all summer and autumn.

Left: Slow-growing *Streptocarpus saxorum* is a charming little plant, with dark felty-textured foliage and delicate purple flowers. It has a naturally compact habit and needs shade, high humidity and a temperature of 13°C(55°F) during the winter.

Right: *Saxifraga stolonifera* has 'pups' at the end of thin 'threads'. This near hardy plant is suitable for an unheated conservatory. Plants turn redder in sun.

Below: The dark foliage of *Columnea* 'Apollo' sets off the pale yellow and bright orange flowers. A winter rest will encourage a greater profusion of flowers.

Hoyas in hanging baskets

Hoyas (wax flowers) have beautiful, thick-petalled fleshy flowers. Plants flower best when slightly potbound; avoid moving the pot after buds form. Do not overwater or remove the dead flowers.

Above: *Hoya lanceolata bella makes a rather stiff plant with drooping horizontal stems. When grown in a hanging basket, they form an umbrella-like shape, which is best seen from below.*

Right: *The large, spectacular flowers of Hoya lanceolata bella have a bad habit of dripping thick sticky honeydew. Do not put polished furniture underneath them and wipe up drops regularly.*

The stems are a mass of glossy green leaves.

Left: *Hoya carnosa 'Tricolor' has long stems and large leaves, and makes a much bigger plant than Hoya bella. Train it round a hoop or a hanging pot and back up the supports.*

1 Almost fill a terracotta bowl with special cactus mix. Make your own mix by adding 25% fine grit to soil-based potting mix.

2 Start with a tall, upright cactus. To handle prickly plants, wrap folded paper round the stem close to the base and hold the ends.

3 Plant a prickly pear and a small globular flowering cactus. Their contrasting shapes add more interest to the display.

4 Choose plants with a different spine formation or colouring, as here. Separate plants of similar shape with contrasting kinds.

5 Before getting too far with the planting, choose some suitable decoration. These pieces of gnarled driftwood make a pleasant change from the usual pebbles or chunks of quartz used in cactus bowls.

CREATIVE CACTI DISPLAYS

Cacti and succulents are naturally drought-tolerant sun-lovers. A group of contrasting shaped plants in identical pots makes an interesting arrangement for a shelf; or use large, striking terracotta pots to house big specimen plants. Bold ethnic decorated pots also suit cacti or succulents, as an alternative to plain terracotta. But one of the prettiest ways to display cacti and succulents is to group them in bowls or shallow terracotta pans (with drainage holes in the base). Ideally, keep cacti and succulents in separate containers, as the latter often need less strong sun but more water than true cacti. Cacti tend to be rather angular, so to avoid rather stilted groupings, make full use of the range of plant shapes, spine sizes and colours, and both hairy and bald bodies for maximum interest. Some of the smaller species of cacti will flower reliably every spring or summer while they are still young, so include a few of these (rebutia, mammillaria and some notocacti are best) for seasonal colour. Use natural decorations that suggest a desert setting; chunks of mineral rock, pebbles or decorative gravel or – as here – gnarled driftwood (available from florists). Both cacti and succulents can stand outdoors in summer; an occasional shower of rain actually helps keep them clean. (If they become dusty, brush between the spines of prickly subjects with a soft paintbrush.) Feed sparingly and water regularly in summer, but keep almost dry in winter, when cacti should be kept frost-free and succulents at 3-8C°(37-47°F).

6 Tuck more plants between the pieces of driftwood. Folded paper is useful for planting species with hooked spines that otherwise snag your fingers and sleeves.

7 When the bowl is well-filled with plants, top up the cactus mix with fine gravel. The easiest and safest way to work the gravel between the plants is to pour it slowly and carefully from a fold of paper.

Creating a still-life with succulents

Succulents are available in a huge variety of shapes and sizes, some with exotic flowers, others with striped or spotted leaves. Their range of forms and leafier appearance make them easier than cacti to arrange attractively. Always select plants that need similar growing conditions.

8 The finished bowl is ideal for a sunny window, but could stand outdoors for the summer. The plants are closely planted for immediate impact and will need more space after a year or two.

1 Part-fill a terracotta bowl (with drainage holes) with cactus mix. Do not damage the roots as you remove plants from their pots.

2 Sit the biggest, most striking plant in the centre. Angle the others outwards around the edge for a natural display.

3 Support rosette-shaped plants with a stone to prevent neck rot. In the wild, they often grow vertically in rock faces.

4 Use as many plants as will comfortably fit into the bowl to make a generous-looking display with immediate impact.

Cleistocactus jujuensis

Opuntia
microdasys rufida

Parodia leninghausii
(Notocactus
leninghausii)

Rebutia
spinosissima

Mammillaria
polythene

Mammillaria
plumosa

Notocactus
ottonis

Mammillaria elongata
'Cristata'

Mammillaria bocasana

Aloe squarrosa

Aeonium
tabuliforme

Haworthia attenuata

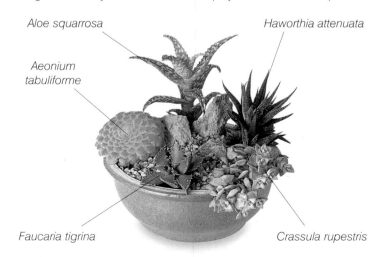

Faucaria tigrina

Crassula rupestris

AN INDOOR RAINFOREST

Exotic-looking plants in the conservatory create a lively rainforest-style display. True tropical plants will need living room temperatures even in winter, so efficient heating is essential. They also need high humidity, so choose furnishings that will not be spoiled by moist air. A plain tiled floor and hardwood, plastic or cast aluminium furniture are ideal. Most tropical plants need shading from strong direct sun, so blinds or shading may be needed in summer. An authentic jungle look requires plenty of plants. Choose those with large leaves, such as palms, monstera and philodendrons, and include caladium and maranta for their colourful variegations. Add exotic flowering plants, such as anthurium, bird-of-paradise flower (strelitzia) and frangipani (plumeria), for extra colour. Go for large specimens backed up by distinctive arrangements of small plants, perhaps grouped around a small water feature with tropical water lilies, or hanging from walls. Orchids, bromeliads and indoor ferns all suit this style, as they enjoy the conditions. Without enough heat for true tropical plants, it is still possible to create a similar effect by choosing plants that have a jungly character but are much less tender than they look, and enjoy summer humidity and indirect light.

Try mimosa (acacia), *Cupressus cashmeriana,* pittosporum, bamboos and fatshedera. All thrive at about 7°C(45°F) in winter. Use exotic-looking flowering houseplants to decorate the conservatory in summer when it is kept warm by the sun – African violets and streptocarpus, plus climbers such as stephanotis – but bring them indoors when the weather gets cooler by autumn. Make the most of exotic-look plants that can be raised annually from seed, such as coleus, strobilanthes, datura, and asarina (climbing snapdragon).

Growing conditions

Temperature
Summer max: 30°C(86°F)
Winter min: 7°C(45°F)

Humidity
High in summer, lower in winter

Light/Shade
Shade plants from strong direct sun

Watering/Spraying
Mist and water well in summer; less in winter

Feeding
Add weak liquid feed to water occasionally

Right: The prayer plant, *Maranta leuconeura kerchoveana*, is so called because of its odd habit of folding its leaves up at night. The rustling noises this causes can be quite disconcerting.

Curcuma

Philodendron 'Burgundy'

Codiaeum variegatum 'Petra' (croton)

268

Above: The flowers of *Anthurium*, (the flamingo flower or painter's palette), are very long-lived. The plant needs constant warmth and high humidity.

An indoor pool

One way of ensuring sufficient constant humidity in a conservatory for rainforest plants is to include a small pool – maybe just a basin of water for floating plants and a few waterlovers grown in pots in dishes of water. Water plants need good light, so put them in a sunny area. In a bright spot, add a tropical water lily; these have pink or blue flowers held 15cm(6in) out of the water, and bloom all summer and autumn.

Left: Water lettuce (Pistia stratiotes) is a floating pond plant often used outdoors in summer. It does not survive winter outside, but is happy in a bowl of water in a conservatory all year round.

Stephanotis floribunda

Aglaonema 'Silver Queen'

The flower heads are like the spokes in an umbrella, giving this plant the common name of umbrella plant.

Right: Cyperus albostriatus (sometimes seen as C. diffusus) is a graceful and compact plant for a conservatory pool or a large pot standing in water. It needs room temperature in winter.

Hibiscus rosa-sinensis

BROMELIADS

Bromeliads are a large family of plants related to pineapples. They include some groups popularly known as urn plants, airplants and Spanish moss. The basic bromeliad plant shape resembles a pineapple top, although some of the airplants look like bizarre shaving brushes or starfish. Their striking architectural shapes make them ideal for modern 'designer' interior schemes. Bromeliads generally have small, weak root systems used for little more than clinging to tree bark in the tropical rainforests where they live. The plants enjoy conditions similar to those needed by orchids – steady warmth, shade from direct sunlight and high humidity – but they are less demanding to grow. Bromeliads take in water mainly through their foliage. The urn plants have a vaselike depression in the middle of a rosette of thick waxy leaves, which acts as a permanent reservoir. In the wild, this may house tree frogs and other wildlife. To water them, top up the 'vase' during the summer and spray them occasionally to increase humidity. Keep the potting mix just moist. In winter, leave the vase empty but water the mix enough so that it never dries right out. Grow urn plants in pots or shake the roots free of soil and wire them to driftwood to make a bromeliad 'tree'. Alternatively, wire them to cork bark in the same way as orchids and hang them from trellis on a wall. Spray the plants over once or twice daily, especially when they are grown out of soil, as it is vital that the air around them does not dry out. Drape Spanish moss around bromeliad displays; it looks decorative, and the textured stems of this rootless bromeliad also absorb water like a sponge, so it acts like a living air conditioner.

Above: *Guzmania,* such as this cultivar 'Claret', are grown for their bright red bracts. Cultivate them in pots or grow them epiphytically, wired to branches or cork bark, and keep warm and humid.

A bromeliad display

Set a large piece of twiggy driftwood (from florists) in a large pot of plaster or cement. Buy a mixture of bromeliads suitable for growing without soil, such as guzmania, neoregelia, nidularium and tillandsia. Take them out of their pots and carefully remove most of the soil. Drape the roots over a branch, tuck a little moss or Spanish moss around them and bind in place with florist's wire. Mist spray daily. Add very weak liquid feed regularly during the summer and top up the urns frequently.

Left: In the case of all bromeliads with a central urn, keep the potting mix barely moist (as plants have little root), but keep the urn topped up with water. Add a few drops of liquid tomato feed in summer.

Right: *Aechmea fasciata* (the urn plant) is one of the most popular bromeliad species; the flowers last up to six months. Even when not in bloom, the silver-green marbled leaves look stunning.

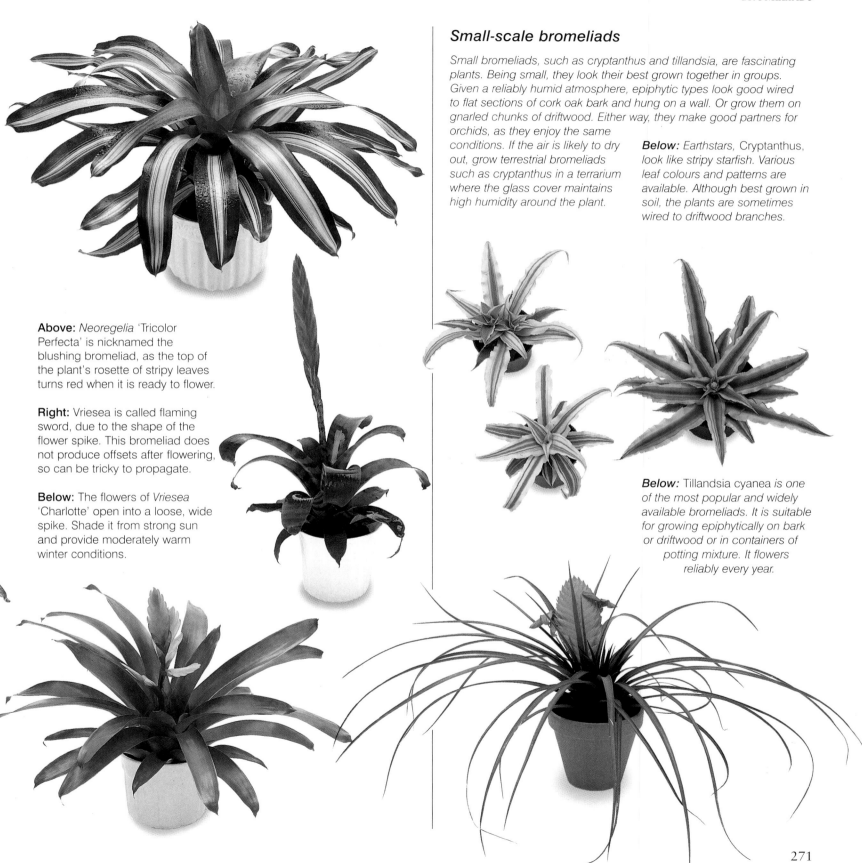

Small-scale bromeliads

Small bromeliads, such as cryptanthus and tillandsia, are fascinating plants. Being small, they look their best grown together in groups. Given a reliably humid atmosphere, epiphytic types look good wired to flat sections of cork oak bark and hung on a wall. Or grow them on gnarled chunks of driftwood. Either way, they make good partners for orchids, as they enjoy the same conditions. If the air is likely to dry out, grow terrestrial bromeliads such as cryptanthus in a terrarium where the glass cover maintains high humidity around the plant.

Above: *Neoregelia* 'Tricolor Perfecta' is nicknamed the blushing bromeliad, as the top of the plant's rosette of stripy leaves turns red when it is ready to flower.

Right: Vriesea is called flaming sword, due to the shape of the flower spike. This bromeliad does not produce offsets after flowering, so can be tricky to propagate.

Below: The flowers of *Vriesea* 'Charlotte' open into a loose, wide spike. Shade it from strong sun and provide moderately warm winter conditions.

Below: *Earthstars, Cryptanthus, look like stripy starfish. Various leaf colours and patterns are available. Although best grown in soil, the plants are sometimes wired to driftwood branches.*

Below: *Tillandsia cyanea is one of the most popular and widely available bromeliads. It is suitable for growing epiphytically on bark or driftwood or in containers of potting mixture. It flowers reliably every year.*

271

Tillandsia tricolor

Tillandsia usneoides
(Spanish moss)

Tillandsia butzii

Tillandsia stricta

Tillandsia bulbosa

Tillandsia argentea

Tillandsia juncea

AIRPLANTS

Tillandsias, or airplants, are part of the huge bromeliad family. Where they grow wild, in parts of South America, airplants use their tiny roots only for clinging onto tree bark or rocks. They take in water through tiny scales covering the rosette of leaves. (The plants have no stems either.) This odd way of life is possible because airplants live in the rainforest where the humidity is constantly very high. The fact that they do not have much root – and in fact can live perfectly well without any roots at all – gives them a great advantage as houseplants, as they do not need to be grown in pots or soil. They are perfectly happy lodged in driftwood, in shells, on chunks of mineral ore or ornaments, although they can also be wired to driftwood or cork bark or tied to nylon cord to make hanging mobiles. Both these and Spanish moss, a trailing species with no roots at all, need humid air around them; daily mist-spraying is vital. Occasional weak liquid feeds can be added to the water for all bromeliads, but only feed them lightly. Use Spanish moss or reindeer moss for decorating groups of bromeliads. Reindeer moss is a species of lichen sold in a dried state. When rehydrated, it produces pretty blue-green fronds. Given daily mist-spraying, the spongy texture of these mosses holds moisture that is slowly released into the air, thus maintaining high humidity, which benefits other plants grown around them.

1 Choose an attractively gnarled chunk of wood (cleaned tropical 'driftwood' is sold in florist's shops). Choose the biggest plant and wedge the base of it firmly in place in a natural crevice.

2 Sit airplants with a wide base like this into natural depressions in the log. They look more natural when placed at a slight angle rather than completely level.

3 Continue adding more plants; smaller or relatively leafless species often look better when grouped in twos or threes.

4 If necessary, glue the plant in place with a hot glue gun. Put a blob of glue on the wood and press the plant firmly into position.

5 If using special airplant glue, place a blob on both the base of the plant and the wood, press and hold together till set.

6 To soften the angular shape, drape over strands of Spanish moss, allowing it to fall between the plants and into hollows in the wood.

7 Tiny plants at the front create foreground detail, important in a display like this where plants are too stiff to spill out over the edges.

Growing airplants

Give airplants bright filtered light, high humidity and a temperature of 10-30°C(50-86°F). Sudden deaths are normally due to prolonged periods of dry air and neglect.

Right: *A collection of small airplants makes a good mobile. Choose a gnarled section of branch, clean it well and strip the bark if it looks better. Make a hook from a piece of wire, then glue, tie or wedge the plants in place.*

Airplant flowers

Left: *A flower may appear in the centre of a plant, and when it is over, offsets grow around the parent plant, which slowly shrivels and dies. Leave the 'pups' attached to the old plant to grow on for a while before detaching them. Alternatively, leave them as a clump for a spectacular display.*

Tillandsia magnusiana

Watering and feeding airplants

Right: *Mist-spray airplants once or twice daily. Brown leaf tips are a sign that the air is too dry. Feed airplants about once a month, using any very well-diluted liquid or soluble houseplant feed, or a proper airplant feed. Add this to the water used to mist spray.*

CITRUS FRUITS

Citrus are very rewarding conservatory plants, with glossy evergreen foliage and scented flowers. Depending on the amount of winter warmth, these can be out at the same time as fruit in all stages of ripeness. Although citrus plants can be raised from pips, the results are variable and may not fruit for many years or until they reach a large size. To be certain of regular heavy crops from relatively small plants, choose named varieties grafted onto special rootstocks. Some named citrus varieties are usually available in garden centres, while specialist nurseries carry a huge range.

In summer, citrus plants are best stood outside in the open air. They can be left in the conservatory provided ventilation is good enough to keep the temperature at about 24-27°C(75-80°F), but pests such as scale insect are more active under cover. During the summer, they need frequent watering and regular feeding. Bring them inside in autumn, when the nights start to get cool. The plants are frost tender, so some heating is needed. In a free-draining mix kept barely moist, all kinds can be maintained at 5°C(40°F) since they are just 'ticking over'. Hardier types, such as Meyer's lemon, mandarin orange and kumquat, are not a problem if kept frost free. Avoid widely fluctuating temperatures in both summer and winter, since this is a common cause of plants shedding leaves. They may also drop blossom and even immature fruit.

Below: The calamondin orange *(Citrus mitis)* produces many 2.5cm(1in)-diameter bitter oranges that remain on the plant for a long time even when fully ripe.

Citrus fruits from the conservatory

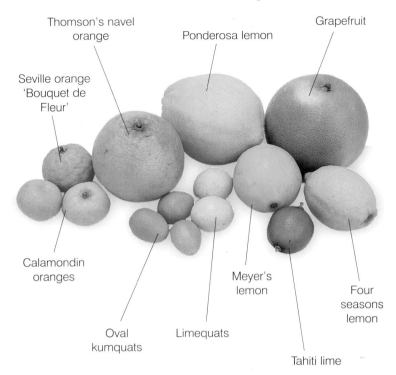

Thomson's navel orange

Ponderosa lemon

Grapefruit

Seville orange 'Bouquet de Fleur'

Calamondin oranges

Meyer's lemon

Four seasons lemon

Oval kumquats

Limequats

Tahiti lime

Left: Four seasons lemon *(Citrus limon* 'Four Seasons') is a popular variety for commercial crops. It is also known as 'Everbearing' for its prolific nature.

Above: The variegated calamondin orange is even more decorative. The flowers of both are strongly perfumed and often appear at the same time as the fruit.

Above: The pink flower buds of four seasons lemon are an attractive feature of the plant. They open into fragrant white flowers.

Left: Tahiti lime *(Citrus latifolia* 'Tahiti'). A compact variety with large sweet seedless fruit; it is the best variety for home growing.

Below: *Citrus aurantium* 'Bouquet de Fleur' is one of the group of bitter oranges with very aromatic fruit, grown to produce essential oil of Neroli, used in eau de cologne.

Above: *Citrus aurantium* 'Bouquet de Fleur' has very heavily scented double flowers. For this reason, the plant resembles gardenia, but is much easier to grow.

Below: A standard kumquat makes a decorative evergreen tree for a conservatory heated enough to keep frost at bay. The fruit can be candied or used for decoration.

Growing conditions

Temperature
Summer max: 30°C(86°F)
Winter min: 5°C(40°F) for most; some 10°C(50°F)

Humidity
Reasonable level in summer; low in winter.

Light/Shade
Good light; shade plants lightly from strong direct sun while inside; give full sun when stood outdoors.

Watering/Spraying
Water freely in summer but avoid waterlogging; water sparingly in winter to prevent potting mix becoming bone dry.

Feeding
High-nitrogen liquid feed at quarter strength weekly from mid-spring to late summer; none in winter.

Caring for citrus plants

Citrus are not difficult to grow. Use plastic rather than clay pots. If you want to achieve the Mediterranean combination of citrus and terracotta then use a plastic pot inside a terracotta one. Water plants thoroughly (tap water is fine) then wait until the potting mixture is starting to dry out before watering again. Give plants enough water so that it runs through the pot, then allow plants to drain before replacing them in their saucers. Do not leave them standing in water. Repot in spring, but only when the old pot is filled with roots; move to a pot one size bigger.

Below: *For growing citrus plants, use a potting mix made up of about 20% perlite and 80% free-draining soil-based mix, with slow-release fertiliser added (see the maker's advice for the correct rate).*

Perlite

Soil-based potting mix

Topdressing citrus plants in containers

1 Citrus plants grown in containers do not need to be repotted every year, as they grow best when the pot is just about full of roots. Instead, topdress in spring; first, scrape away the top surface of the mix to a depth of about 2.5cm(1in).

2 If the exposed potting mix looks compacted, loosen up the next layer with the points of a dinner fork, taking care not to break any roots. Then replace with fresh potting mix to just below the rim of the pot. This will keep the plant growing well.

GROWING ORCHIDS IN THE CONSERVATORY

The conservatory or sun lounge is an area designed for relaxation and there are several good reasons for growing orchids here. To begin with, the central heating system can be taken directly from the house and run at very little extra cost. Secondly, the more time you spend among the orchids the better you can care for them, quickly spotting any problems and dealing with them as they arise. And finally, because this is a place to relax in, you will ensure that your conservatory is comfortable – neither too hot nor too cold – and these conditions will also suit the orchids. Place staging around the sides of the conservatory and install a system that will hold moisture under the plants. If you have a tiled floor, any water sprayed or spilled can be left to dry naturally without causing damage. Use the central area for table and chairs, and a tall plant if there is space. Control temperatures by shading and ventilating, and install tailor-made blinds that can be lowered to keep out the direct sun and to keep in warmth on winter nights. You can grow a wide range of orchids in a conservatory, but it may not be easy to create different temperature zones, so choose either all cool varieties or intermediate and warm ones. If you have plenty of headroom, try a few large specimen plants, such as cymbidiums or *Epidendrum ibaguense.*

Above: *Laeliocattleya* Barbara Belle 'Apricot' is a good example of the most popular type of cattleya. The large blooms are among the most flamboyant of orchids.

Above: One of the many lovely hybrids of miltoniopsis, the popular pansy orchids. These colourful hybrids are ideal for beginners.

Above: The most popular and free-flowering of all the vandas is *Vanda* Rothschildiana, one of the finest examples of a blue orchid.

Right: An unusual feature of the paphiopedilums is a lip modified into a pouch, which has given rise to the name 'lady's slipper'.

Left: Although their colours are limited, there is abundant variety in phalaenopsis. This is a spotted variety, *Phalaenopsis* Babette.

Below: Cymbidiums are the most widely grown orchids and available in a wonderful range of hybrids. This hybrid of *C. devonianum* is Sea Jade 'Freshwater' AM/RHS.

Above: The decorative hybrids of *Dendrobium nobile* bloom along the length of their canes. Colours range from white and yellow, through shades of pink and red.

Below: This selection of modern hybrids shows a *Vuylstekeara* (left), deep pink *Odontioda* Marie Noel, pale pink *Odontioda* Aloette x Flocalo and the superb yellow *Odontioda* La Hougie Bie.

Buying orchids

Before buying orchids, it pays to visit a specialist orchid nursery to discover the range of plants available and seek expert advice. Orchid society meetings can be the source of a good bargain. Orchids are available either as young plants needing several years to bloom, as first-time flowering plants or as large, mature specimens in full bloom. Look for healthy plants that are not in need of immediate repotting and check that the foliage is clean and free from virus. If the plant is in flower, check the blooms are fresh, so that they last for many weeks.

Above: *A conservatory furnished with phalaenopsis, cattleyas, miltoniopsis and dendrobiums. The roof is shaded outside with green emulsion paint and blinds can be lowered to protect plants against direct sun.*

Right: *Provide staging that can accommodate the orchids, with a moisture tray underneath. This purpose-built slatted staging allows the moisture from a water-soaked gravel bed to rise around the plants, creating the humidity that is vital for good results.*

Dropping on

1 Ease the orchid from the pot by squeezing it until the plant becomes loose and lifts out. Otherwise, cut the pot carefully away. Notice the healthy roots here.

2 Select a clean pot 5cm(2in) larger in diameter than the original one. For good drainage, add just sufficient crocking material to cover the base of the pot.

3 Position the plant carefully in the new pot. Leave room at the front for it to grow forward by placing the oldest pseudobulbs against one side of the pot.

4 Firm the mix by pressing it with your fingers around the rim of the pot. Dampen the bark chippings before adding to the pot.

5 If the potting has been firm, you should be able to lift the plant as shown here without the pot falling off. If this test fails, firm the potting mix again using more pressure. Label the plant clearly for future reference.

POTTING ORCHIDS

The majority of orchids in cultivation are epiphytes that need an open, well-drained potting mix. The most popular growing medium is non-resinous tree bark. Bark chippings come in different grades for large and small plants, are easy to handle and almost impossible to overwater. Osmunda fibre is very useful for growing orchids on cork bark. Repot adult orchids every other year, ideally during the spring when the new growths are up to about 10cm(4in) long and before they have started to make their new roots. Repot plants while they are on the dry side. After repotting, do not water them for a few days to allow trimmed or broken roots time to heal, but you can spray the foliage and potting mix to prevent moisture loss. Dropping on is the easiest method of repotting an orchid. It simply involves taking a plant from its outgrown pot and placing it in a larger one without disturbing the rootball. Dropping on is ideal for young plants, and also for larger ones that are not ready for division. Be sure to use a potting mix that matches the one in which the plant is already growing.

Orchids root quickly into bark mix. It decomposes slowly, releasing most of the nutrients required. A little extra artificial feed helps to keep plants healthy.

A young plant potted in fine bark can be 'dropped on' every six months for successive years while the bark remains in good condition. Chunks of bark provide space for air around the roots.

Loosely packed rockwool and polystyrene granules provide an inorganic mix that encourages quick root growth, but you must supply all the nutrients. Wear a face mask to filter out dry fibres in the air.

A mix made up of Finnish peat. Added foam rubber pieces and polystyrene provide more space and aid swift drainage when watering.

Repotting

1 This vigorous system contains living and dead roots. There are several pseudobulbs, but the plant is too small to divide; there are no surplus back bulbs to remove.

2 Remove the crocks and old potting mix. Tease out the roots and shake the plant to release the mix. You may need to cut some roots to separate them.

3 The dead roots at the back are dry and hollow. Cut them away. Trim live roots to about 15cm (6in). If left long, they will snap and cause rotting.

Place a handful or two of mix on top of the crocking to bring the plant to the correct level in the pot. Fill in with mix while holding the plant steady.

4 Use a new pot 5cm(2in) larger than the old one. Position the plant with room in front for new growth. Fold the roots underneath until the plant rests just below the rim.

Growing orchids on cork bark

Epiphytic species often grow better on cork and it is easier to contain orchids with a climbing habit. You can save valuable bench room by hanging them at either end of your greenhouse or conservatory.

1 Insert wire through the bark and make a hook. Place dampened osmunda fibre or sphagnum moss on the cork.

2 Position the back bulbs at the bottom end, leaving plenty of room at the top for future pseudobulbs to grow.

3 Use two or three lengths of wire to hold the plant with its fibre pad in place. Do not let the wire press into the pseudobulbs.

4 Spray the plant and the fibre straightaway. Keep both moist to encourage new roots, which will appear very soon.

Orchids in a hanging basket

Left: *Line a basket with netting to retain the planting mix. Position the plant diagonally across the basket to give it maximum room, tucking the roots underneath. Orchids that like plenty of light do well hanging in the roof of the conservatory.*

Buried aerial roots may not survive. New roots from young growths will soon appear. One or two older leaves will drop off, but will soon be replaced.

279

CARING FOR ORCHIDS

Orchids need watering and spraying throughout their growing period. Some grow all year round, while others rest in winter. Plants often bloom while resting. Resting orchids require just enough water to keep the pseudobulbs from shrivelling. A plant is resting between the formation of its last pseudobulb and the appearance of the next new growth, which may take a few weeks or several months. Orchids with short resting periods should be watered all year; do not let them dry out. Spraying is another way of providing moisture, but does not take the place of watering. Daily spraying during spring and summer helps to cool the foliage during hot weather, deters pests and maintains humidity around the plants. Water and spray in the early part of the day when the temperature is rising. The leaves should be dry by the time the temperature starts to drop towards nightfall. Avoid spraying buds and flowers. Orchids will benefit from a light feed during their growing season. Those that grow all year round need less feed in winter and more in summer. Apply the feed directly to the roots or spray it over the foliage. Use a specially formulated orchid feed according to the instructions. Feed the orchids at every second or third watering. The clear water will wash out any residue and prevents potentially harmful overfeeding.

Feeding orchids

Above: For orchids growing in bark, light feeding will supplement natural nutrients. In rockwool, an inert growing medium, regular feeding is important.

Watering and spraying

Above: Indoors, use a spray bottle to mist the plant with water or a feed. When spraying foliage, avoid getting water onto the flowers; it can cause damp spots to appear.

Above: If a plant has become too dry, place it in a bowl of water to soak for up to one hour. You may need to hold it down at first. Do not let water get into new growths.

Left: Use a spouted watering can to flood the surface of the planting mixture, giving the plant plenty of water at one application. Most of it will run directly through the potting mix.

Above: In tropical rainforests, many orchids grow on trees and are drenched with rain each day. In a conservatory, you can use a spray lance to imitate this effect.

Caring for leaves

Left: Remove yellow leaves when they are 'ripe' enough to pick easily. This is safer than cutting, which can spread virus disease.

Below: Use leaf wipes or clean water to sponge foliage that has become dulled with hard water or residue from insecticides.

Cleaning up bulbs

1 Remove the dried and sharp spiny bracts by splitting one at a time down each side of the pseudobulb and pulling away.

2 Once the bracts are stripped away, the back bulbs not only look better but will also receive more light to speed up ripening.

Repairing cymbidium leaves

Right: If cymbidium leaves are damaged, you can repair them by twisting green string between each leaf and tying occasional knots. In time, the string can be removed and the leaves will be able to support themselves.

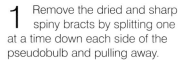

Staking methods

Staking keeps flower spikes upright or semi-arching and prevents heavily budded spikes from snapping under their own weight.

Staking an odontoglossum

2 *Successful staking starts when the flower spike is young. Some orchids need minimum support; others need training for as long as they continue to develop.*

1 *Twist string loosely between the cane and spike so that the growing spike can continue to develop. Move the string higher as necessary.*

Staking a paphiopedilum

1 *Take a length of green string and loop it behind the flower at the very top of the stem. Twist the string and pull it gently towards the cane until it is tight enough.*

2 *When the bloom has been open for a few days and has set, put the last tie in place behind the flower. If you tie it back too soon, the bloom will droop forward.*

Staking a cattleya

Above: *Hold open the split end of a cane lodged in the planting mix. Lift the bloom and lower the stem into the top of the cane.*

Left: *Once the bloom is held by the cane, you can lift or lower it. By twisting the cane you can turn the bloom to the left or right.*

Whitefly

Right: Whitefly resemble tiny white moths that congregate on the backs of young leaves and only fly if the plants are disturbed. The young whitefly are 'scales' stuck tight under leaves, which rarely respond to chemical sprays, so biological control is the best way of dealing with them.

Left: The biological control against whitefly is a tiny parasitic wasp, *Encarsia formosa*, which lays its eggs inside whitefly scales. Wasp larvae feed on the developing whitefly and the scales turn black. *Encarsia* is supplied as cards of whitefly scales containing wasp eggs. Hang these on the plants.

A HEALTHY CONSERVATORY

Being warm and sheltered and the source of a good food supply, the conservatory environment is one in which pests can flourish and be very difficult to eliminate. Chemical sprays are particularly undesirable as they percolate into adjacent living rooms, so use alternative strategies. Firstly, prevent unhealthy plants spreading pests and diseases by checking them over thoroughly before you buy them. Reject any with visible pests or diseases and if you are unsure of likely symptoms (such as grey mould) also reject any with brown leaves, spots or physical damage. Even if they are not actually diseased, such plants are unlikely to have been well cared for in the past. Put all new plants into quarantine for two or three weeks before placing them in the conservatory. Keep them by a window in the house or somewhere else quite separate from the conservatory to see if any pests appear or disease symptoms develop. Alternatively, treat them straightaway with a spray of pesticide and/or fungicide. Once in the conservatory, make sure that the plants are not overcrowded, which makes it easy for pests and diseases to spread and also prevents good air circulation, which is essential for good health. Check plants regularly – easiest done while you are watering them – and wipe off insect pests or pick off diseased leaves by hand immediately.

Right: Many conservatory plants dislike draughts, but in very hot weather, ventilators and blinds may not be enough to keep the temperature below 30°C (86°F). In this case, it is useful to use a fan to keep the plants cooler so that they do not suffer. This is a small fan with a clip that you can reposition easily.

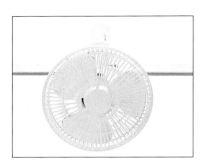

Scale insects

Above: Scale insects are like tiny limpets that cling to leaves of many kinds of conservatory plants. Their hard covering makes them difficult to control.

Left: The best way to control scale insects is by using systemic insecticides, but the insects remain attached to the plant even after they are dead. Remove them individually with cotton buds as shown here.

Left: Products such as pesticides are sold ready-mixed in 'trigger' operated containers that form their own spray gun. These are ideal as no mixing is needed and you do not need to buy a sprayer. These products remain effective over a period of months when stored as directed by the manufacturers.

Right: Dilute the fungicide with water as directed, using the bottle cap as a measure. Avoid getting the solution onto your hands and do not mix products. Spray plants thoroughly until droplets run off the leaves. Mix fresh spray each time; do not store diluted chemicals.

Red spider mite

Right: Using a lens you can see the small red spider mites on the underside of a leaf. They pierce the leaves and suck out the cell contents, causing discoloration.

Mealy bug

Right: Mealy bugs – small, grey, crawling insects covered with a white mealy powder and waxy threads – weaken plants by sucking sap. Treat plants with systemic insecticide and remove dead insects after a few days with a cotton bud.

Powdery mildew

Left: One of the most widely seen diseases under glass in late summer and autumn is powdery mildew, a mould that can affect pot plants. Use a systemic fungicide.

Left: The biological control for red spider mite is an even tinier predatory mite called *Phytoseiulus persimilis* that eats them. Open and hang the pots on the affected plants so emerging mites are close to their 'food'.

Aphids (greenfly)

Aphids can be green, cream, brown, pink, grey or black. They feed by puncturing plant tissues to suck the sap, and in doing so often spread plant viruses.

Right: Large numbers of aphids will attack buds, flowers and young growths, turning them yellow and, in severe cases, causing die back and deformation.

Left: *Blackfly are less of a problem in conservatories than greenfly, however they are attracted to certain types of plants and can breed rapidly. Remove them by hand or use suitable insecticides.*

Right: The biological control for aphids is Aphidoletes, a gall midge that lays its eggs near aphids and the small orange larvae that emerge feed on them. Midge pupae are delivered in small tubs; empty the contents in a pile on damp paper covered by pots close to affected plants. The affected aphids turn into brown 'shells', as shown below.

A bubbling water feature provides the focal point in a courtyard garden.

PART ELEVEN

CONTAINER WATER FEATURES

Potted water features are the latest development in container gardening. Choose from potted pools and lily ponds, dwarf bog gardens or mini-fountain features – all in containers. Better still, group them together or use them all round the garden to reap all the benefits of regular ponds, but without the problems.

1 For a potted bubble fountain, you will need a large plastic pot, a plastic hanging basket that fits inside it upside down, a small submersible pump and smooth pebbles.

BUBBLE FOUNTAINS

Fountain features make striking and unusual ingredients for a container garden. Team a bubble fountain, like either of the ones shown here, with two or four 'potted ponds' of different sizes to make a complete patio water garden. (As in all container displays, they will look best if an uneven number of elements are grouped together.) It is the ideal way to add moving water to a display of potted 'water lily ponds', since these plants cannot be grown under fountains – they do not thrive if the tops of their leaves keep getting wet. And in a garden used by small children, a feature filled with pebbles where there is no standing water – however shallow – is a safer option.

Be sure to set up a potted fountain carefully. The container must hold enough water so that the submersible pump is constantly covered with water. Adjust the jet so that the water trickles back into the pot and is continuously recycled – if too high, much of the water will go over the sides of the container, which will soon empty itself until the pump runs dry and is damaged. The reservoir of water will, in any case, need topping up at least once a week, since natural evaporation will gradually lower the water level. Make sure that the stones and pot, plus other ingredients, are all perfectly clean when you set the feature up – any dirt and grit will soon clog the pump. And remember that electricity and water make a dangerous combination, so consult a qualified electrician if you need practical guidance.

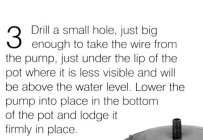

2 Make a hole in the base of the plant basket so that the nozzle of the fountain fits tightly when pushed through it. Push the nozzle through until both the base of the basket and pump are flush.

Thread the wire through the hole and reconnect it to the plug at the other end.

3 Drill a small hole, just big enough to take the wire from the pump, just under the lip of the pot where it is less visible and will be above the water level. Lower the pump into place in the bottom of the pot and lodge it firmly in place.

4 Put a ring of the largest pebbles around the edge of the plastic hanging basket to keep it in place. The basket is now acting as a cover for the pump.

5 Part-fill the pot with water until you can just see the level. The aim is to provide sufficient water in the base to feed the pump as it returns through the stones.

6 Continue filling the container with smooth pebbles. You can buy pebbles or cobbles in various sizes from a garden or aquarist centre. Leave the pump nozzle exposed.

7 Fit the fountain head over the nozzle. Various types are available that will give a bell fountain effect, as here, or a spray pattern. Use more pebbles to hide the base of the tube.

The bell fountain is a good spray pattern for outdoors, as the wall of water stands up to a breeze. A fountain that makes a fine spray has tiny droplets that blow away, creating a one-sided effect.

8 Switch on the pump and adjust the height of the fountain head as necessary, moving it up or down slightly, so that the bubble stays within the container and does not splash water over the edge.

A small pebble water feature

1 Use a tiny pump that will work in a small quantity of water. Attach clear plastic tubing to the nozzle and sit the pump in the pot.

2 Drill a hole under the pot rim, thread the wire through and reconnect the plug. This will leave the rim of the container clear.

 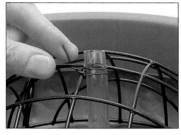

3 Remove the chains from a wire hanging basket and fit it firmly inside the pot. It should cover the pump and not slip.

4 Wire the tip of the nozzle to the frame to hold it securely. The nozzle alone will produce a clean fountain-shaped water jet.

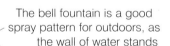  

5 Part-fill the container with water, making quite sure that the pump is completely covered, with 5cm(2in) to spare.

6 Hide the pump and basket pump cover under a layer of smooth clean pebbles; choose a size in proportion to the pot.

7 When the pump is switched on, a simple fountain effect trickles water over the pebbles. Adjust the pump valve as needed to make the fountain jet a suitable height.

1 Line the tub with butyl pond liner. Drape the material loosely inside and arrange the slack in folds. Put 2.5-5cm (1-2in) of well-washed gravel into the bottom of the tub to bed the marginal plants into later.

MARGINALS IN A BARREL

Marginal pond plants make fascinating container subjects. Any container that holds water is suitable, but a wide half barrel is best as it has a large water surface that makes the most of the plants' reflections – one of their best assets. Marginal plants are the sort that can be grown in 0-30cm (0-12in) of water (measured over the top of the pot). This includes all the popular water irises, marsh marigolds and rushes, as well as many of the plants commonly grown as bog garden plants, such as zantedeschia. Avoid plants that merely grow in damp soil; although they are sometimes sold mistakenly as marginal plants, subjects such as hosta and astilbe do not enjoy standing in water above their necks and do not last long under these conditions. Marginal plants are often imposing specimens that grow quickly; to keep them at a suitable size for a half barrel, lift them out and divide them every spring, just as they are starting into growth. Once planted up, keep the barrel topped up with water. Remember that in hot weather it can lose 2.5cm(1in) of water each week due to evaporation.

2 Half-fill with water to weight the liner down into the bottom of the container. Rearrange the folds so that surplus material is evenly distributed around the edge.

3 Trim away the excess liner, leaving enough spare to allow for turning over the edge. Make small tucks to even out large folds in the material around the rim.

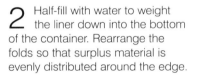

4 Turn the liner edges under, smoothing out tucks in the material to flatten them down as you work. Use waterproof tape, ideally black, to secure the liner firmly inside the rim of the container.

5 Begin adding plants; choose a mixture of striking flowering and foliage marginal plants that contrast well in shape. Leave them in the net-sided pond pots that they are growing in when you buy them.

6 Upright, reedlike shapes are typical of many waterside plants. These are *Butomus umbellatus (*flowering rush) and *Typha minima* (miniature bulrush).

7 Pickerel weed has striking heart-shaped leaves and blue flowers from early midsummer to early autumn. It works well with the tall linear leaves of the other plants.

8 Three plants are enough, as they will make quite a bit of new growth over the summer. Top up with water to the rim of the container and check that the tape holds the edge of the liner firmly.

9 Finally, float a handful of azolla over the surface. In full sun, this lacy-leaved plant turns bright red. Alternatively, use other floating plants, such as water lettuce or water hyacinth.

Repotting marginal plants

Marginals, bog garden and water plants are sometimes sold in pots that are far too small. Often they are a good buy as they are priced according to the size of the pot, not the size of the plant. Simply move them to a bigger pot when you get them home. When your own plants outgrow their containers after a year or two, repot them in spring.

1 If a plant is too potbound to knock out of its pot in the usual manner, cut away the pot, taking great care not to cut through the roots. Peel away the remains of the pot and discard it.

Butomus umbellatus
(flowering rush)

Typha minima
(miniature bulrush)

Pontaderia cordata
(pickerel weed)

Azolla (fairy moss)

10 Choose a sunny site for the barrel, perhaps standing on paving slabs in a low border or herb garden. Best of all, group it with other containers planted with a watery theme in a patio or courtyard.

2 Put 2.5cm(1in) of pond plant mix or garden soil with no added fertiliser into the bottom of a special net-sided pond pot. Sit the plant in the centre of the pot.

3 Pot it firmly, using more of the same mix to fill round the roots. If you find the mix trickles out through the holes in the pot, line the pot with hessian.

4 Tap the pot to consolidate the potting mix and then cover the surface with 2.5cm(1in) of well-washed gravel. This weights down the soil, preventing it from floating away when the pot is put into the water.

1 Use a waterproof wooden barrel, or line it first with thick black plastic or butyl rubber pond liner. Half-fill it with water and add a tall, strikingly shaped, leafy plant.

2 Choose a second plant that complements the first; foliage types look good all season. Slowly submerge the planting baskets until they sit on the bottom.

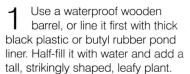

3 As there are going to be fish in the pond, add a spray of Canadian pondweed, *Elodea canadensis,* to oxygenate the water. Being evergreen, it keeps working in winter, too. Anchor the clump down with a clean pebble.

4 Top up the pond to just below the rim of the barrel. Now there is only the water lily to plant; if the barrel is overfilled at the start, water will spill over the edge each time a new plant is added.

CREATING A MINIATURE WATER LILY POND

If you do not have room for a conventional pond, then a potted pond could be just the answer. They make great patio features. Put the container in position first, as it will be difficult to move once filled. Normal tap water is fine, but if possible fill the tub and allow it to stand for 48 hours before introducing plants. This allows much of the chlorine to disperse. When choosing plants, opt for those with a long season of interest. A single miniature water lily could be used alone; it will quickly fill an 45cm(18in) diameter barrel with foliage, and flowers all summer. Or add up to two other plants, as we have done here. Choose good foliage plants to contrast with the lily; go for bold architectural shapes that will look good all summer. Or why not make a group of potted ponds? Use matching containers in various sizes, each with a different planting theme. You might have a water lily pond, a marginal plant pond of water irises, zebra rush and miniature bulrush, a potted bog garden, a 'pond' of fountain and pebbles, and a floating garden of water hyacinth, azolla and water lettuce. If you want fish, choose the largest container possible and only a few small fish, or there will not be enough oxygen in the water for them.

5 Lower the water lily slowly, protecting the leaves and flowers, which become weak and floppy out of water. They easily tear if snagged on the edge of the barrel. Stand the pot on the bottom of the barrel.

6 Four small fish are plenty for a barrel this size. Float their bag on the surface for 30 minutes so that their water reaches the same temperature as that in the tub.

7 Open the neck of the bag underwater, allowing the fish to swim out in their own time. Do not tip them out as this might injure or frighten them.

Caring for fish in a barrel

Always add a small bunch of oxygenating water weed, and plant lilies or other floating plants to give fish shade and shelter. If possible, delay introducing fish for several weeks to give the plants time to settle down first. Feed the fish daily from late spring to early autumn; although they will probably find plenty of 'wild' food – mosquito larvae and daphnia – in their 'pond', feeding makes them tame. Do not feed fish in winter. Prevent the water from freezing by installing a small pond heater or move the pond under cover. Avoid adding water snails as they breed profusely and eat the plants, especially water lilies. Ramshorns snails, which have coil-shaped shells, are much less destructive.

Water lilies in potted ponds

'Potted ponds' are relatively small, with water less than 30cm(12in) deep, so choose only the most miniature water lily varieties, otherwise the plants will look out of scale and soon spill out over the sides. Water lilies need sun, or the flowers will not open and the plants do not thrive.

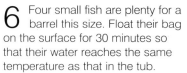

Scirpus zebrinus (zebra rush)

Cyperus involucratus (umbrella plant)

Nymphaea 'Marliacea Chromatella' (water lily)

8 After a few hours, the lily leaves shrug off water and emerge floating on the pond surface. Water lily flowers only open fully in direct sun, so make sure the pond is correctly sited from the very start.

Below: N. 'Laydekeri Purpurata' is another very good water lily for a small patio tub. The small, marble-patterned leaves set off deep pink flowers all summer.

Above: N. pygmaea 'Helvola' is a very free-flowering variety with tiny, pale yellow flowers and red-marbled olive-green leaves. Good for shallow ponds as well as tubs.

Below: The pale golden flowers of Nymphaea 'Marliacea Chromatella' become a deeper yellow in strong sun. Speckled leaves are an added bonus.

291

1 Choose a large half barrel and line it with a butyl pond liner to prevent leaking and to protect the wood from rotting. Cut the butyl liner loosely to shape, leaving some slack for sinkage when soil is added.

A BOG GARDEN IN A TUB

Bog garden plants make ideal subjects for containers. This is a good way of growing them if you garden on dry soil, where they would not be happy in the open ground. It is perfect for a small garden, since many bog garden plants are large and invasive, spreading rapidly given a free root-run, so that they soon become a nuisance. Use a watertight container; if yours has drainage holes in the bottom or leaks, simply line it with butyl rubber pond liner or heavy duty black plastic before filling and planting. Since the soil will be kept permanently damp, this type of container suits all sorts of bog garden plants, including houttuynia and *Lobelia cardinalis*, as well as border plants that enjoy moist to boggy conditions, such as hostas, lythrum and astilbe. Since space is limited, restrict yourself to plants with a long summer flowering season and those with good architectural foliage. Those that have both, such as zantedeschia, are doubly valuable. Bog garden plants are often sold growing in special net-sided pond pots. They are best left in their pots; the roots are intended to grow out through the sides so that you can lift them out later if they grow too big and you want to replace them. Otherwise, the whole container becomes over-run with roots, and you have to empty the whole tub and replant it all at once.

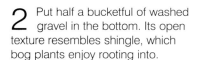

2 Put half a bucketful of washed gravel in the bottom. Its open texture resembles shingle, which bog plants enjoy rooting into.

3 Fill the container to just below the rim with pond planting mixture or garden soil with a high clay content but no added fertiliser.

6 Choose plants that contrast well with each other. Use drooping or trailing plants round the sides and shorter plants towards the front to make the best possible display in a small space.

4 Place a tall plant at the back. This *Lobelia cardinalis* 'Queen Victoria' has purple foliage and tall spikes of red flowers in mid- to late summer. It looks striking even when not in flower.

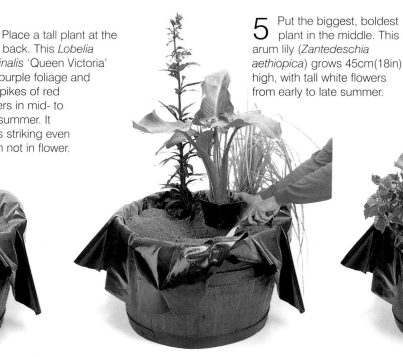

5 Put the biggest, boldest plant in the middle. This arum lily (*Zantedeschia aethiopica*) grows 45cm(18in) high, with tall white flowers from early to late summer.

7 A trailing plant will cascade down at the front. This is *Lysimachia nummularia* 'Aurea', a gold-leaved form of creeping Jenny, that also has yellow summer flowers.

8 Top up the soil level to within 2.5cm(1in) of the rim. Add at least a full watering can of water, leaving the soil boggy.

9 Water again after 30 minutes if the soil is no longer boggy. Roughly level it; add 2.5cm(1in) of washed gravel over the surface.

10 Add a few smooth round pebbles. When watering in future, trickle water over the pebbles to avoid soil splashing up.

11 Neatly trim the excess butyl liner with sharp scissors. Roll the edges over and tuck out of sight below the gravel.

Maintaining a bog garden

Every two years, when the plants outgrow their space, you will need to empty out the barrel and replant it. Do this in early spring. Otherwise, just top up the tub regularly with water. Avoid using fertiliser, since bog plants grow naturally in impoverished conditions and overfeeding will make them grow lanky and out of character. Cut back dead flower spikes regularly to encourage new shoots. Protect the container from freezing solid in winter by lagging it with several layers of bubble plastic tied round with string. In cold climates, move the container into a frost-free greenhouse or shed. The plants will be dormant then so light is not essential.

12 These plants will look good all summer. They die down in winter but come up the following year. They will thrive in a sunny spot on a patio, by a pond, fountain or potted pond.

Lobelia cardinalis 'Queen Victoria'

Zantedeschia aethiopica

Milium effusum 'Aureum' (Bowles' golden grass)

Houttuynia cordata 'Variegata'

Caltha palustris alba

Lysimachia nummularia 'Aurea'

Lobelia syphylitica

Planting an astilbe in a metal bucket

A tall, narrow, metal flower bucket suits a tall, graceful plant such as astilbe. The plant can be left in its pot or removed – it will only be left in place for one summer as it will soon grow too big.

1 Fill the base of the container with gravel to act as 'ballast' to keep it upright, and to provide some drainage.

2 Position the plant on top of the gravel bed, so that it rests 2.5cm(1in) below the rim of the container.

WATER PLANTS IN BUCKETS

Since shiny metal buckets hold water, have reflective surfaces that suggest water and are normally used for water, what could be more natural than to plant them with waterside plants? A group of matching containers in different shapes and sizes, planted with marginal and bog garden plants, makes a brilliant display that looks good in an informal cottage-style garden, outside a back door, or by an outbuilding. Choose a good background; stand the display on a base of gravel, cobbles or pebbles; it looks good in front of a pond, a large glass door or a white-painted wall where sunlight will be reflected between the various surfaces to create a sparkling effect. Suitable plants include those that grow naturally in shallow water or boggy ground that never dries out. To make a good display, plant some containers with a single large specimen foliage plant and others with a group of smaller flowering plants, then team them together. All water plants associate well together, but for a more 'designed' look, allow one colour, say yellow, to run through the scheme in each container. It only takes a small amount in each to 'link' the display together visually, since they are already in matching containers. Ideal plants would be compact or slow-growing subjects with a long flowering season. In practice, however, few water plants fall into this category. It is best to choose plants with a long flowering season, and either plant them out in a damp part of the garden after one season in containers, or else to divide and replant them the following spring.

Planting up a metal trough

1 Part-fill the trough with good-quality potting mix. There is no need to add gravel for drainage, as the trough is too shallow and only waterloving plants will be used.

2 Choose a mixture of tall, upright plants with contrasting shapes, textures and colours, but of roughly similar height. Knock them out of their pots and plant them in a row.

3 Plant several of the same kind of low, spreading plant along the front and at each end of the container. Here we have used a purple-leaved form of ajuga.

294

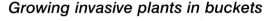

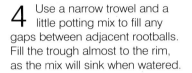

4 Use a narrow trowel and a little potting mix to fill any gaps between adjacent rootballs. Fill the trough almost to the rim, as the mix will sink when watered.

5 Trickle water around each plant to settle the mix around the roots. Add more water, leaving the mix wet but not sloppy. Keep it wet; bog plants dislike drying out.

Growing invasive plants in buckets

Some waterside plants spread quickly when grown in the open ground, and can become difficult to control. Growing them in containers keeps them within bounds, yet is an easy way to give them the conditions they enjoy. When the plants get too big, tip them out and divide them in spring. Repot a healthy piece back into fresh mix in the same container.

1 *Place a layer of clean gravel in the bottom of a watertight bucket to give it a firm base and to support the finished display.*

2 *If the plant is large, stand it in its pot in the bucket. If it is small, fill the bucket with potting mix and plant as normal.*

Below: Arrange the three finished containers close together to create a 'themed' display. A background of pebbles, gravel, water or a reflective surface such as glass would suit them ideally.

Astilbe arendsii hybrid

Houttuynia cordata 'Chameleon'

Phalaris arundinacea 'Picta'

Mimulus luteus

Lobelia cardinalis

Ajuga reptans 'Braunherz'

Glyceria maxima 'Variegata'

SUITABLE PLANTS

Cyperus (umbrella plant), *Caltha palustris* (marsh marigold), *Filipendula ulmaria* 'Aurea' (golden dropwort), *hosta*, *Iris laevigata* (Japanese water iris), *Iris versicolor*, *Lysimachia nummularia* (creeping Jenny), *Lysimachia punctata* (loosestrife), *Juncus effusus* 'Spiralis' (corkscrew rush), *Mentha aquatica* (water mint), *Mimulus* (monkey musk), *Scirpus zebrinus* (zebra rush), *Typha minima* (miniature bulrush), *Zantedeschia aethiopica* (arum lily)

1 Line the barrel. Trim off some of the excess but leave plenty around the edges to allow for it to settle as you add water and bricks.

2 Stand the pump on a hard brick for stability and to raise it up to the right level. Add more bricks to support pots and stones.

A WATER GARDEN IN A WOODEN BARREL

A miniature pool in a barrel, pot or other suitable container can have all the features of a large pond: water lilies, marginal plants, fish and even a tiny, sparkling fountain. Any waterproof container is suitable, from a large cut-down barrel to a small terracotta or plastic patio pot. The only real proviso is that the container has not been treated with any poisonous or fungicidal chemicals that might damage plants and fish. Make sure that it is painted inside with a sealant and line it with butyl rubber or plastic pond liner to ensure that it is watertight. Remember that once filled with water, a few plants and an ornament or fountain, the feature is going to be extremely heavy, so decide on its final position while it is empty and plant it up in situ. If you are going to have to move it, place the container on a low platform with lockable casters for mobility. A water feature in a tub makes an excellent focal point for a dull corner of the garden or patio, where it might be raised up on such a platform or a few bricks for extra prominence. Alternatively, stand it on a bed of pebbles or gravel, or surround it with large stones and pots of lush plants to reinforce the watery effect. To show off the tub at its best, position it against a suitable backdrop, such as a wall, fence or plain greenery. Large pebbles or a wall behind are also useful for installing concealed spouts for moving water effects to enhance the feature.

3 Add some cobbles to fill in the spaces between the bricks. These will help to stabilise the piles of bricks and will also stop the pump moving around once the feature is operating.

4 Add a top layer of bricks to support the large stones and plant pots of the final display. Build the bricks up in stable patterns to avoid problems later on.

5 Now add the large stones that will form the visible part of the feature. Rounded boulders not only look attractive but will also stand continuous immersion in water.

6 Add water until it reaches the base of the boulders. This will leave enough expansion room to add the plants and final stones. Do not dislodge the pump.

7 If you want to neaten things up a bit, you can now trim off more of the pond liner. The weight of the water will have pushed the liner into its final position.

8 Add the plants, potted into plastic mesh pond baskets. Plan the planting in advance. Adding this low-growing water forget-me-not *(Myosotis palustris)* towards the front will work well with the tall water buttercup at the back of the barrel.

Routine care

Like any other type of water garden, this one is not entirely maintenance-free. Over the course of a year in the open, algae will grow on the stones, plants will outgrow their space and the fountain and pumps will get dirty and slimy. Since the feature cannot be left in place over winter due to the risk of freezing, take the opportunity to dismantle it in late autumn. Clean the stones, fountain fittings and pump housing (do not dismantle the pump, but do clean or replace the filter). Scrub out the inside of the barrel and, if necessary, treat the outside with wood preservative. Plant the water plants out into the garden or put them in net pots and place them in a normal pond. You can divide them in spring and replant some pieces back into the new barrel water garden then. Store all the 'hardware' under cover where it will remain dry, ready to be used again the following year.

9 With the planting complete, you can fill in any spaces with more stones. Another boulder here creates an even better display.

Lysimachia thyrsiflora

Ranunculus flammula (water buttercup)

Iris versicolor 'Blue Light'

Myosotis palustris

10 Add cobbles and some pebbles to match the boulders. This helps the feature to look more like the bank of a natural stream.

11 Neaten the edge of the liner. Fit a three-tier spray fountain head or, as here a bell-shaped head. Be careful not to pull out the central tube of the pump when changing heads.

Epimedium x *youngianum* 'Roseum'

Primula veris

297

NOVEL WATER FEATURES

Given a little imagination, all sorts of novel water features are possible. Use them all round the garden to add detail and interest. In a conservatory, a fountain feature adds a glitzy 'finishing touch' to a collection of exotic tropical plants. The moving water creates beneficial humidity that the plants will enjoy, while the sound suggests a tropical stream, adding ambience to the dramatic shapes of giant flowers and architectural foliage, and so contributing to the jungly illusion. Outdoors, a simple fountain makes a good addition to a shady garden, as the moving water adds sparkle and reflects light; it looks particularly good amongst damp-loving plants, such as hostas, ferns and astilbes. For a more sophisticated grouping, team a classical fountain and statue with ivies and euonymus, or a helxine (soleirolia) 'lawn'. A water feature in which the water gurgles over large pebbles, or that operates a bamboo 'deer scarer' (a regular feature of Japanese gardens) adds an extra dimension of sound to a garden designed primarily for relaxation, so you might consider placing one on the patio or close to a garden seat. Another big attraction of water features is the variety of garden wildlife that comes to bathe and drink. If using water in a deep container, such as a tub, make sure that these visitors are able to get out as well as in. Water features that do not involve standing water, such as fountains coming up through millstones or cobbles, are safest for both small children and wildlife. They also have the big advantage of not harbouring mosquitoes, which need still water to breed successfully.

Right: The fountain causes the water in this jar to overflow constantly, sending a thin film of moisture down over the sides, from where it is caught in a reservoir underneath and recycled via a submersible pump.

Below: A pump makes an authentic feature for a cottage-style garden, and teams well with a display of marginal water plants in the larger barrel.

Left: The bright blue of this bowl is very appropriate for a potted lily pond; use only the smallest miniature water lilies (*Nymphaea pygmaea*) in this type of display. They will flower all through the summer.

Right: Water features need not be highly sophisticated; this angled pipe running into an animal drinking trough works well with a display of plants that enjoy cool, humid, shady conditions.

Below: A touch of humour spices up even the plainest containers. A display like this is perfect for a shady corner as it makes you look twice – and the fountain adds light, sound and sparkle.

Right: Water features such as this millstone are safe to use as a feature in gardens where small children play unattended, as there is no standing water for them to fall into, yet birds can still drink and bathe, but mosquitoes cannot breed.

Containers of water without plants

A container of water on its own contrasts with surrounding plants, which might be grown in other pots or in the ground. Use running water for greater interest by installing a small submersible pump. To combat algae, you could add a liquid pond water treatment to the water in the pot, but may prefer not to do so if wildlife use the water. The best plan is to dismantle the pond at the end of summer, before the first frosts, and scrub everything clean before putting it away for the winter.

Above: *This stone pot overflows continuously through flanges in the sides. The water is then recycled from the collection container underneath by a small pump inside.*

Right: *The lion's mask is a very popular fountain design. You could stand a small water plant in a pot in the trough underneath, but it would look just as good surrounded by decorative foliage.*

A windowbox overflowing with a wide range of useful and attractive herbs.

PART TWELVE

HERBS IN CONTAINERS

Herbs are ideal for containers. Grow them in tubs, planters and hanging baskets to make the most of everything they have to offer, from fresh sprigs for cooking to exquisite fragrances, decorative flowers and foliage. And make the most of their portability to bring them wherever they are needed, at any time of year.

1 Choose herbs with a variety of foliage shapes and textures. Place a few crocks in the bottom of the trough.

2 Add a 5-15cm(2-6in) drainage layer of washed gravel or pea shingle. Top up with planting mixture.

3 Supporting the rootball lightly between your fingers, plant the herbs, maintaining a pleasing balance of appearance, height and habit.

CULINARY HERBS IN A TERRACOTTA TROUGH

A trough or windowbox is the perfect way to grow a selection of culinary herbs in the minimum of space. The kitchen windowsill is an obvious site, providing the window opens conveniently enough for regular access to your mini-garden. Make absolutely sure that the windowbox is firmly secured; use strong brackets or ties and check these periodically for wear or weathering. The box might be homemade from new or old wood, painted to match window frames or shutters; or it might be lightweight plastic, antique stone or terracotta. If the windows provide too exposed a site, why not plant up an indoor windowbox, perfect for a few of the more tender species such as basil?

Choosing the right blend of herbs for your containers can be great fun. Even taking into account soil compatibility and whether the plants need sun or shade, there is plenty of scope to create pleasing contrasts of colour, foliage and size. Regular cropping or trimming is important to ensure that the herbs remain small and leafy. Keep the box adequately watered and apply a liquid feed during the growing and cropping season. The soil soon runs out of essential nutrients in the confines of a box, especially where plants grow prolifically and where rain washes constantly through the soil. A mulch of small pebbles conserves moisture and reduces the effect of heavy rains.

Herbs in the kitchen

The flavour of fresh herbs is far more delicate than that of dried ones, so use them generously in the kitchen. Generally speaking, add them at the end of the cooking period for maximum effect. Mint, basil and tarragon change their flavour once dried, so do not expect them to taste the same as before. Add herbs to soups and salads or tie them into tiny bundles to add to home-made stocks and stews.

4 Top up with soil, making sure it settles between the plants without any air gaps. To allow for watering, do not fill to the top of the box.

5 A sprinkling of gravel or small stones on top of the soil around the plants not only looks attractive, but also helps to slow down moisture loss.

Other herb displays

Experimental cooks often prefer to grow a variety of herbs in small quantities; growing them in pots and other containers is the ideal way to do this. Keep herbs close to the kitchen for maximum convenience; if you only want a few sprigs, you may not want to bother going out into the garden. If you cut from them a great deal, keep spare pots of herbs in the garden to bring in when the first batch need a rest.

Left: *The kitchen windowsill is the perfect place for herbs. Besides being handy, their fragrance acts as a living air freshener and many kinds also deter flies.*

Chives *(Allium schoenoprasum)*

Culinary thyme *(Thymus vulgaris)*

Sorrel *(Rumex acetosa)*

French tarragon *(Artemisia dracunculus)*

Sage *(Salvia officinalis)*

Parsley *(Petroselinum crispum)*

Oregano *(Origanum vulgare)*

6 This trough includes a useful blend of flavours for the cook. If you use plenty of herbs in cooking, reduce the number of plants in the box to two or three bigger plants.

Above: *A mixture of fragrant, flowering and culinary herbs in a windowbox makes an attractive, useful display that brings a breath of country air into the room every time you open the window.*

Planting up a parsley pot

1 Place a few crocks or broken pieces of china in the bottom of the pot so that the drainage holes do not become blocked.

2 Fill the pot with potting mix to just below the level of the planting holes. In taller pots, these might appear at various heights.

3 Insert the plants through the holes and press them into the mix. Cover the rootball and make sure the plants are the right way up.

PARSLEY, MINT AND BAY

Parsley, mint and bay are probably among the most used herbs in the kitchen and excellent subjects for growing in containers. Cropping parsley by the handful rather than the sprig can quickly outstrip supply, so try growing several plants in a multi-pocketed strawberry barrel, which suits parsley just as well and is perfect for backyards and patios. A partly shady spot is ideal for parsley and be sure to provide plenty of moisture. Parsley is a biennial and the leaves taste best in the first year, becoming bitter and rather coarse in the second, so try to sow a fresh supply each year in spring and late summer. The seeds can take at least six weeks to germinate, but this can be speeded up by soaking them overnight in warm water. Sow a packet of seeds in a small pot and keep at a temperature of about 21°C(70°C) – a warm windowsill is ideal. When they germinate, leave the plants unthinned for a dense growth of fresh parsley.

Members of the mint family are available in a wonderful variety of types and scents, but many people are afraid to grow them on account of their vigorous habit, which may threaten to swamp neighbouring plants. Growing mint in containers restricts the creeping rhizomes, but still produces a useful crop for a range of culinary uses.

Bay will thrive in a sunny, sheltered position in light, well-drained soil, but it requires indoor winter protection in cooler climates. Bay leaves are the main attraction of the plant, being large, shiny, deep green and aromatic. They can be picked and used at any time, but dry well, too, the flavour actually strengthening and becoming more mellow.

4 Place the final plant in the top of the container, making sure that it is planted at the correct height to grow right out of the top.

5 After firming with potting mixture, sprinkle a handful of small stones or gravel on the surface to reduce moisture loss.

6 The pot will provide plenty of fresh parsley for picking within a very small planted area. To maintain good growth, pinch off the flower stalks as they appear.

Left: Curly-leaved parsley makes an attractive container plant; sow or plant a potful in spring. The same plants will keep going until late autumn, but replace them annually, as they run to seed in their second year.

Versatility of mint

Red raripila (Mentha x smithiana)

Spearmint (Mentha spicata)

Below: Growing a whole collection of mints in a variety of terracotta pots of different sizes is an ingenious way of displaying their range of colour, shape and texture.

Pennyroyal (Mentha pulegium 'Upright')

Variegated apple mint (Mentha suaveolens 'Variegata')

Spicy ginger mint (Mentha x gracilis 'Variegata')

Peppermint (Mentha x piperita)

Planting and keeping a bay tree in a pot

Bay trees in pots can look particularly attractive when trained and shaped to grow into pyramids, balls and other topiary shapes. It is a useful way of removing leaves required for the kitchen and you can dry surplus leaves. Water potted bay trees every day during the growing season, especially in hot weather. In winter, only water them when the soil feels really dry. From spring until the end of the summer, feed them every week with a nitrogen feed to encourage healthy new leaves.

1 Cover the drainage hole with a crock and fill the pot with a soil-based mix. Lower the bay gently into the new container.

2 Keeping the bay upright, continue filling the pot with more potting mixture. Try to avoid getting any soil on the foliage.

3 A layer of small stones or gravel on the soil surface retains moisture, discourages weeds and also looks pleasing.

4 Stand the finished pot in a sunny, well-sheltered spot and be sure to bring it under cover at the first signs of frost.

1 Drape the mesh inside the basket. Fit a circle of plastic cut from an old potting mix bag into the base, black side down.

2 Fill the basket loosely with soil-based potting mixture. As the basket fills, the netting sinks into the shape of the basket.

A BASKET OF EDIBLE HERBS

Fresh culinary herbs make tasty and healthy ingredients, but often they are grown in the vegetable plot at the end of the garden, which makes snipping a few sprigs a nuisance, especially if you are in a hurry or the weather is poor. The solution is to grow them close to the house, where they are always handy. Herbs can be grown in all sorts of containers, but where space is short a hanging basket is the ideal choice. And by combining culinary herbs with a few decorative types – which can often be used for garnishing as well – you can create a stunning and useful display. A large basket is best, as there will be enough room to grow a good selection of your favourite herbs. Start by choosing the herbs that you use regularly in cooking, such as basil, thyme, chives, mint and oregano. Choose interesting varieties of each, such as lemon thyme, Greek oregano (a specially fiery-tasting form), curly mint or red-leaved basil 'Dark Opal', which is decorative as well as edible. Herbs that you use in very large quantities are best grown in separate containers or in beds in the garden, so that you do not strip the display completely for the kitchen, but you can still include one or two here for 'emergency' use. Snip small sprigs from the plants little and often; it encourages plants to grow bushier and improves their appearance. Turn the basket round once a week so that no plants are always shaded by others, and all grow evenly.

3 When the basket is full, trim the mesh. Leave a 2.5cm(1in) rim to stop potting mix spilling out; this will soon be hidden by the plants as they grow and trail over the edges.

4 Place the most striking or colourful plants in the centre. This is red orache, which makes a colourful, unusual salad ingredient.

5 Add borage, red clover and purple basil. Both the borage and red orache usually grow tall, but in a container they are naturally dwarfed. Nip out the tops of the stems to make them bushier and to delay flowering.

The mesh used to line this hanging basket is the sort sold for use as windbreak material. It provides free drainage (ideal for herbs) and a pleasant green background.

6 Choose plants that look decorative as well as being edible. The herb being planted here is annual sage; its colourful bracts can be used sparingly in salads or garnishes. Both its flavour and aroma are quite strong.

7 Calendula flowers look pretty in salads and summer drinks or sprinkled over rice. Separate the petals from the green calyx first or use whole heads as ornamental buffet decorations.

8 Heartsease is another popular edible flower. Whole blooms are good for garnishes and salads. They can also be crystallized.

In summer, many of the herbs will cascade over the sides, making a fuller display.

9 A herbal basket is best planted in early summer, as some plants are frost-tender. In the autumn, remove the hardy herbs and replant them in the garden, or prune and pot to replant in another container with fresh annual herbs the following year.

Garnishing herbs

It is worth adding a few unusual herbs to a basket – ones that you only use occasionally and which add a touch of colour. These need not only be leafy herbs; petals of calendula and red clover can also be sprinkled in salads. Rocket, buckler-leaved sorrel and golden purslane are all useful salad leaves and handy for garnishing. The flowers of rocket can be used in salads as well, and have an unusual hazelnut taste. Include a few scented herbs such as pineapple sage (whose leaves smell exactly as you would imagine), and lavender. Plant them all closely together so that the basket is well filled from the start, to allow for cutting.

__Left:__ Add herbs to an edible hanging basket display – here, variegated sage grows with tumbler miniature tomatoes and 'Lollo Rossa' lettuce. French marigolds add a decorative touch and also deter whitefly.

EDIBLE HERBS

Edible herbs have a huge number of culinary purposes. We are all familiar with using popular herbs such as sage, rosemary and thyme for cookery (they also dry and freeze well), but many soft-leaved kinds, such as chives, buckler-leaved sorrel and rocket, can be used as salad leaves and garnishes. Fragrant herbs can be used to flavour herbal oils and vinegars, and edible flowers such as heartsease can be candied for decorating cakes and trifles. Burn dried woody herb prunings, particularly of sage, rosemary and thyme, on the hot coals of the barbecue to add an aromatic flavour to meat while it is cooking. And use large leaves of French sorrel to wrap herby minced meat as an alternative to stuffed vine leaves or choux farci. Any good book on culinary herbs will have lots more ideas and recipes for using everything you can grow in your containers.

The herbs featured here are the ones planted in the basket shown on pages 306-307. The final view of the basket is shown at left.

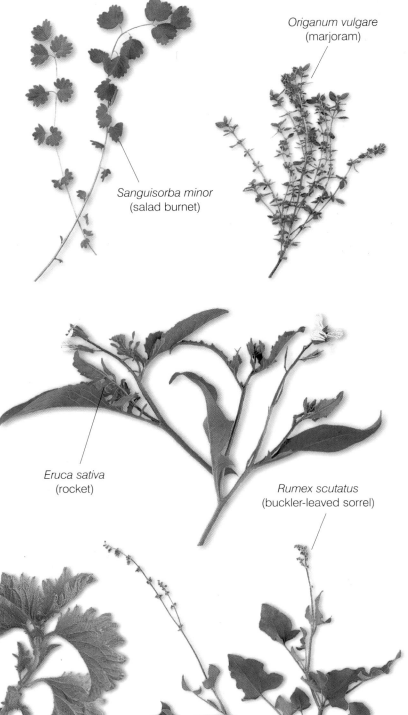

Origanum vulgare
(marjoram)

Sanguisorba minor
(salad burnet)

Eruca sativa
(rocket)

Rumex scutatus
(buckler-leaved sorrel)

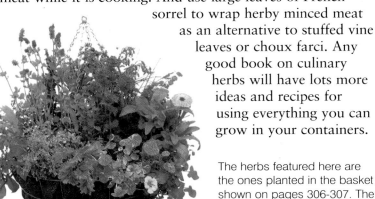

Calendula officinalis
(pot marigold)

Atriplex hortensis
var. *rubra*
(red orache)

Ocimum basilicum var.
minimum 'Napolitano'
(lettuce-leaf basil)

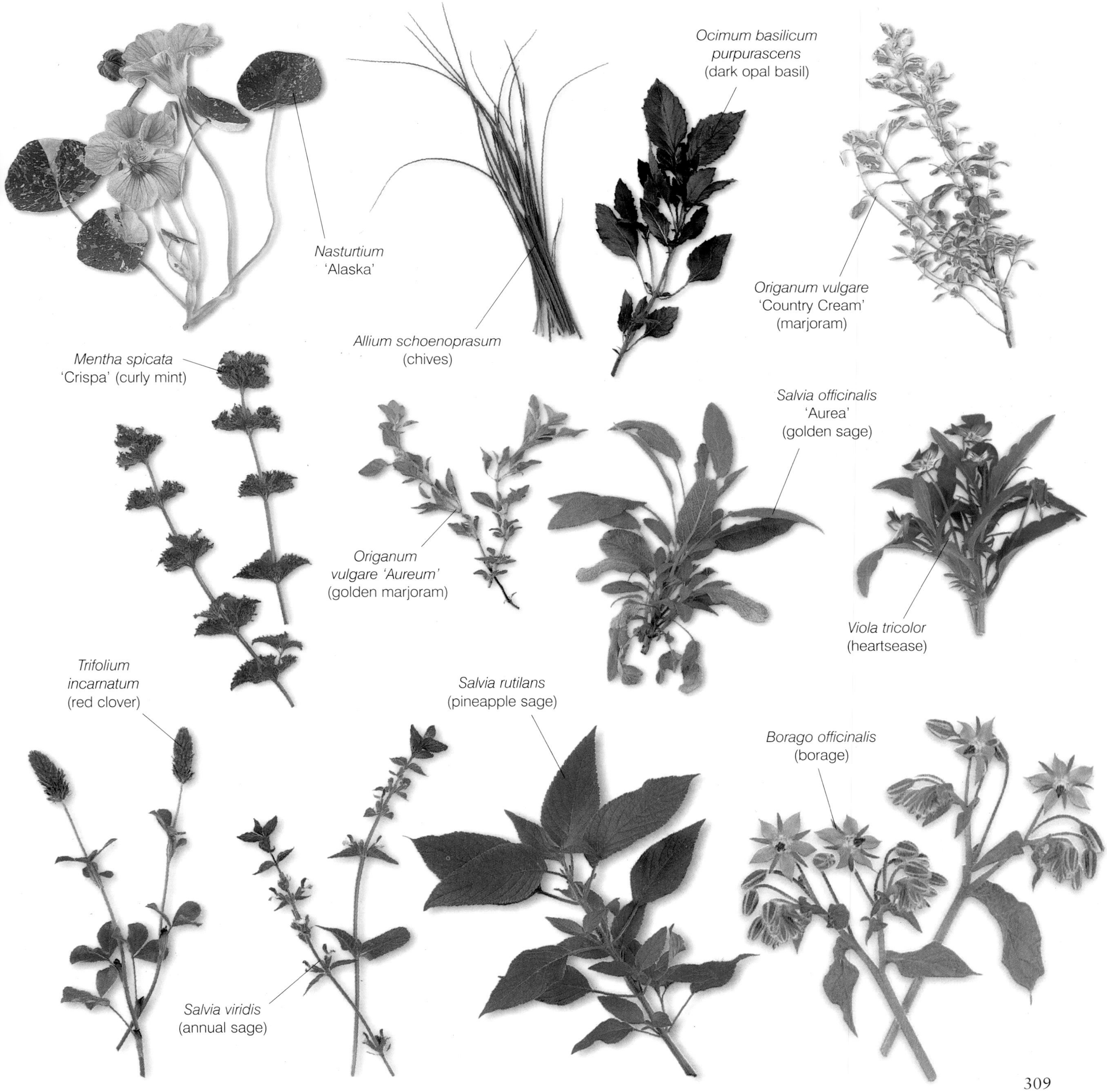

Ocimum basilicum purpurascens (dark opal basil)

Nasturtium 'Alaska'

Allium schoenoprasum (chives)

Origanum vulgare 'Country Cream' (marjoram)

Mentha spicata 'Crispa' (curly mint)

Salvia officinalis 'Aurea' (golden sage)

Origanum vulgare 'Aureum' (golden marjoram)

Viola tricolor (heartsease)

Trifolium incarnatum (red clover)

Salvia rutilans (pineapple sage)

Borago officinalis (borage)

Salvia viridis (annual sage)

309

1 Cover the drainage holes with crocks and add 2.5cm(1in) of gravel for drainage. Add potting mix to just below the rim of the pot.

2 Put in each plant without breaking up the rootball. This is a variegated, scented-leaved pelargonium, 'Lady Plymouth'.

3 Scoop out a hole for each herb, planting the outside row close to the edge of the tub. This scented-leaved pelargonium is called 'Chocolate Peppermint'.

A POT OF SCENTED HERBS

Aromatic herbs enjoy hot, sunny, dryish conditions, which concentrate their scents, and a well-sheltered spot where their perfumes can linger on the air. Place a large container such as this on the patio, by a doorway or outside a window that is often left open in summer. Alternatively, put it by a sunny seat anywhere in the garden. Since it is the leaves that are scented, aromatic herbs are perfumed all the time, but the leaves need to be bruised lightly to release their fragrant oils, so brush them lightly with your hand. Choose sweetly scented herbs; those with citrus, rose and spicy scents have the most pleasant perfumes; save culinary or medicinal herbs for elsewhere. Scented-leaved pelargoniums offer the greatest range of fragrances, including pine, balsam, rose, cinnamon, peppermint, orange and lemon. Neither these nor aromatic herbs in general have colourful flowers, but offer a range of foliage shapes, textures and sizes. If more colour is needed, keep to the herbal theme by including a few edible flowers, such as heartsease or compact nasturtium. Other herbs to use in this way include eau-de-cologne mint (also a good culinary plant) and pineapple sage, which has brilliant red spikes of narrow tubular flowers above strongly pineapple-scented leaves. Otherwise, add a few related flowering plants that are happy in similar conditions and will not outgrow the display. Miniature pelargoniums, rockery pinks or *Salvia grahamii* (which itself has blackcurrant-scented leaves) are good choices. Many scented herbs are not frost hardy, so bring scented-leaved pelargoniums, *Salvia grahamii, Lippia citriodora* and pineapple sage indoors for the winter months.

4 Since aromatic herbs have little flower colour, make the most of plants that contrast with each other in leaf shape and texture. This lemon verbena (*Lippia citriodora*) has strongly lemon-scented foliage.

5 As the container begins to fill up, be sure to include at least one good prostrate plant to soften the edge. This is *Pelargonium tomentosum*, which has soft, furry, strongly peppermint-scented leaves.

A display of thymes

There are dozens of different thymes, both creeping and upright. The plants have pretty pink or mauve summer flowers, and the foliage is highly aromatic. Thyme is used in cooking – it has a strong resinous flavour – and also medicinally, due to its natural antiseptic action.

Below: Where space is short, group several thymes together in a multi-pot, using low spreading kinds in the pockets and a taller variety in the top. Trim to keep the shape tidy and use the sprigs in cooking.

Thymus x *citriodorus*

Thymus 'Annie Hall'

Thymus albus

Thymus 'Doone Valley'

6 Fill the container well. This is *Salvia officinalis* 'Tricolor', a red, cream and green-variegated form of culinary sage (also edible).

7 Fill gaps between rootballs with potting mix. This provides extra root-room as plants grow, and also prevents rapid drying out.

8 Water well to settle the mix around the roots. If it sinks slightly, top up to within 2.5cm (1in) of the rim, but do not overfill.

The various plant perfumes combine to create a living potpourri.

9 The plants soon fill the container; finger-prune wayward stems. To concentrate the fragrance, grow in full sun, avoid over-watering and place the container where you can brush gently against the plants as you go past them.

SCENTED HERBS

Today, we can indulge in the luxury of growing scented herbs for pleasure. They can be grown in pots at the kitchen window, or outdoors in patio tubs close to the back door, a garden seat, or under windows to perfume the air. Grouped with pretty but unscented flowers, they lend their fragrance to everything near them. However, back in medieval times when aromatic herbs first became popular, their use was far more serious. Sweet-scented herbs were strewn on the floor mixed with the rushes used as temporary floor covering to mask domestic odours. Strong-smelling kinds were added to repel fleas. Both were necessary precautions, as it was considered good manners at the time to throw bones and other inedible bits of meat onto the floor for scavenging dogs to eat. In the streets, the gentry carried pomanders with them – oranges stuffed with cloves and other strong-smelling spices to kill the smells caused by open-air drains. And since hanging cupboards had not been invented, clothes and bedlinen were stored laying flat in chests – when put away damp, they would soon start to mildew and smell. To counteract this, ground orris root (the dried and powdered root of a species of iris) was sprinkled in between layers to absorb moisture and add a delicate scent of violets. In upper class establishments several centuries later, dried herbs and spices were mixed with orris root to make potpourri. Modern potpourris may contain added ingredients like pine bark, pine cones, curls of orange peel and dried rose petals, but essential oils of herbs and spices are still used to refresh them when the natural aromas eventually fade.

The herbs featured on these pages are the ones planted in the container of herbs on pages 310-311. The final view of the container is shown left.

Above: Pick lavender on a sunny morning after the dew has evaporated and as the buds are beginning to open. Leave the stems long when harvesting and drying; cut them shorter later on.

Scented-leaved pelargonium 'Lady Plymouth'

Scented-leaved pelargonium 'Chocolate Peppermint'

Mentha x piperita citrata 'Chocolate'

Lavandula
'Twickle Purple'
(lavender)

Salvia officinalis
'Tricolor'
(tricolor sage)

Pelargonium
'Atomic Snowflake'

Pelargonium crispum
'Variegatum'

Origanum
'Country Cream'
(marjoram)

*Pelargonium
tomentosum*

Helichrysum italicum
(curry plant)

Mentha suaveolens
'Variegata'
(variegated apple mint)

Aloysia triphylla
(Lippia citriodora)
(lemon verbena)

SCENTED-LEAVED PELARGONIUMS

P. citriodorum and *P. c.*
'Variegatum': (lemon)
P. fragrans: nutmeg
P. quercifolium: resin
P. 'Attar of Roses': rose
P. 'Clorinda': eucalyptus
P. abrotanifolium:
southernwood
P. filicifolium: balsam
P. graveolens: rose
P. odoratissimum: apples
P. tomentosum: strong
peppermint
P. 'Mabel Grey': lemon
P. 'Prince of Orange':
orange

1 Choose a container capable of holding a large volume of potting mix. Place crocks over the drainage holes and cover the base with 2.5cm(1in) of gravel so excess water can run away quickly.

A MEDICINAL HERB POT

True herbal medicine should be left to trained practitioners, but since many culinary and decorative herbs have mildly beneficial effects, it is fun to use them as a natural tonic or for minor problems. Red sage has natural antiseptic properties; an infusion makes a good gargle for treating sore throats. Use an infusion of rosemary for rinsing hair to make it shine, or add it to the bath for a scented herbal bath. In cookery, the herb is believed to improve the memory. Thyme is a mild antiseptic too; make an infusion for coughs or upset stomachs. Any of the usual culinary herbs, chopped in small quantities into salads or used in normal cooking, have a mildly therapeutic influence. For instant first aid, grow aloe vera, also known as the burn plant. Cut a piece from one of the thick succulent leaves and squeeze the clear gel inside onto burns, scalds or sunburn. Houseleeks have been used in much the same way, with the juice from the leaves applied to burns and skin complaints – it was once believed to cure warts. To maximise their therapeutic properties, grow herbs in a warm sunny spot and avoid overwatering them, as this 'dilutes' beneficial oils etc., in the foliage. When planted in normal soil-based potting mix, plants should not need feeding for about three months. Then use a general-purpose liquid plant feed (preferably organic) at about half the normal dilution rate.

2 Add a soil-based potting mix to within 5cm(2in) of the rim. Soilless mixes retain more water, which can lead to roots rotting.

3 Tuck the outermost plants up against the edge to use every bit of space in the container. This plant is variegated lemon balm.

4 Continue to add more plants. Place them close together, but try to make sure that neighbouring plants have contrasting shapes, leaf colours and textures to create a decorative appearance. This is houseleek, or sempervivum.

5 Aim to fill the container well; once you start picking, plants are unlikely to grow faster than they can be used. Plant prostrate kinds around the edge of the display to make best use of space.

6 Top up any gaps with potting mix. For an ornamental look, surface the top with a thin layer of pea-gravel or granite chippings.

7 Water well to settle the mix and allow surplus water to drain away. Leave the tub until it is nearly dry before watering again.

8 Keep the container regularly fed and watered. Snip off sprigs from the back of the plants or take shoots hidden behind other plants to avoid spoiling the display.

Herbal teas

Several herbs make pleasant herbal teas; use chamomile, hyssop or black peppermint in this way. The latter is good for digestion, while chamomile tea is very relaxing and often used as a caffeine-free bedtime drink. If you do not find it quite to your taste, sweeten the tea with sugar or, better still, a mild-flavoured honey.

Left: *To make herbal tea, shred a handful of fresh leaves into a teapot. Add boiling water to cover and allow to stand for 5-10 minutes. Bottled or filtered water produces a tea with good colour and flavour. This is lemon balm tea.*

Right: *Some pots have a separate compartment for the tea leaves. To make chamomile tea, infuse fresh or dried flower heads in boiling water. Chamomile tea is said to prevent nightmares and relieve nausea. It is also used as a skin cleanser.*

Herbs that repel flies

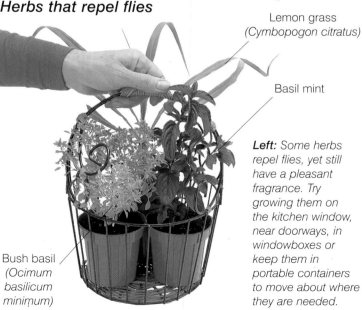

Lemon grass (Cymbopogon citratus)

Basil mint

Left: *Some herbs repel flies, yet still have a pleasant fragrance. Try growing them on the kitchen window, near doorways, in windowboxes or keep them in portable containers to move about where they are needed.*

Bush basil (Ocimum basilicum minimum)

MEDICINAL HERBS

The use of herbs in medicine dates back many thousands of years. Traditionally, monks cultivated well-stocked herb gardens, to which local people travelled in search of cures. As people began to keep their own gardens, they grew and used herbs to treat their own minor problems. In case of more serious illnesses they consulted the 'wise woman' – an old woman with a more extensive knowledge of herbal remedies. Medieval cottagers were highly superstitious and many wise women also dabbled in lucky charms and love potions, which frequently earned them the reputation of being witches; many lived alone with only a cat for company, which added to the myth. Nowadays, people still use herbs for their tonic properties and to make refreshing healthy drinks; herbal teas, being caffeine-free, are very popular. Today, herbal practitioners are highly trained and often work in conjunction with medically trained doctors. While it is fascinating to know how herbs were used in the past, and it adds considerably to their conversation value around the garden, it is not advisable to treat yourself with herbs for anything beyond minor problems.

The herbs featured on these pages are the ones planted in the container of herbs on pages 314-315. The final view is shown again at left.

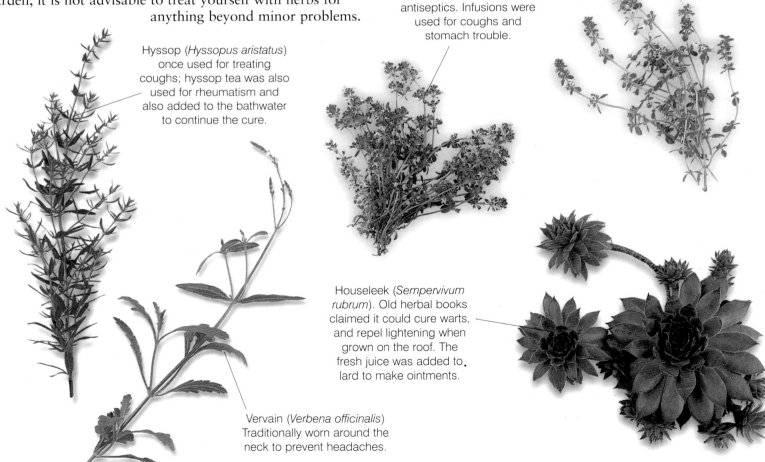

Thymus 'Golden Lemon'

Thymus 'Annie Hall'. All thymes are natural antiseptics. Infusions were used for coughs and stomach trouble.

Hyssop (*Hyssopus aristatus*) once used for treating coughs; hyssop tea was also used for rheumatism and also added to the bathwater to continue the cure.

Houseleek (*Sempervivum rubrum*). Old herbal books claimed it could cure warts, and repel lightening when grown on the roof. The fresh juice was added to lard to make ointments.

Vervain (*Verbena officinalis*) Traditionally worn around the neck to prevent headaches.

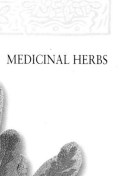

Chamaemelum nobile · 'Flore Pleno'. Chamomile tea, made from the dried flowers, is mildly sedative – a relaxing bedtime drink. Also used as a final rinse when washing blonde hair.

Salvia officinalis 'Purpurascens', Red, or purple, sage is a natural antiseptic. Infusions were used as a mouthwash and gargle. Aids digestion of rich or fatty food when used in cookery.

Gold variegated sage (*Salvia officinalis* 'Icterina') can be used in the same way as red sage, but probably less effective. Good as a garnish.

Rosmarinus officinalis Prostratus Group. Rosemary contains natural antiseptics; add an infusion to the bath for healthy skin. Use as a final rinse when washing dark hair to give shine. The aroma aids relaxation. Also claimed to improve the memory.

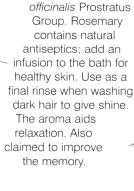

Variegated lemon balm (*Melissa officinalis* 'Variegata'). Melissa tea is used for stomach trouble. It also makes a refreshing summer drink. Fresh leaves are used in salads or cooked with fish.

Heartsease (*Viola tricolor*) is so-called because it was once used for treating heart problems. Also used in love charms. The flowers are edible and can be used in salads.

Burn plant *(Aloe vera).* The fresh gel, squeezed from the leaves, is used for minor skin irritations, psoriasis, sunburn and scalds.

Black peppermint (*Mentha*) has a strong peppermint flavour unsuitable for mint sauce, but used as a digestive tea.

A cascading display of ripening strawberries in early summer.

PART THIRTEEN

FRUIT AND VEGETABLES

Many kinds of fruit and vegetables thrive in containers, allowing previously unproductive patios, paving and paths to be turned into oases of luscious edible produce. And if your garden soil, situation or growing conditions make it impossible to cultivate crops, then this is a practical and decorative way of doing so.

1 Make a support to stabilise the tower of pots by screwing a length of wooden pole to a flat base and sit the biggest pot over it.

2 Part-fill the pot with any good-quality potting mix. Leave a deep depression in the middle where the second pot will rest.

3 Put six strawberry plants around the edge of the pot, spreading the roots out as much as possible and then firming lightly.

4 Set the second pot in place. This should be sufficiently smaller to allow room for the first tier of plants to develop freely.

5 Firm the pot down until level and part-fill with more mix. As before, put most round the edges and leave a depression in the centre for the smallest pot.

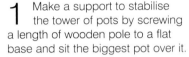

Use the same variety throughout or plant different varieties on each tier.

STRAWBERRIES IN POTS

Strawberries make excellent subjects for hanging baskets, windowboxes, growing bags, tubs and troughs. High-rise containers, such as strawberry pots with planting pockets in the sides, are a particularly good space-saving way of growing them in small gardens. Unlike many edible crops, strawberry plants are neat and compact, and are also highly decorative with their apple-blossom-like flowers in spring followed by cascading green strawblets. Containers of strawberries are pretty enough to keep on a patio or next to a back door. They associate nicely with tubs of flowers, or can be added to a herb garden or potager-style vegetable garden to give height to a ground-level display. When grown in containers, ripening strawberries are far more easily protected from birds. Drape containers with netting or crop protection fleece from the time the first green fruit appear; this way, birds will not get into the habit of trying to steal your crops. Prevent slugs and snails spoiling the fruit by smearing crop protection jelly round the base of containers to prevent them climbing up. A strawberry container can be started any time in autumn or spring. 'Loose' strawberry runners are available in autumn and should be planted straight away so that the roots do not dry out. If you have access to a strawberry bed, you could also dig up spare runners from established plants in autumn to replant in containers. Small potgrown plants are also sold in spring right up until the time plants carry green fruit, however, the earlier in spring you plant them the better.

6 Plant four strawberry plants around the edge, but not directly above those in the lower pot, so the fruits hang down evenly.

7 Fit the smallest pot in place, taking care to keep the tower upright to prevent toppling once the plants are heavy with fruit.

8 Put two plants in the top and fill to the brim with mix. Fill any gaps between the lower plants with mix to prevent plants drying out.

9 Pour gravel into the saucer for extra stability and to hide the base plate. To move the tower, lift and steady using the 'handle'.

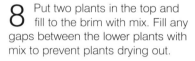

10 Water each tier thoroughly. Moisture will drain down from the top pot, so after the initial watering, it will need more than the others. Feed weekly with half-strength liquid tomato fertiliser.

11 By early summer, the plants will have grown and filled the container with bunches of swelling green fruit cascading down over the 'tiers'. Soon, the first fruit will start to ripen.

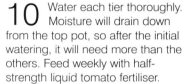

Protecting your strawberries

Many kinds of wildlife enjoy ripe strawberries, and can spoil the fruit by making holes in it. Slugs and snails are easily deterred by growing strawberries in pots, since the containers are raised above ground level and therefore harder to reach, but use slug traps or bait if they are still a problem. Birds are the greatest hazard, so use nets draped over a support to keep them a safe 'beaks-distance'·from ripening fruit.

1 As the first green fruits reach full size, put up a frame to support the fruit net. This is a circular perennial plant support, which fits nicely over the pole through the centre of the planter.

This is black plastic netting. You can buy various types of netting that would be suitable.

2 Tuck the netting loosely around the plant and hold it down with bricks to prevent birds getting in underneath. This way it can easily be lifted when you want to pick the fruit – which you should do daily.

Stand in a sheltered sunny spot and keep well watered.

Routine care of potted fruit

Each spring scrape away the top 5cm(2in) of mix and replace with fresh. Every three years, repot fruit back into the same pot with fresh potting mix, after shaking most of the old material from the roots.

Keep well watered at all times in summer; if plants dry out the fruit can drop.

In hot weather, protect roots from overheating by covering pots with thick matting, mulching materials like bark chippings, or surround them with containers of flowers.

Feed regularly throughout the growing season with full-strength liquid tomato feed; fruit needs plenty of potash and in pots all the nutrients need topping up often

In winter, protect the pots from freezing solid by plunging them to their rim in a garden bed or moving pots under cover during periods of severe weather. Raise the containers up on 'feet' to prevent waterlogging.

Tie tall plants up to trellis or fencing to stop them blowing over in a windy spot.

APPLES IN CONTAINERS

If you do not have room in the garden for fruit trees and bushes, grow them in containers instead. They take up far less room this way since the pot tends to dwarf the plants, though you still get a good crop of fruit. Put the pots in a sheltered sunny spot and grow several varieties of the same sort of fruit together to ensure good pollination, or choose self-fertile varieties. Large pots 38-45cm(15-18in) in diameter are quite adequate for tree fruit, while 30-35cm (12-14in) pots are big enough for bush fruits. Fruit can be planted into containers at any time of year, though spring is best, as it is the start of the growing season. Plant into rich soil-based mix with added gravel to weight the pots down; otherwise, being rather top-heavy, fruit trees tend to blow over easily. Trees like apples can either be trained as dwarf versions of normal tree shapes, or upright cordons – the latter take up much less room. (Ballerina trees naturally grow into single stems without any pruning or training.)

Choose a strong healthy apple tree growing on a dwarfing rootstock. It should have four or five vigorous branches well spaced out round the trunk, giving it a nice, evenly shaped 'head'. Add 10% gravel by volume to the soil-based potting mix.

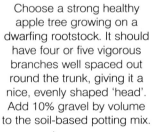

1 Buy a pot at least 38-45cm (15-18in) across, or use a large half barrel. Part-fill it with soil-based potting mix and some gravel – this will make the pot more stable.

2 Knock the tree gently out of its original pot. If the roots are coiled thickly round, tease a few out from the mass before placing it in the middle of the new container.

3 Fill round the rootball with the soil and gravel mix so that the tree is growing at the same depth as in its previous pot. Leave about 2.5cm(1in) clearance for watering.

4 Push a strong stake down to the bottom of the pot next to the tree trunk. It should be long enough to go to the point where the branches join the main stem.

Above: 'Bramley's Seedling' is well known as a brilliant cooking apple, but if you enjoy a tart-tasting apple, let it ripen well on the tree, pick a red-flushed fruit and eat it thinly sliced straight from the tree.

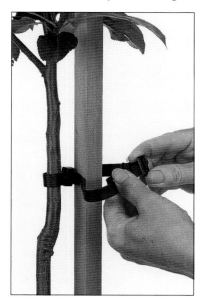

5 Secure the trunk with a proper tree tie, fitted just below where the branches join. Position the rubber 'buffer' between the stake and trunk to prevent chaffing.

6 Water the tree in well. Give as much water as the potting mix will hold, then allow the surplus to drain away before moving the tree to a sunny sheltered spot.

Apple varieties suitable for containers

Any varieties of apples can be grown in containers, but choose those growing on moderately dwarfing rootstocks. To find out which of the hundreds of varieties you like best, go to an open day or apple-tasting event. These are often organised by specialist fruit growers.

Above and left: 'Gala' is one of the most popular modern eating apple varieties. You can expect a good crop from a dwarf tree in a pot, and they start bearing fruit within a few years of planting.

Left: Ballerina apple trees naturally grow into upright shapes with lots of short fruiting spurs along the trunk. They do not grow branches and need no pruning. If you cut the top off, they develop normal branches, however.

Right: The ballerina apple tree variety 'Bolero' has crisp green fruits that ripen on the tree in early autumn. Eat these straight after picking – do not store them.

Planting a morello cherry tree

1 Cover the drainage holes of a large pot with crocks. Make sure you can still move the pot once it is filled with potting mixture.

2 Add 5cm(2in) of soil-based potting mix. Leave room for the rootball plus a gap of 2.5cm (1in) at the rim for watering.

3 Remove the tree from its old pot. Tease out overcrowded roots. Sit the tree in the centre of the new pot. Push in the canes.

4 Add more soil, firming it down gently. If any roots are visible on the surface, add a little more but do not bury them deeply.

5 Water the plant well in. A clay pot will dry out faster than a plastic one, so check daily. Do not allow soil to dry out.

6 A fan-trained fruit tree takes up less room than a normal tree. Stand the pot against a wall or tie the tree to a trellis or fence. The shelter they provide leads to earlier ripening fruit, and makes the crop easier to protect from birds.

OTHER FRUIT TREES

A fruit garden takes up valuable space in a small plot; if this is a problem, then growing in pots is the solution. Many tree fruits, particularly those grown on dwarfing rootstocks, make good patio pot subjects as they have pretty spring blossom as well as fruit. Pots are also a good way of housing fruit bushes, such as redcurrants and gooseberries; the only kinds that do not do well in pots are cane fruit – raspberries and the blackberry family. Peaches and cherries are best grown as dwarf trees or fan-trained; this is a handy way of growing them against a wall, where it is easier to protect the fruit from birds. Bush fruit – redcurrants, blueberries and gooseberries – can be grown as bushes, much like normal shrubs. For a more decorative effect, train gooseberries as standards, and redcurrants as double cordons against a wall. Blackcurrants are not generally suitable for containers as they make large vigorous plants, but the more naturally compact varieties, such as 'Ben Sarek', do well. Blueberries make very good container plants, especially where garden soil is chalky, since they need acid soil. Grow them in large pots of ericaceous mixture. Other heathland fruits, including cranberries, can also be grown this way.

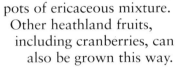

Above: Morello cherries are sour cherries used for cooking rather than eating raw. They are ready to pick in midsummer.

Planting up a fruit bush

1 Snip open film plastic pots and pull them off. If the plant is in a rigid pot, knock it gently out without breaking the rootball.

2 Tease out the largest, thickly coiled roots. If not potbound, do not break up the rootball. Sit the plant centrally in the new pot.

3 Fill the gap around the edge with more potting mix, barely covering the surface of the rootball. Leave a 2.5cm(1in) gap round the rim for watering later on.

4 Finally, water well in. Soft fruit bushes are heavy feeders, so start feeding them after the first week, using diluted tomato feed.

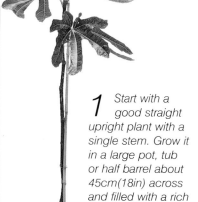

Above: Whitecurrant fruits are like strings of pearls dangling from the branches. They are ornamental enough to include in a shrub border where space is short.

Creating a standard fig tree

Figs crop heaviest when their roots are restricted by growing in a pot; they need heavy feeding and watering throughout the growing season, but can be kept almost dry in winter when they lose their leaves.

1 Start with a good straight upright plant with a single stem. Grow it in a large pot, tub or half barrel about 45cm(18in) across and filled with a rich soil-based mix.

2 Nip out the growing tip to encourage branching from the top of the plant.

3 After 'finger pruning', rub soil onto the cut. 'Bleeding' could weaken the plant.

4 To form a neat head, stop the side shoots when they reach 7.5-10cm (3-4in). Repeat each time new side shoots reach 15cm(6in).

5 Fruits appear as little green swellings. Pick them when they change colour and feel soft. They ripen from late midsummer to autumn.

1 A good way of preventing an opened bag from spreading is to cut off the end beyond the heat seal to form a ring of plastic.

2 Slip the ring over one end of the unopened bag and move it into the centre. Do not be rough with the strap if it is not very wide.

RAISING TOMATOES IN A GROWING BAG

One of the best ways of growing tomatoes, in a greenhouse and outdoors, is in a growing bag. Tomatoes are susceptible to root diseases at the best of times and greenhouse plants are especially vulnerable. Growing bags are free of pests and diseases and the plastic isolates plant roots from any diseased soil. Both cordon (single stem) and bush varieties grow well in bags. Generally speaking, grow one less plant of a bush variety than a cordon, because a bush type takes up more room. Follow the general rules for watering growing bags; wait until the surface of the soil has dried out and then give at least 4.5 litres(1 gallon) of water at a time. Feeding is not necessary for the first few weeks, but once the first fruits are pea-sized, feed according to the instructions on the bag or the feed packaging. To allow sun and air to reach the bottom fruits, remove the leaves from the base of the plant up to the lowest truss that has fruit showing red. Tomatoes dislike high growing temperatures, so make sure that the greenhouse is adequately ventilated and shaded. Too much heat leads to excessive water loss and this can cause problems, notably blossom end rot.

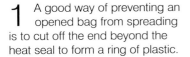

3 Make a V-shaped cut at each end of the growing bag, with the point of the V towards the centre. Join the points of the two Vs with another straight cut running under the strap.

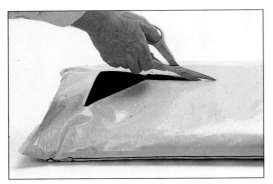

4 Fold under the edges of the single planting compartment. The planting mixtures are formulated to produce the best results in growing bags. They are not general-purpose mixtures.

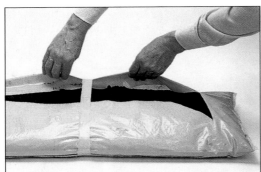

5 The planting mixture will have worked its way out of the corners. Push it back and along the sides, so that the surface is slightly dish shaped.

6 Scoop out a planting hole in the growing bag. This usually means going right down to the bottom to get it deep enough.

7 Firm the plant gently into place. Never push the soil down too hard or you run the risk of it becoming waterlogged.

8 Put in three plants per bag in a greenhouse. Outdoors, plant four single stem, or three bush plants per bag.

9 Apply up to 7 litres(1.5 gallons) of water at the first watering. Later waterings can be slightly less.

10 Being a bush variety, the side shoots have not been removed. After a few weeks, there are plenty of flowers and the promise of a good crop.

Above: As the fruits mature on this bush variety, they provide an array of attractive colours, ranging from pale green to bright red.

Buy new bags for planting tomatoes the following year.

When to plant out tomatoes

Do not plant out tomatoes until you see yellow petals in the bottom truss of flower buds. This takes about ten weeks from sowing seed. Plant out in an unheated greenhouse about three weeks before the last expected frost; outdoors, about a week after the last expected frost.

Left: *This tomato is too young to plant out. Extra growth induced by putting it into new soil will lead to an unfruitful bottom truss.*

Right: *Here, the first flower is open and the tomato is ready to plant out. Never pull a plant from its pot. Turn it upside-down, tap the rim on a bench and let the plant drop into your hand. The rootball should be full of healthy roots.*

Ghost spot

This form of grey mould (botrytis) affects tomatoes, particularly those growing in a greenhouse, where a lack of ventilation can lead to high temperatures and excessive humidity. Make sure that ventilation is adequate and if necessary use a systemic spray to control the condition. Spraying will not remove spots from the affected tomatoes, however.

1 Line a large hanging basket. This thick coco-fibre liner acts as insulation, keeping the potting mix at a more even temperature.

2 Make an inner lining from black plastic to hold water. Press the plastic into the base of the basket and trim it roughly.

3 Loosely fill the basket with potting mixture and firm the mix down gently into the base of the basket. The weight will settle the liner down into all the curves of the container, stopping it 'shrinking' later.

TOMATOES AND FRENCH MARIGOLDS IN A BASKET

Several kinds of edible plant make very attractive hanging baskets, especially when teamed with complementary ornamental flowers. Marigolds attract beneficial insects that will help prevent pests attacking tomatoes, so you should not need to spray, which is ideal for organic gardeners. A container arrangement is a good way of growing a few edibles in a small garden and is pretty enough to keep by the back door. Compact, bushy tomato varieties are ideal basket crops, as they have a naturally prostrate growth habit and it is not necessary to remove their side shoots. However, to get a good crop they need a little more care than normal hanging basket plants. Fluctuating moisture levels and soil temperatures, commonly found in hanging baskets, must be evened out, otherwise the tomatoes will not set fruit or may develop physiological problems that spoil the crop. To avoid these variations, try using a large container (which holds more potting mix than a small one and takes longer to heat up or dry out) and insulate it with a thick liner. To keep moisture levels even, add water-retaining gel crystals to the potting mix and water up to twice daily in hot weather. A sunny spot and frequent feeding with a high-potash liquid tomato feed are essential for tomatoes. As the plants grow, the tomatoes will trail down naturally around the sides of the basket forming a fruiting 'fringe', with the marigolds in the top. For best results, leave the tomatoes on the plants until they are completely ripe so that they develop their full flavour, and deadhead the French marigolds every week.

6 Space three tomato plants evenly around the basket. Fill the spaces in between them with a few French marigolds.

4 Trim the edges of the liner; the plants will soon hide any rough edges. The vital thing is that the basket holds plenty of water.

5 Choose a compact bush tomato variety. Remove it from its pot and plant it angled out over the edge of the container.

7 Water the container well. Use diluted liquid tomato feed to encourage heavy fruiting and avoid excess leafy growth, thus making a more decorative and productive container.

French marigolds
(*Tagetes patula*)

Bush tomato
Tumbler F1

8 As the tomatoes begin to swell, the plants hang down below the rim of the basket, making picking easy. Harvest the ripe tomatoes regularly (shown at right) and deadhead the marigolds to keep this combined display going all summer.

Companion planting

Some gardeners claim that companion planting – the deliberate pairing of certain plants – prevents pests and disease without using chemicals. It is certainly true that by cultivating a wide range of nectar-rich flowers, such as herbs and old-fashioned hardy annuals, beneficial insects, such as hoverflies, are attracted to the garden. These then stay and breed, and their larvae – and in some cases also the adult insects – feed on plant pests. However, the claims for companion planting have not been proven; what works for one person does not always give good results for another. Some common plant combinations are:

Below: The pretty blue flowers of borage are believed to improve crop yields of fruit and vegetables by attracting beneficial butterflies and bees to pollinate them.

Borage, thyme and hyssop
Attract bees, which improve crop yield in strawberries.
Chamomile
Said to repel insect attacks, thus improving crop yields.
Chives
Said to prevent black spot on leaves and deter aphids.
Dill and fennel
Attract hoverflies, which then go to work on aphids.

Above: Nasturtium is said to keep pests away from the vegetable garden, partly owing to the way it attracts aphids to itself. It also repels ants and whitefly. The young leaves and flowers are delicious in salads.

Garlic
With its strong odour, it is thought to be beneficial to roses.
Mint
The pennyroyals have been found to be good fly and midge repellents.
Rosemary and thyme
Said to mask the scent of carrots, which deters carrot fly.
Sage
Believed to repel the cabbage white butterfly.

Below: The nectar-filled flowers of calendula (pot marigold) will attract hoverflies that eat aphids. May deter nematodes in the soil.

329

1 To 'chit' potatoes (which means cause them to sprout) stand them in a warm, dark place in small pots or on an egg tray, with the eyes (buds) pointing upwards. Chitted potatoes grow away faster.

GROWING POTATOES AND BROAD BEANS IN TUBS

You can grow all kinds of potatoes in containers, but it is more practical to grow early (new) potatoes or 'specialist' varieties that are difficult to find in the shops. Early varieties can be produced even sooner by planting the tubers six weeks earlier than recommended and keeping the container in a frost-free greenhouse or conservatory until after the last frost. Then move the container outdoors. Expect to gather the crop in early midsummer, leaving the container free to be planted up with flowers or other edibles, such as herbs. It is also possible to enjoy 'new' potatoes later in the season by storing a few seed potatoes of an early variety in a cool, shady spot and planting them after gathering the first crop of earlies. These will be ready to harvest from autumn onwards. However, remember to bring the container back into a frost-free growing environment before the first frosts, as potatoes are not hardy. Specialist gourmet potatoes with a fine flavour include both early and maincrop varieties. 'Belle de Fountenay', 'Pink Fir Apple' and 'Linzer Delikatess' are especially tasty. Early potatoes are ready to pick when the first flowers appear on the plants. There is no need to pull up the whole plant; just feel round for the largest potatoes and leave the others for a bit longer. Do not pull up maincrop potatoes until the foliage starts to turn yellow, but, again, you can take a few potatoes before this stage. Keep potatoes well fed and watered during the growing period and buy new seed potatoes the following year.

2 Used soil-based potting mix or old growing bag mix is fine for potatoes. New potting mix can lead to rather too much top growth.

3 Fill the pot or tub with potting mix until it is one third to half full. Firm it down gently. This tub is about 45cm(18in) in diameter.

4 Lay in the chitted seed potatoes, leaving 15-20cm(6-8in) between them. This will produce a good crop without the risk of overcrowding the potatoes.

5 Cover the potatoes with about 2.5cm(1in) of potting mix and level the surface. There will be enough nutrients left in the old potting mixture, so there is no need to feed them yet.

6 Water the container well and stand it in a warm place. When the first shoots appear above the surface of the potting mix, increase watering and give a liquid feed once a week.

The benefits of container-grown potatoes

Potatoes are very susceptible to soil pests, such as wireworms, which are a common problem when old grassland or turf has been dug up to make a vegetable garden. Many soil pesticides cannot be used where potatoes are to be grown, as they cause a flavour 'taint', and in any case, few people like to use pesticides on crops they are going to eat. Growing in containers enables you to raise clean, good-tasting crops without problems. If burrowing rodents are likely to be a problem, stand the base of the container on fine mesh wire netting before filling it. You can use old growing bag potting mix for potatoes in containers. Pull out all the old roots and plant debris, such as dead leaves. Mix used for growing tomatoes would be fine for potatoes. Make sure that the first crop has not suffered from disease or soil-borne pests.

Broad beans in a tub

Broad beans make splendid plants for growing in containers of all sorts on a sunny patio. Be sure to use dwarf-growing varieties that are short and sturdy and generally need no support. Because dwarf varieties are not sufficiently hardy to withstand the winter outdoors, and will become drawn if grown in any heat, sow them in the early spring. Keep them outdoors, so that the flowers are adequately pollinated by bees.

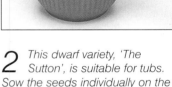

1 *Fill the container almost full with a good multipurpose potting mix. Firm it down gently to prevent later compaction.*

2 *This dwarf variety, 'The Sutton', is suitable for tubs. Sow the seeds individually on the surface about 10cm(4in) apart.*

3 *Push the seeds about 4-5cm(1.5-2in) down into the mix. Move some soil back over the seeds and firm in gently.*

4 *Water thoroughly. Do the initial watering in easy stages but do not stop until some drains out of the base.*

Right: Use an early variety; they have the shortest growing season and are ready the soonest. This one is 'Arran Pilot'. To see if the potatoes are ready for eating, scrape away the soil to expose a few tubers.

7 Fine foliage is the forerunner of a delicious crop. If you can obtain, or save, seed tubers, you could grow potatoes all year.

Right: *The young plants grow away well and flower. When grown outside (cooler than under cover), this variety should need no support. The plants stay short and are suited to growing in containers.*

1 Cut two compartments in a growing bag. Fold the edges under for strength. The raised sides prevent excess spillage.

2 Space out three aubergines evenly in a standard-sized growing bag. They will grow to make large plants.

3 The top of the rootball should be just below the soil. Firming in the plants excludes air gaps and ensures good water absorption.

4 Water with at least 4.5 litres (1 gallon) of water. This should be all that is needed for 10-14 days. Do not feed at this stage.

GROWING AUBERGINES, COURGETTES AND PEPPERS

Sow aubergine seeds singly in small pots. Leave the sowing until early to mid-spring or be prepared to keep them warm. Do not overdo the heat, though, or the seedlings will become drawn, weak and useless. Aim at a temperature in the range of 15-20°C(60s°F). For best results, plant them out into a growing bag in a greenhouse or conservatory when they have made a good root system. Feed and water as for tomatoes. Never be tempted to take too many fruits from a plant or the size will suffer; four is ample.

When grown in a greenhouse, aubergines are especially susceptible to attacks of red spider mite. Although the plants are fairly well able to stand up for themselves, the mite will spread to other species, with disastrous results. There is no reliable chemical control for the microscopic mites, but the predatory mite *Phytoseiulus* produces excellent results if you introduce it as soon as the leaves start to become speckled in the summer. This form of biological control is becoming widely available. In addition to this, you should keep the atmosphere in the greenhouse moist and reasonably cool, which in itself discourages the mite. Whitefly can also be a nuisance but they seldom reach the plague proportions they do with tomatoes. Yellow sticky traps hung above the plants will usually control them, but if they fail, the parasitic *Encarsia* wasp will do the trick.

5 When the stem is 15-20cm (6-8in) tall, nip out the top to encourage side shoots and to prevent the plant getting too tall.

6 Nipping out also encourages more flowers. Support the plants with canes once the weight of fruit bends the branches.

Sweet peppers

Sow the seeds in a heated greenhouse or propagator from late winter to mid-spring and prick out the seedlings singly into small pots of multipurpose potting mixture. Plant the seedlings in their final position when the first flowers are visible. The plants should branch out naturally, but if not, nip out the growing point at 30cm(12in) tall. Pick the first few fruits while they are still green to encourage more to form on the plant.

Below: In containers, plant peppers so that finally they will be growing no less than 30cm(12in) apart.

Courgettes in a growing bag

Grow courgettes in a sunny spot and in fertile soil well supplied with bulky organic matter. As they are frost-tender, sow them under cover in mid-spring for planting outside in early summer or outside in late spring where they are to grow. Raise seeds singly in peat pots, water them well, cover with plastic and put them in a warm place to germinate.

1 *If there is little risk of the bag spreading out, cut a single planting compartment and push the mix into the sides and corners.*

2 *Given warmth, young plants grow quickly. When roots appear through the sides of the pot, plant them out or pot on.*

Put two plants in a standard-size growing bag.

3 *Leave the top of the rootball 1.25cm(0.5in) above the soil to help prevent plants rotting at the neck. Water thoroughly.*

7 These plants have been 'stopped', the side shoots are growing vigorously and the first flowers are just showing.

Right: Shiny purple fruits soon start to form. Although they normally need greenhouse conditions in temperate climates, in a good summer, aubergines will succeed outdoors in a sunny, sheltered spot.

4 *A few weeks later the plants are growing well. The slight difference in foliage is a varietal characteristic and not harmful.*

1 Loosely fill a wooden planter (with drainage holes in the base) with rich potting mixture. There is no need to add fertiliser.

2 Choose plants with a low, semi-trailing habit to plant round the edge. This way, light can reach all the plants in the container.

TASTY SALAD CROPS IN A WOODEN PLANTER

Pots of herbs are traditionally grown by the back door where they are convenient for picking, so why not use salad plants in the same way? Nowadays, a whole range of edible leaves are popular as garnishes and ingredients for green salads; planted together, they make a decorative and useful container display. The best 'ingredients' for a container salad garden are those that can be picked little and often: sorrel, purslane, rocket, land cress, salad burnet and cut-and-come-again lettuce, such as 'Salad Bowl'. Planted in spring, the same plants can be picked over lightly for most of the summer. If the container is large enough, add a few hearting salads, such as Chinese cabbage, cos and normal lettuce and radicchio-type chicory. Where available, choose miniature varieties, as they take up less room and are faster-maturing than full-sized varieties. As soon as a plant forms a heart big enough to use, cut the heart, remove any remaining foliage, pull the root out carefully and put in a new plant. In this way, you can obtain quite a regular succession of salads from a very small space, even if you do not have a garden.

3 Floppy plants, such as salad burnet, look specially effective planted in the corners; place them as close to the edge as possible to make full use of the space. Turn plants so that their best sides face forward.

6 French sorrel is a useful leaf-salad, with large, lemon-flavoured leaves. This perennial plant can be cut little and often over several years, but dies down in winter.

4 Add an edible-flowered plant, such as this nasturtium, in the centre, where it will make a focal point surrounded by foliage.

5 Miniature lettuce, such as this baby iceberg 'Blush', are fast-growing and ready to cut when the hearts are the size of tennis balls.

7 Chinese cabbage grow quickly and are safer from slugs and snails in a raised container, but make sure that the potting mix does not dry out, otherwise they are likely to run to seed. Plants form chunky hearts.

8 Plant everything 15cm(6in) apart. Water well after planting, and check daily, as the potting mix will start drying out fast when the tub fills with roots, and in hot weather. Begin liquid feeding after four weeks.

When to plant salad crops in containers

Plant lettuce, nasturtium and perennial crops, such as sorrels and salad burnet, from spring onwards, but wait until early summer before planting tender plants, such as purslane, along with radicchio and Chinese cabbage. In mid- and late summer, you could add other Chinese leaf vegetables, such as Pak Choi and mizuna, as well as a late planting of radicchio, endive and more Chinese cabbage for autumn and early winter use. Alternatively, choose winter salad leaves such as lambs lettuce and winter purslane (Claytonia perfoliata). Given a little protection, some varieties can continue to crop well into winter.

Right: A selection of frilly lettuce makes a novel hanging basket that provides enough leaves for several salads and garnishes. By the time the mini tomato plant is cropping, the lettuce will have been picked, giving it more space to develop.

Radicchio 'Pall Rossa Bello' – firm red hearts with white veins.

Chinese cabbage

Lettuce 'Blush' – a baby iceberg type with red-tinged leaves. Ready to cut when tennis ball-sized.

Purslane (*Portulaca oleracea*) – a succulent plant with fleshy green leaves.

Rocket (*Eruca sativa*) – both flowers and leaves are edible.

Buckler-leaved sorrel (*Rumex scutatus*)

French sorrel (*Rumex acetosa*) – large leaves like thick spinach with pronounced lemon-herbal tang.

Nasturtium 'Alaska' has pretty variegated foliage.

Salad burnet (*Sanguisorba minor*) – foliage has a faint taste of cucumber.

9 Although the tub will soon look crowded, plants around the edge will spread outwards over the sides, while plants such as sorrel and purslane are picked regularly, leaving more room for others.

Above: *Once the planter is in full growth, it provides a harvest of fresh salad. Both leaves and flowers of nasturtium are edible.*

A stone urn overflowing with spring flowers dominated by tulip 'Apricot Beauty'.

INDEX

Page numbers in **bold** indicate major text references and main features. Page numbers in *italics* indicate annotations and captions to photographs. Other text entries are shown in normal type.

P

A note about plant names

The joy of gardening is burdened with a bewildering variety of plant names. Common names are often only relevant in a particular area of the world, whereas scientific (or Latin) names should form a universal language that successfully straddles the worlds of botany and horticulture. Unfortunately, plants commonly available in the gardening hobby are occasionally renamed by well-meaning botanists. Invariably, a plant you have come to know under one name seems to have acquired a new one that is nothing like the original. In this book, we have tried to reflect the latest scientific plant names, but each book can only present a snapshot of the current situation. If you are new to gardening, you may find this confusing, but you will soon learn to recognise the plants and enjoy them for the colour and beauty they bring to your garden – whatever they are currently called.

CREDITS

Picture credits

The majority of the photographs featured in this book have been taken by Neil Sutherland and are © Quadrillion Publishing Ltd. The publishers wish to thank the following photographers for providing additional photographs, credited here by page number and position on the page, i.e. (B)Bottom, (T)Top, (C)Centre, (BL)Bottom left, etc.

Peter Blackburne-Maze: 323(TL)
Eric Crichton: 19(CL, Steve Williams), 24(CR), 25(TL, Penny Sinclair), 27(CL, Rupert Golby), 28(Jim Keeling, Whichford Pottery), 54(T, Jim Keeling, Whichford Pottery), 75(TL, RHS Chelsea 1995), 75(TR, Daphne Foulsham), 75(BL, RHS Chelsea 1992), 77(TL, David Stevens, RHS Chelsea 1997), 77(BR, RHS Chelsea 1991), 80(BR, Esther Merton), 82(BR, David Stevens, RHS Chelsea 1993), 83(C), 103(BR), 107(TR), 119(BL, Jim Keeling, Whichford Pottery), 147(TR, Mrs. Kenison), 205(CR, RHS Wisley), 231(TL, RHS Wisley), 232(Bunny Guiness), 237(C, Wyevale Garden, RHS Chelsea 1995), 299(BL)
Flower Tower Co.: 153(TR, CR, BR)
John Glover: 13, 14(BR), 15(TL), 22(BL), 27(TL), 55(TR,CR,BR), 57, 74(CR, BL, BR), 75(BC, BR), 76(BL), 77(TR, CR), 78(BL), 79(TL, TR), 80(BL), 81(CL), 83(TL), 86(TC, BL), 89, 107(CR), 133(TR), 134, 139(CR), 141(BR), 146(TL), 150(BL), 168, 181(CL, BR), 187(TL), 199, 213(TR, C, BR), 230(BC), 231(TR), 250, 254(T), 298(BL, BR, TR), 300, 303(CR, BR), 307(TR), 318, 324(BR), 335(CR)
W.E.Th. Ingwersen Ltd., Sussex: 207(TR)
Paul Goff: 248(T), 249(BL)
International Flower Bulb Centre: 174(BL), 201(BR)
Andrew Lawson: Title page, 17(C), 54(BL), 55(BL), 74(TR), 76(BR), 79(BR), 133(BR), 223(BR), 299(TR)
S&O Mathews: 20(TR), 24(BL), 56, 78(TR, BR), 82(TR), 85(BL), 87(BL), 103(TR), 135, 139(BR), 147(CR), 261(BR)
Clive Nichols Garden Pictures: Copyright page (Photographer Graham Strong), 12 (Photographer Graham Strong), 16(C, Bourton House, Glos.), 18(TL, Photographer Graham Strong, 19(BR, Photographer Graham Strong), 21(TC, TR Photographer Graham Strong), 22(TL, Photographer Graham Strong), 22(C, Designer Emma Lush), 23(CL, Designer Elisabeth Woodhouse), 55(TL, Photographer Graham Strong), 76(C, Photographer Graham Strong), 77(BL, Photographer Graham Strong), 80(TR, Photographer Graham Strong), 84(TR), 101(TL, Photographer Graham Strong), 106(TR), 147(BR, Bourton House, Glos.), 171(TL, Photographer Graham Strong), 175(TL, Photographer Graham Strong), 185(TL, Bourton House, Glos.), 198(Designer Simon Shire), 217(C, Photogrpaher Graham Strong), 217(BR, Photographer Graham Strong), 223(CR, Photographer Graham Strong), 230(T, Photographer Graham Strong), 230(CL, Photographer Graham Strong), 231(BR, Photographer Graham Strong), 299(TL, Designer Roger Platts), 305(TL), 336(Photographer Graham Strong)
Potterton & Martin: 207(CR, BR)
Geoffrey Rogers: 81(TL), 113(TC), 123(TR, BR), 171(BR), 176(BL), 188(TR), 189(TR, C), 229(TR, BR), 230(BR), 231(BL), 291(C, CR, BR), 299(BR)
Derek St. Romaine: 81(TR), 83(BR), 84(BL), 255(BL), 299(CL), 323(TR)

Acknowledgments

The publishers would like to thank the following people and organisations for their help during the preparation of this book:

Neil Allen; Angus White at Architectural Plants, Horsham, West Sussex; Diana Grenfell at Apple Court, Lymington, Hampshire; Bressingham Plant Centre, Diss, Norfolk; Bridgemere Garden World, Nantwich, Cheshire; Brinsbury College, Pulborough, West Sussex; Brogdale Horticultural Trust, Faverhsam, Kent; Burnham Nurseries, Newton Abbott, Devon; June Carter; Shelley and Jonathan Choat; Amanda Dennis at The Citrus Centre, Pulborough, West Sussex; Clifda Steels Ltd., Canvey Island, Essex; Country Gardens at Chichester, West Sussex; June Crowe at Rose Cottage, Hartley, Kent; The Flower Auction Holland, Naaldwijk; The Flower Tower Company Ltd., Bridgwater, Somerset; Grosvenor Garden Centre, Belgrave, Chester; Hadlow College, Kent; The Hillier Plant Centre, Braishfield, Hampshire; Terry Hewitt, Holly Gate Cactus Nursery, Ashington; Hozelock Ltd., Haddenham, Buckinghamshire; Iden Croft Herbs, Staplehurst, Kent; W.E.Th. Ingwersen Ltd, East Grinstead, West Sussex; Kaktuskwekery Ariane, Kwekerij Marienoord bv, Lochristi, Belgium; Little Brook Nurseries, Ash Green, Hampshire; Millbrook Garden Centre, Gravesend, Kent; Murrells Nursery, Pulborough, West Sussex; Terry and Leslie Neale of Neales Aquatic Nurseries, Fawkham, Kent; John O'Dell, Oast House Nursery, Ash, Kent; Rosie and Robin Lloyd at Pots and Pithoi, Turners Hill, West Sussex; Premdor Crosby Ltd., Halstead, Essex; Reads Nursery, Loddon, Norfolk; The Royal Horticultural Society Garden at Wisley, Surrey; Russell's Garden Centre, East Wittering, West Sussex; Secretts Garden Centre, Milford, Surrey; Philip Sonneville nv, Lochristi, Belgium; Springhead Nurseries, Gravesend, Kent; Stapeley Water Gardens, Nantwich, Cheshire; Sussex Plants Ltd., East Sussex; Treasures of Tenbury Ltd., Burford, Worcestershire; T.H.Waters, Gravesend, Kent; Andre Whelan at B & A Whelan, Sheerness, Kent; Vesutor Air Plants, Billingshurst, West Sussex.